New Directions in Surveillance and Privacy

New Directions in Surveillance and Privacy

Edited by

Benjamin J. Goold and Daniel Neyland

WILLAN
PUBLISHING

Published by

Willan Publishing
Culmcott House
Mill Street, Uffculme
Cullompton, Devon
EX15 3AT, UK
Tel: +44(0)1884 840337
Fax: +44(0)1884 840251
e-mail: info@willanpublishing.co.uk
website: www.willanpublishing.co.uk

Published simultaneously in the USA and Canada by

Willan Publishing
c/o ISBS, 920 NE 58th Ave, Suite 300
Portland, Oregon 97213-3786, USA
Tel: +001(0)503 287 3093
Fax: +001(0)503 280 8832
e-mail: info@isbs.com
website: www.isbs.com

First published 2009

ISBN   978-1-84392-363-3 hardback

British Library Cataloguing-in-Publication Data

A catalogue record for this book is available from the British Library.

FSC
Mixed Sources
Product group from well-managed
forests and other controlled sources
Cert no. SGS-COC-2482
www.fsc.org
© 1996 Forest Stewardship Council

Project managed by Deer Park Productions, Tavistock, Devon
Typeset by GCS, Leighton Buzzard, Bedfordshire
Printed and bound by T.J. International Ltd, Padstow, Cornwall

Contents

Acknowledgement   *vii*
List of abbreviations   *ix*
Notes on contributors   *xi*

Introduction: Where next for surveillance studies?
Exploring new directions in privacy and surveillance
Daniel Neyland and Benjamin J. Goold   *xv*

Part 1: Regulation

1   The limits of privacy protection   3
     James B. Rule

2   Building it in: the role of privacy enhancing
     technologies (PETs) in the regulation of surveillance
     and data collection   18
     Benjamin J. Goold

3   Regulation of converged communications surveillance   39
     Ian Brown

4   From targeted to mass surveillance: is the EU Data
     Retention Directive a necessary measure or an
     unjustified threat to privacy?   74
     Marie-Helen Maras

Part 2: Technologies and techniques of surveillance

5   Surveillance, accountability and organisational failure:
    the story of Jean Charles de Menezes   107
    Daniel Neyland

6   Perceptions of government technology, surveillance
    and privacy: the UK Identity Cards Scheme   133
    Edgar A. Whitley

Part 3: Surveillance futures

7   'Ten thousand times larger...': anticipating the expansion
    of surveillance   159
    Kevin D. Haggerty

8   Since *Nineteen Eighty Four*: representations of surveillance
    in literary fiction   178
    Mike Nellis

Index   *205*

Acknowledgements

Many thanks to the Oxford Institute for Science, Innovation and Society for their funding of the seminar series on which this book was based. The Institute was established in 2004 at the University of Oxford through the generosity of the James Martin Trust, and seeks to investigate how science and technology will shape society in the next century, and inform the education of business leaders and policy and decision makers worldwide. http://www.sbs.ox.ac.uk/research. We are also grateful to the University of Oxford Centre for Criminology for its support during the course of the seminar series.

Benjamin J. Goold and Daniel Neyland
2009

List of abbreviations

AC	Assistant Commissioner
ACLU	American Civil Liberties Union
APIG	All Party Parliamentary Internet Group
ATCSA	Anti-Terrorism, Crime and Security Act
CCTV	closed circuit television
CNIL	Commission Nationale de l'Informatique et des Libertés
CO19	Central Operations Specialist Firearms Unit (of the Metropolitan Police)
CRIS-E	Client-Registry Information System – Enhanced
DNA	Deoxyribonucleic acid
DRI	Digital Rights Ireland
DRM	Digital Rights Movement
DSL	digital subscriber line
ECHR	European Court of Human Rights
EDRI	European Digital Rights
EEA	European Economic Area
EHRR	European Human Rights Report
EWCA	England and Wales Court of Appeal
FBI	Federal Bureau of Investigation
FISA	Foreign Intelligence Surveillance Act
FISC	Foreign Intelligence Surveillance Court
FLOSS	Free/Libre/Open Source Software
FSA	Financial Service Authority
GCHQ	Government Communications Headquarters
GPS	Global Positioning System
HMSO	Her Majesty's Stationery Office

HMRC	Her Majesty's Revenue and Customs
IEEE	Institute of Electrical and Electronics Engineers
IMEI	International Mobile Equipment Identity
IMSI	International Mobile Subscriber Identity
IP	Internet Protocol
IPCC	Independent Police Complaints Commission
IPS	Identity and Passport Service
ISSA	Information Systems Security Association
ITAA	Information Technology Association of America
LSE	London School of Economics
MEP	Member of the European Parliament
MPA	Metropolitan Police Authority
NAO	National Audit Office
NIR	National Identity Register
NSA	National Security Agency
OECD	Organisation for Economic Co-operation and Development
OGC	Office of Government Commerce
PACE	Police and Criminal Evidence Act
PDA	personal digital assistant
PETs	privacy enhancing technologies
PGP	pretty good privacy
PIN	personal identification number
PNR	passenger name record
P3P	platform for privacy preferences
QC	Queen's Counsel
RAE	Royal Academy of Engineering
RIPA	Regulation of Investigatory Powers
SAS	Special Air Service
SOCA	Serious Organised Crime Agency
SO12	Specialist Operations Department of the Metropolitan Police
TNIR	Temporary National Identity Register
TOR	The Onion Router (anonymity network)
UKIPS	UK Identity and Passport Service
VoIP	Voice over Internet Protocol

Notes on contributors

Ian Brown is a research fellow at the Oxford Internet Institute and an honorary senior lecturer at University College London. His research is focused on public policy issues around information and the Internet, particularly privacy, copyright and e-democracy. He also works in the more technical fields of information security, networked systems and healthcare informatics. His recent research grants include £2m from the Engineering and Physical Sciences Research Council to investigate individuals' conceptions of privacy and consent across a range of contexts and timeframes. During 2009 he is undertaking a study for the European Commission on updating the European data protection framework.

Benjamin J. Goold is a university lecturer in law and a fellow and tutor at Somerville College, and a member of the University of Oxford Centre for Criminology. His major research interests are in the use of surveillance technology by the police and the relationship between individual privacy rights and the criminal law. In recent years, he has served as a specialist legal advisor to the House of Lords Inquiry into Surveillance and Data Collection, and as an independent advisor to the UK Identity and Passport Service. He also writes on aspects of the Japanese criminal justice system and is a member of the Oxford University Faculty of Oriental Studies and an associate member of the Nissan Institute of Japanese Studies.

Kevin D. Haggerty is editor of the *Canadian Journal of Sociology* and book review editor of *Surveillance and Society*. He is Associate

Professor of Sociology and Criminology at the University of Alberta and a member of the executive team for the New Transparency Major Collaborative Research Initiative. He has authored, co-authored or co-edited *Policing the Risk Society* (Oxford University Press, 1997), *Making Crime Count* (University of Toronto Press, 2001) and *The New Politics of Surveillance and Visibility* (University of Toronto Press, 2006).

Marie-Helen Maras is a recent graduate from the University of Oxford. At the University of Oxford, she completed her DPhil in Law in October 2008, MPhil in Criminology and Criminal Justice in November 2007, and MSc in Criminology and Criminal Justice in July 2006. She also has a Bachelor of Science in Psychology, a Bachelor of Science in Computer and Information Science, and a Masters in Industrial and Organisational Psychology. Marie has taught seminars at the University of Oxford on 'Security and the War on Terror' and the 'Burdens of Seeking Security' on the MSc in Criminology and Criminal Justice. In addition to her teaching and academic work, Marie served in the US Navy from 1997 to 2004. She gained extensive law enforcement and security experience from her posts in the military as a Navy Law Enforcement Specialist and Command Investigator. Her main research interests include terrorism, counter-terrorism, security and surveillance.

Mike Nellis is Professor of Criminal and Community Justice in the Glasgow School of Social Work, University of Strathclyde. He is a former social worker with young offenders, trained at the London School of Economics in 1977/8 and between 1990 and 2003 was himself closely involved in the training of probation officers at the University of Birmingham. He was awarded his PhD from the Institute of Criminology, University of Cambridge in 1991. He has written extensively on the changing nature of the probation service, the promotion of community penalties and the cultural politics of penal reform (including the educational use of prison movies and offenders' autobiographies). A longstanding interest in the electronic monitoring of offenders has taken him more deeply into the surveillance studies field.

Daniel Neyland works on a broad portfolio of projects focused on issues of governance and accountability (including surveillance technologies, the global textile trade, electronic waste, vaccines for neglected diseases, airports and security, traffic management, and household recycling). He has published widely including a 2006 book entitled *Privacy, Surveillance and Public Trust* (Palgrave Macmillan, 2006) and a methodology text: *Organizational Ethnography* (Sage, 2007). He has a forthcoming book on *Mundane Governance*.

James B. Rule is Distinguished Affiliated Scholar at the Center for the Study of Law and Society, University of California, Berkeley. His first book on privacy and personal information was *Private Lives and Public Surveillance* (Allen Lane, 1973); his most recent is *Privacy in Peril* (Oxford University Press, 1997). In addition to these subjects, his writings include books and articles on the role of social science in the improvement of social conditions; the causes of civil violence; cumulation and progress in social and political thought; and computerisation in organisations. He also writes for *Dissent* magazine, on whose editorial board he serves. He lives in Berkeley, California and Aniane, France.

Edgar A. Whitley is Reader in Information Systems in the Information Systems and Innovation Group of the Department of Management at the London School of Economics and Political Science. He is the research co-ordinator of the LSE Identity Project and represented the project at the Science and Technology Select Committee review of the scheme. He has written extensively about the Identity Cards Programme for both academic and trade audiences and is a frequent media commentator on the scheme. He is also the co-editor for the journal *Information Technology & People* and an associate editor for the journal *MIS Quarterly*. His research draws on his interests in social theory and its application to information systems, and recent publications include work on FLOSS (Free/Libre/Open Source Software), international students and academic writing, and the technological and political aspects of the UK Identity Cards Scheme.

Introduction

Where next for surveillance studies? Exploring new directions in privacy and surveillance[1]

Daniel Neyland and Benjamin J. Goold

Surveillance is now so prevalent in modern society that it touches almost every aspect of our daily lives. Our homes, our workplaces and even the public spaces in which we socialise, play and shop, are now brimming with a multitude of sophisticated data collection systems and complex surveillance technologies. Although many people may not be fully aware of the extent to which they are being monitored, most now regard surveillance as an inescapable – if not necessarily desirable – part of life in the early twenty-first century. While we can argue about whether we are already living in a 'surveillance society', it is abundantly clear that the spread of surveillance has dramatically altered the way in which our societies function and are experienced by ordinary people.

To date, academics and others interested in the nature and effects of surveillance have sought to understand this phenomenon through a variety of disciplinary lenses. Drawn together under the banner of surveillance studies, writers in sociology, philosophy, criminology, political studies, geography and urban studies have all offered their own unique insights into surveillance, and have together produced a diverse and impressive body of work on the subject. Indeed, to describe surveillance studies as multi-disciplinary is to do it something of a disservice: it is at its heart pragmatic and eclectic, and has shown an admirable willingness to embrace new and often divergent perspectives in its efforts to understand the complexities of surveillance.

It is in keeping with this spirit that the following volume – and the seminar series on which it was based – was conceived. Conscious of the fact that as disciplines mature, there is always the danger of them being constrained by the emergence of an accepted orthodoxy or canon of key ideas, this book aims both to celebrate the diversity of the field and to provide a home for new and emerging ideas about surveillance and privacy. As even the most casual glance at the table of contents will reveal, this is not a book that embraces any single theme, or one which takes a narrow view of the nature or significance of surveillance. Instead, it seeks to provoke by presenting readers with a range of radically divergent yet sympathetic perspectives, ranging from the philosophical and legal to the literary and futurist. Here, the hope is that readers will find their assumptions about the field tested and their curiosity provoked. Furthermore, because the chapters in this collection all seek to anticipate how surveillance and our responses to it might develop, hopefully they will provide a rich source of ideas for future research and writing in the field of surveillance studies, and help to ensure that it retains its intellectual diversity and dynamism.

New directions

In order to provide a space for pushing current writing in new directions, this collection is organised around three main themes. The first of these investigates the possibility of regulating surveillance activities and offering privacy protection. This involves questioning the strength of current protections (Rule), the possibilities of developing regulation more suitable for rapidly expanding technological systems (Brown and Goold) and the justification and necessity of giving up civil liberties in return for apparent protection (Maras). The second theme of this collection focuses on technologies and techniques of surveillance. It investigates the possibilities of rendering surveillance accountable (Neyland) and newly emerging public configurations of opposition to surveillance (Whitley). Finally, the third theme of the collection is focused on the future of privacy and surveillance. Here we find an analysis of future-oriented surveillance fiction (Nellis) and a search for possible future directions in surveillance activities (Haggerty). The following sections will provide a brief analysis of why we as editors think these themes are provocative, challenging and relevant for surveillance and privacy scholars.

Regulation of surveillance and privacy protection

One trend in recent privacy and surveillance writing has been to focus on regulation. Questions have been raised regarding the possibility, likelihood, range, time frame and logistics of protecting privacy from surveillance. But regulation has not been narrowly conceived, with discussions ranging across, amongst many other things, codes of conduct, laws, policies and privacy enhancing technologies. Much of this discussion takes place simultaneously with suggestions that privacy has died (see for example, Garfinkel 2000), is dying (see for example, Sykes 1999; Whitaker 2000; Rosen 2001) and/or that we already live in a transparent society (Brin 1998).

Claims regarding the death, end or destruction of privacy are frequently founded on one of the following arguments. First, it is claimed that an interconnected global flow of data, people and technology has emerged in recent years that has shifted 'us' into an era of so many privacy concerns that the term itself has become defunct. There are just too many variations on what a privacy concern could be for the term privacy to be able to cope (Sykes 1999). Second, it is suggested that the same flows have led to a situation where there are no longer any spaces, actions or forms of information which can be considered immune from collection, storage, analysis and further mobilisation. In this sense privacy as a concept is dead (or dying) as traditional material boundaries prove to be an insufficient impediment to activities of data scrutiny and management (Brin 1998). Detailed consideration of these claims suggests a variety of problems.

First, the proposal that society is now characterised by an interconnected mass of people, technology and flows of information, what Castells (1996) refers to as the network society, offers a socio-technical gloss to a range of complex and ongoing relations. These relations involve the plaiting and bounding of social and technical entities for the production, mobilisation and direction of forms of information. For example, in a CCTV system we can find staff, monitors, radios, police officers, pens, paper, regulations, codes of practice and fibre optic connections drawn together. Much effort goes into both building and maintaining these relations between people and things. However, it is not straightforwardly the case that such interconnection is all-encompassing. There are breakdowns in relations between people and technologies, and there is a great deal of work done to constitute boundaries that prevent potential relationships between people and technologies from emerging. For example, local populations could be invited to engage with CCTV cameras through opening up systems of surveillance. In practice, local populations do not receive such an invitation. Furthermore, these relations do not stand still. New technologies are frequently introduced, along with new ways of working, new subjects of focus, and new ways to use old data.

Hence, we need to pay close attention to the kinds of relations in play between people and surveillance systems, and to what those relations open up and what they close down. Rapidly adopting metaphors of the network society, as if everyone and everything is now related and that all relations are equal and operate smoothly, risks a socio-technical gloss which opens up the space for making grand claims such as privacy is dead. Indeed rather than heralding a death of privacy, these relations, their openings and closures, inspire many new ideas, discussions and demands of privacy.

A second problematic feature of the death of privacy arguments relates to the 'we' or 'us' which, it is claimed, is now experiencing a global flow of information, ending boundaries to data collection, storage and analysis. Who is the 'we' that might be experiencing such a phenomenon? As in Bennett and Raab (2003), both Haggerty and Maras argue in their respective chapters that our social experiences of privacy are not evenly distributed. Those in need of state welfare are involved in the submission, collection and use of information that otherwise would not be required. Those with credit cards and those who have access to the internet and telephones, as well as those who pay bills, shop in areas covered by CCTV, and are required to carry ID cards, may each engage in a range of observable activities, the traces of which are collected, stored, analysed and further mobilised. However, these are by no means global experiences and are by no means universally experienced even by those who do participate. The claim that everyone participates in such activities and that these participants share the same experiences is simplistic. Research on technology (see for example Bijker, Hughes and Pinch 1989; Bijker and Law 1992; Grint and Woolgar 1997 amongst others) provides multiple examples of the variety of experiences which engagement with the 'same' technology can bring. In light of this, careful consideration is required of what is meant by privacy in relation to specific technological systems, when and for whom.

A third feature of death of privacy arguments involves the claim that the rise in number and scope of systems designed to collect, store, categorise and analyse information on the population has led to an explosion of privacy concerns so diverse that the term privacy is no longer appropriate or meaningful. This implies that at a previous time there was a universal, agreed-upon definition of privacy that has now somehow become obsolete. This does not appear to be the case. Privacy has consistently formed a focus for questions. What might be an appropriate form of privacy? What types of information should be held on the population? Which freedoms should the population be expected to concede in order to meet the demands of the state? These questions constituted the basis for the (successful) 1952 challenge to abandon the use of wartime identity cards in the UK, and have been reiterated on every occasion since when successive governments have proposed some new identity card system.

In this sense privacy has always been a focus for multiple concerns and, although there are more technologies available to gather information, it is not clear that the types of privacy concern have significantly altered or become obsolete. Indeed, Rule in this collection makes the case that a liberal democratic consensus on privacy protection principles is broadly recognisable. Although experiences of privacy invasion may be highly variable across different contexts, we can still find much discussion of the appropriate means to protect privacy against surveillance. According to Whitley (this volume) we may only now be witnessing the emergence of a popular, public uptake of privacy issues. Hence in place of the dissolution of privacy, we find instead a mounting discussion of privacy and the development of new modes of privacy legislation. For Rule, this has led to the development of a consensus of privacy protection principles (although this consensus is not without problems, notably that the diverse experiences of privacy may not match a narrowly constituted consensus, see below). This may now mean that privacy – at least in policy terms – has greater coherence and resonance than ever before. For example, although the Human Rights Act (1998) is subject to multiple interpretations, it does for the first time establish a right to privacy in the United Kingdom.

This suggests current writing on privacy and surveillance displays a combination of both scepticism (that privacy might already be dead or at least on its way out) and hope (that there might be a form of regulation which could be more effective in protecting privacy from surveillance). How then, can we tackle this simultaneous scepticism and desire for change? Rule takes us through a natural history of privacy as a topic of controversy. In line with some of the sceptics, Rule suggests that privacy is an intractable problem. The lack of any natural limit to innovation in the technologies of information collection, mobilisation and techniques of utilisation, suggests the problem of privacy is not about to be solved in any single, straightforward manner. At the same time, privacy does not die. Instead, it is continuously subject to change in line with technological developments, new and imaginative ways to exploit existing data, and in response to changes in legislation.

If the problem of privacy is intractable and ever changing, what are the prospects for protection? The authors in this volume posit a range of possible responses. For Brown, the massive expansion of communication technology provides a compelling need for privacy protection to keep up. Brown suggests that policies have slipped behind the social, political and technological landscape. Writing in a similar vein, in his chapter Goold questions the effectiveness of regulatory regimes that rely solely on legal rules and sanctions, and argues instead for an approach that embeds organisational restraint and a respect for privacy via privacy enhancing technologies (PETs). Finally, for Maras, concerns over privacy protection in relation to data retention suggest a profound change in social order. We are now called upon to sacrifice civil liberties and need to ask what we might receive in return, whether or not our sacrifices are necessary and on what grounds our sacrifices might be justified. Privacy protection appears some distance from cognisance of these issues. For Rule the lack of any natural limit to privacy invasion requires a normative stance. Questions to ask include what kinds of information should different organisations collect, and what ought organisations be allowed to do with information?

This suggests both that privacy has not died, and that protection against surveillance has not become any less poignant a matter of social and political interest. However, as Goold reminds us, identifying the most appropriate means of privacy protection is neither straightforward nor universal. Furthermore, Rule's critique of liberal democratic privacy protection principles is an apt demonstration of the limitations of universality. A single set of privacy protection principles suitable for all occasions is unlikely to prove adequate. Lee (1999) refers to this as the tension between the general and the particular. The general refers to those sets of principles, codes and laws which might be deemed relevant to any incident. The particular refers to the work done to translate the general into something relevant for each specific incident where the general is invoked. For Lee (1999), this translation can lead to a tension whereby disputes follow on from any particular translation of a general principle. In relation to privacy, how might general privacy protection principles be enacted in particular situations, who would decide on whether or not a particular translation of a general principle is suitable and what might the consequences be of movement between the general and the particular?

These are all questions considered by authors in the first section of the collection. Rule suggests that the current liberal democratic consensus on privacy protection principles (what we might term the general) run into a multitude of problems across specific incidents (the particular) when they are applied. For Brown the general lags behind the particular. For Goold, (general) privacy protections must be designed into (particular) surveillance systems, as well as mandated by law. For Maras the general have unexplored and problematic social consequences when translated into particular instances of policy implementation. A challenge set down by these authors is how we might sidestep or get beyond some of these tensions.

Technologies and techniques of surveillance

A second trend in privacy and surveillance writing in recent years has been a detailed analysis of the technologies and techniques of surveillance. Arguments have been put forward regarding the need to get close to what goes on in surveillance systems, to generate further insights into public understanding of surveillance, and to explore the extent to which such detailed explorations can aid in the development of normative understandings of privacy and surveillance. Getting closer to the activities of surveillance has involved up-close, often ethnographic, studies of, for example, CCTV control rooms (see for example, Norris and Armstrong 1999; and Goold 2004). This has provided a rich and nuanced picture of what surveillance in practice looks like and has initiated debates regarding the extent, likelihood, threats to and prospects for privacy protection.

Within this focus on the techniques and technologies of surveillance, developing a public understanding of surveillance has been hitherto a somewhat neglected concern both practically and theoretically. Firstly, in the UK there has been a lack of clear public participation in debates regarding privacy and surveillance (with the exception of the proposed ID card scheme). Where consultation does happen, for example in the introduction of new CCTV systems, it seems to be on a small scale and without clear consequences. Secondly, this absence of participation and consultation seems to have evinced very little interest in the privacy and surveillance studies community. These notable absences tie in with research in the field of public understanding of science and technology which has frequently involved a focus on what have been termed deficit models (see for example Irwin 1995). The first deficit model suggested that policy-makers treated knowledge held by members of the public as inferior to that held by apparent experts.[2] The focus for these models has shifted more recently to a deficit in participation or trust (that there are too few opportunities for public participation in scientific and technological debates and an absence of trust in science, Gregory 2001), and to a deficit in legitimacy of public engagement (that science is afforded a licence to operate beyond, despite or regardless of public participation, Gregory 2001).

Each of these deficit models could be said to apply to public participation in surveillance and privacy debates. For example, it is not clear that public consultation on potentially privacy-infringing technologies treats public knowledge as having potentially equal status with expert knowledge. This suggests a frequent policy buy-in to deficit in public knowledge models. It is also not clear that public participation in the introduction of new technology such as CCTV systems in the UK operates to the same extent as the introduction of other technologies, such as new ID cards. This signals a deficit in opportunities for participation in relation to some technologies. It might also be said that such participatory activities lack legitimacy, with consultations, for example, carried out in order to adhere to government guidelines, rather than with a view to incorporating a strong public voice into developments.

Beyond these deficit models, it has also been argued (Neyland 2006) that public participation in privacy and surveillance debates could be characterised by a deficit of concern. It is often the case that local residents living near CCTV systems in the UK assume that the system is operating for their benefit (or at least is not operating to their detriment), and that there is some notable authority overseeing CCTV on their behalf (Neyland 2006). However, this deficit of concern may be slowly changing. In his chapter on ID cards in this collection, Whitley suggests that attempts to introduce ID cards in the UK have shifted the tenor of the public debate around privacy and the limits of surveillance. According to Whitley, media stories of ID cards and their associated challenges have coincided with an increase in other stories of privacy and surveillance, including breaches, challenges and their social consequence. This increase in media attention might be a signal that the deficit of concern is diminishing. It could also signal a move toward greater public engagement in normative debates over the appropriate extent of surveillance and the value of privacy.

Normative questions are also helpful insofar as they challenge our belief in the straightforward utility of detailed, empirical studies of surveillance technologies and techniques, and can instead inform our understanding of what surveillance and privacy protection ought to look like. The tension generated by such normative questioning has been noted over many years of philosophical and social scientific work, and is traceable (at least) as far back as the work of Hume (1740). Hume famously argued that there is no logical connection between questions regarding the nature of what something is and questions regarding the nature of what something ought to be. This division between 'is' and 'ought' later became known amongst philosophers as Hume's guillotine (Black 1964). For philosophers, the cut of the guillotine is a matter of logic. For social scientists, however, the cut presents more of a practical challenge: namely, how to develop policies and practical solutions to problems from our empirical observations of the social world? (Woolgar and Neyland forthcoming).

In surveillance studies, the work required to get from observation to prescription requires us to translate up-close studies of the features of surveillance in practice into recommendations for possible remedial action. Here Neyland looks at two aspects of this challenge in relation to the accountability of surveillance systems. Neyland argues that legal processes aimed at ensuring surveillance actors and systems are held to account are inevitably complex and messy. This suggests that establishing what happened in a particular instance of surveillance – the 'is' in Hume's dichotomy – is far more challenging than it may first appear. Furthermore, beyond determining what has happened and who has done what to whom in a particular surveillance episode (in this case, the mistaken police shooting of Jean Charles de Menezes in London as a suspected terrorist), there are numerous questions concerning who should be held to account for those actions, and with what outcomes. This latter question of 'ought' is made more complex by continuing disputes regarding what has happened, whether or not the form of accountability is appropriate, and multiple interpretations of the outcome of the accountability process.

Whitley and Neyland's chapters offer insight into the challenge of getting close to the technologies and techniques of surveillance, and of using that closeness to engage with normative debates. Whitley's chapter could, for example, be read as an illustration of the advantages of greater public participation in surveillance debates, while Neyland's chapter demonstrates some of the limitations (and need to get beyond) current accountability dependencies. However, as

Latour (2004) has cautioned, moving from matters of fact to matters of concern is not straightforward. Normative engagements do not get any easier when we turn our attention to the future.

Futures of privacy protection

A third focus for surveillance studies introduced by the chapters of this book is that of the future. We can find a broad range of future-oriented writing across the social sciences from futurology to scenario planning. The purposes of this future orientation may vary from concerns with planning and strategising, through mapping, to concerns with the present and a desire to invoke questions such as how can we know more about what to do now, given what we think might happen next? This appears to be an under-explored area in surveillance studies. However, its potential utility is clear. Engaging with possible futures of privacy and surveillance enables a continuation of normative challenges (how should we engage with the future of surveillance, what would we want the future of privacy to look like?) and epistemological challenges (how could we know what the future holds?). Beyond normativity and epistemology, we are also faced with a methodological challenge: how might we research people, events, places, policies and technologies which are not happening yet (and may never come to fruition)?

Nellis strides out on a new and distinct methodological path by engaging with future-oriented writing about surveillance. What worlds are imagined and have been imagined by writers of fiction? Nellis takes us on a tour of the different genres and conventions for surveillance-based fiction, and surveys the fictional portrayals of future surveillance societies. Through Nellis' work, we are provided with a rich normative backdrop beyond our conventional contemplations, through which we are confronted with various new and provocative questions. This offers an alternative take on Leavis' work which suggests the importance of the arts and literature as having a critical function in opposing dominant views of our time. Leavis (1962: 28) argues that society needs a 'creative response to the challenges of our time' and that literature is essential in 'maintaining the critical function' (1962: 29). Hence we have the opportunity to ask whether writing about futures of surveillance can be seen as one of the sets of resources through which readers of texts orient their contemplation of surveillance activities? Through fiction can we see the ways in which surveillance concepts are becoming part of the world?

Haggerty also explores possible futures in a different but equally distinctive manner. In place of a focus on writing about the future, Haggerty instead focuses on current practices and tries to extrapolate from them and imagine what the future of surveillance might look like. Some of the futures suggested by Haggerty appear alluringly straightforward. For example, Haggerty suggests the current expansion of surveillance activities, technologies, information storage capabilities and capacities, is likely to continue and lead to more surveillance in the future. However, we should caution against any counter expectation that knowing the future of surveillance is simply a matter of extrapolation from today's newspapers. That there might be more surveillance tells us nothing of the modes, effects or consequences of expansion. For Haggerty, examining and predicting possible modes of future surveillance also involves an exploration of cognitive issues, conditional choices and stigmatisation. Each of these has a contemporary counterpart. It is through tracing out the bases for these contemporary actions that we might find traces of likely future consequences. Coming to terms with the epistemologies of surveillance (the nature of knowledge production and usage through surveillance) might give us a basis for navigating through the (at least in theory) limitless bounds of possible future actions.

In this sense, the future cannot be determined in a straightforward manner, but neither should it be left beyond our consideration. The future instead becomes a malleable boundary object (Star and Griesemer 1989), an object that is a locus for multiple representative practices that move through a more focussed passage point. As Star and Griesemer (1989: 387) argue: 'Scientific work is heterogeneous, requiring many different actors and viewpoints. It also requires co-operation ... Boundary objects are both adaptable to different viewpoints and robust enough to maintain identity across them'. Hence the futures of privacy and surveillance can be seen as boundary objects, or as organising focal points around and through which a range of entities are gathered, occasionally producing incompatible renderings of our likely future and occasionally producing interpretations wildly off target. That our capacity to predict may be limited should not, however, limit our attempts to engage with the possible futures that may lie ahead of us.

Conclusion

The field of surveillance studies continues to expand at a rapid pace, and with it so too does academic interest in questions of privacy and the limits of surveillance. This collection aims to provide a home for innovative new thinking and perspectives on surveillance, and to introduce new themes into existing discussions and debates. It also hopes to act as a guard against the emergence of any premature or comfortable consensus within the surveillance studies community. As the community continues to expand it becomes increasingly important to defend the eclecticism and intellectual curiosity that has helped to make surveillance studies so interesting, important and relevant. Put simply, we believe that one of the great strengths of the discipline is the fact that it operates as a broad church, and in providing a forum for new and challenging writing in the field, we hope this collection will help to keep the doors of that church as wide open as possible.

Notes

1 Many thanks to Inga Kroener for her helpful and insightful comments on an earlier version of this chapter.
2 This kind of model has been challenged by assertions that lay knowledge could be seen as a useful input to debates even if predicated upon a distinct epistemology (Wynne 1996).

References

Bennett, C. and Raab, C. (2003) *The Governance of Privacy – Policy Instruments in Global Perspective.* Hampshire: Ashgate.

Bijker, W. and Law, J. (eds) (1992) *Shaping Technology/Building Society: Studies in Sociotechnical Change.* London: MIT Press.

Bijker, W., Hughes, T. and Pinch, T. (1989) *The Social Construction of Technological Systems: New Directions in the Sociology and History of Technology.* London: MIT Press.

Black, M. (1964) 'The gap between "is" and "should"', *The Philosophical Review*, 73(2): 165–181.

Brin, D. (1998) *The Transparent Society: Will Technology Force Us To Choose Between Privacy and Freedom?* New York: Addison-Wesley.

Castells, M. (1996) *The Rise of the Network Society.* Oxford: Blackwell.

Garfinkel, S. (2000) *Database Nation: The Death of Privacy.* Sebastopol, CA: O'Reilly.

Goold, B.J. (2004) *CCTV and Policing: Public Area Surveillance and Police Practices in Britain.* Oxford: OUP.

Gregory, J. (2001) *Public Understanding of Science: Lessons from the UK Experience* [Online]. Available at: http://www.scidev.net/en/features/public-understanding-of-science-lessons-from-the.html [accessed 26 November 2008].

Grint, K. and Woolgar, S. (1997) *The Machine at Work: Technology, Work and Organisation*. Cambridge: Polity Press.

Hume, D. (1740) *A Treatise of Human Nature: Being an Attempt to Introduce the Experimental Method of Reasoning into Moral Subjects*.

Irwin, A. (1995) *Citizen Science*. London: Routledge.

Latour, B. (2004) 'Why has critique run out of steam? From matters of fact to matters of concern', *Critical Inquiry*, 30, [Online]. Available at: http://mendota.english.wisc.edu/~clc/Latour.pdf [accessed 16 November 2008].

Leavis, F.R. (1962) *Two Cultures? The Significance of C.P. Snow*. London: Chatto and Windus.

Lee, N. (1999) 'The challenge of childhood – distributions of childhood's ambiguity in adult institutions', *Childhood*, 6(4): 455–74.

Neyland, D. (2006) *Privacy, Surveillance and Public Trust*. London: Palgrave Macmillan.

Norris, C. and Armstrong, G. (1999) *The Maximum Surveillance Society – The Rise Of CCTV*. Oxford: Berg.

Rosen, J. (2001) *The Unwanted Gaze: The Destruction of Privacy in America*. New York: Vintage Press.

Star, S. and Griesemer, J. (1989) 'Institutional ecology, "translations" and boundary objects: amateurs and professionals in Berkley's museum of vertebrate zoology', *Social Studies of Science*, 19(3): 387–420.

Sykes, C. (1999) *The End of Privacy*. New York: St. Martin's Press.

Whitaker, R. (2000) *The End of Privacy: How Total Surveillance is Becoming a Reality*. New York: New Press.

Woolgar, S. and Neyland, D. (forthcoming) *Mundane Governance*.

Wynne, B. (1996) 'May the sheep safely graze? A reflexive view of the expert-lay knowledge divide' in S. Lash, B. Szerszynski and B. Wynne (eds) *Risk, Environment and Modernity: Towards a New Ecology*. London: Sage, 44–83.

Part I

Regulation

Chapter 1

The limits of privacy protection

James B. Rule

It would be hard to imagine a more thoroughly inter-disciplinary topic than privacy, and the efforts in legislation and policy to protect it. How to make sense of the demands on personal data in today's world, and what constitutes a reasonable response, are questions too big for any one line of thinking.

One form of analysis required here is obviously that of empirical social science. Like any other state of human affairs, today's pressures for appropriation of personal information require explanation in human terms. And the social, political and economic chemistry of the processes that have brought privacy to the fore since the 1960s are clearly no open-and-shut case. True, some observers (including many who should know better) are willing to bypass this question with a kind of intellectual shrug – simply stating that 'technology' is to blame for the loss privacy in today's world. Against such views, I want to argue that the demands for personal information from organisations underlying today's privacy controversies stem from fundamental changes in relations between large institutions, both government and private, and ordinary 'private' citizens. To frame any response to privacy issues, we need to understand the changes in social relations, political power and economics implicated in these developments.

A second domain of thinking that must inform any such response is the strictly normative thinking of philosophy – notably, ethics. What essential claims should any individual be able to make to reserve given domains of his or her life as private? Do people have *any* compelling right to withhold information about themselves that should override the rights of others who 'need' to access such information? Warring responses to these far-reaching questions, it turns out, tap tensions between contending traditions of ethical thought that go back centuries – well before anyone thought of committing personal data to large-scale computerised, or indeed written, records (Rule *et al.* 1980).

True, virtually everyone can join in decrying the 'invasion' of privacy. But this is simply because 'invasion' has become a term denoting those demands on personal data held excessive. Faced with the challenge to give account of which demands ought to be acceptable and which should not, we find ourselves in a thicket of conflicting rationales.

I emphasise this multiplicity of considerations in weighing privacy issues, particularly because I mean to return to it at the end of these remarks. Between now and then, I aim to develop the briefest sketch of the evolution of privacy as an issue. Here I seek to put forward my own empirical analysis of the social and economic forces that have made large-scale personal record-keeping such an endemic point of controversy in the world's 'advanced' democracies – and which make solutions to such controversies so problematic and highly-contested. At the end I want to argue that much of this intractability stems from disagreement – or more, perhaps, ambivalence within public opinion as to the proper claims of privacy against other values at stake in public affairs.

I would place the origins of privacy as a public issue to the United States in the 1960s (Rule 2007). Here I understand 'privacy' in a particular sense – that is, the struggles between institutions and individuals over access to and use of personal information on the latter. To be sure, demands for privacy in other senses also figure in public debate – as in claims to 'privacy' (in the sense of autonomy from government control) in matters of birth-control and abortion. And to be sure, privacy in many senses has been a subject of speculation and debate for much longer than 40 years. But about four decades ago the idea took shape that the creation and use of vast datafiles on individuals *by government and private institutions* required state supervision and restraint. At that point, privacy in this sense became a public issue – a matter of claims and counterclaims over prerogatives of organisations to collect information about people, and individual rights to constrain or block such collection (Rule *et al.* 1980).

The first such controversy to trigger action at the federal level in the United States had to do with consumer credit. By the 1960s, American public opinion had registered with dismay that consumers' access to credit – in accounts with merchants, home mortgages, credit cards and the like – depended on the exchanges of personal information that had been largely hidden. When further publicity showed that the contents of these decisive files could readily be erroneous, confused or inappropriate, classic privacy demands arose: *Something must be done,* the refrain went, to protect people's interests in the treatment of 'their' information. In short, institutional treatment of personal data systems was too important to be left – as it had always been in the past – to the discretion of the institutions themselves.

The immediate result of these controversies was passage of the Fair Credit Reporting Act (1970) – a template for much further privacy legislation, including the much better known Privacy Act of 1974, governing treatment of personal information in certain federal government systems. This remains today America's most comprehensive privacy law. Since 1974, the United States has enacted no further legislation guaranteeing privacy rights across different sectors of record-keeping. Instead American law-makers have set down *ad-hoc* rules for specific uses of personal data in specific settings – such as health care files, financial records, and video rentals.

Other democracies, starting a bit later than the United States, have generally established broader privacy rights and – most privacy-watchers would agree – more forceful institutions for their enforcement. Sweden adopted comprehensive privacy legislation, governing treatment of personal information in both public and private systems, in 1973. Following closely in the 1970s were Germany, France, Norway and Denmark. In 1995, the European Community promulgated its Privacy Directive, requiring each member country to follow a single template of privacy rights and procedures in its national legislation.[1]

Today, virtually every liberal democracy around the world has some national privacy code. Some of the most recent countries to adopt such codes are Argentina, India and Taiwan. The great majority of these countries have hewn closer to the European than the US model – establishing broad rights holding for personal data held in many different institutional settings, and creating some form of national ombudsman to defend such rights. But even including the United States as some sort of outlier, one can identify a core of principles as constituting what I am prepared to call a global consensus approach to privacy protection. In the briefest summary, and with no claims to comprehensiveness, let me identify the core of these principles.

1 The keeper of any system of personal records is responsible for the safety, security and integrity of the data so stored.

2 The existence, purposes, and workings of such systems should be readily accessible to public understanding.

3 A single figure (a 'privacy officer' or 'data controller') should be identified publicly as responsible for safeguarding the privacy interests affected by the working of each such system.

4 Information held in such systems must be collected legally and fairly.

5 Individuals must be able to review the content of information held on them in such systems and the uses and disclosures of such information; individuals must be able to obtain redress for inaccurate and inappropriate uses and disclosures of such data.

6 Personal data should only be collected in the form and to the extent necessary to fulfil the purposes of the system.

7 Information held in file should be as accurate and up-to-date as necessary to fulfill the purposes of the system.

8 Information collected for one purpose should not be used or released for other purposes, except under legal requirement or with permission of the individual.

9 Information held in file should be collected with the knowledge or consent of the person concerned.

(Rule 2007: 26)

Other privacy scholars summarising the same array of legislation and policy have produced similar encapsulations of key principles guiding global privacy protection efforts (Bennett and Raab 2003: 26).

These nine points make up, of course, a kind of composite portrait – blurring important details and downplaying differences among the world's many influential privacy codes. But with those limitations acknowledged, I believe that most privacy-watchers would recognise in these nine points the essentials of a global consensus on the requirements of meaningful privacy protection policies.

Indeed, I believe that many commentators would identify in these points what they might regard as the 'mature' response to the dilemmas posed by mass institutional monitoring of individuals' lives. From this perspective, these nine key principles provide a successful template for resolving the most intractable dilemmas in treatment of personal data. This is, to say the least, an optimistic position.

I am not one of the optimists. The pages to follow aim at showing why these precepts seem to me to leave some of the most pressing questions in privacy protection unanswered.

One problem is that, even where officially accepted for many purposes, the precepts are not applied to all forms of personal data collection and use. Above all, they are rarely held binding on the extensive personal data systems maintained by coercive and investigative agencies of the state – law-enforcement, counter-espionage and counter-terrorism agencies, above. Police, tax authorities, and intelligence agencies in most countries would regard it as ludicrous that their surveillance operations should be required to be open to inquiry and challenge from those under surveillance, for example – at least while such investigations are under way. Certainly there are good reasons why such activities should not always be held to the same standards of openness and accountability in handling personal data that are expected, say, of credit reporting agencies. But the idea that privacy protection codes should have *no bearing* on activities of these agencies should certainly give pause.

Secondly, the nine consensus principles imply a kind of parity between isolated individuals and large institutions that ill fits the realities of their relative positions. The underlying idea seems to be that personal data are exchanged in some sort of equal transaction between institution and individual, where each party gains something and gives up something of equal value. This thinking would seem to underlie the notion that personal data should only be collected, as Point 9 notes, 'with the knowledge or consent of the person concerned'. Of course, individuals may refuse their consent to having their names checked against watch lists on boarding air flights, or their credit accounts monitored when they seek credit. But in most cases, such refusal of consent to the demands of monolithic organisations comes at a drastic cost: being excluded from access to air travel or to consumer credit, in these cases. The bargaining positions of individuals confronting such organisations are not enviable.

In fact, 'consent' is a notoriously slippery notion when applied to contexts like these. Very commonly in practice, 'consent' to the most far-reaching appropriation and scrutiny of information about one's self is a condition of access to what most people would consider basic amenities of everyday life – access to consumer credit, for example, or ability to board an airliner, or rental of a car. However one may view the rights and wrongs of the claims made by the institutions for personal data in settings like these, it should be clear that individuals' 'consent' to such demands hardly indicates their assent to the principle underlying the demand – so much as recognition of the marked imbalance of power between the parties.

Thus a major UK bank requires that applicants for accounts sign a consent statement reading:

Where considering your application and where appropriate from time to time during your relationship with us, we will make searches about you at credit reference agencies ... and from the Electoral Register, for the purpose of verifying your identity .... We may use credit-scoring methods to assess applications and to verify your identity and we may also search the Electoral Register ourselves and carry out other identity checks.

Members of the HSBC Group may record, use, exchange, analyze and assess relevant information held about you and your relationships with the HSBC Group. This will include the nature of your transactions, for credit assessment, market research, insurance claim and underwriting purposes and in servicing your relationship with the HSBC Group. This may include information provided by you or someone acting on your behalf which is relevant to your relationship with us.[2]

It is safe to assume that many consumers might prefer not to give their 'consent' to such far-reaching inquiries. But in a world where banking and credit relationships are considered essential elements of a normal life, few will have the appetite to refuse such consent.

Further, even the *idea* that individual consent should be necessary for sharing of personal data among systems is widely disregarded in practice. If practiced consistently, this simple precept would indeed afford meaningful protection for privacy interests: data provided to one organisation for one purpose ought not to be shared without individual assent. But in practice, both government and private interests have readily swept aside such protective firewalls in one setting after another – *vide* the gutting of the US Privacy Act of 1974 provisions that prevented federal agencies from sharing personal data obtained for one purpose with other agencies devoted to other purposes.

Thus personal data collected by telecommunication companies – above all, logs of subscribers' calls and e-mail communications – have increasingly been collected by government agencies. The effort to combat terrorism has served as the official rationale for these expanding demands; but in fact, the revealing personal information maintained in these logs is also being made available for law-enforcement purposes with no particular relation to terrorism. Or in another example: data that consumers 'consent' to provide to credit reporting agencies is widely sold to insurance companies, for use in setting the rates proposed by the latter to their customers. Or, in some countries, data on citizens' current addresses disclosed by them to welfare state agencies – for medical care provision, for example – is supplied to tax authorities seeking to locate reluctant taxpayers. In these and many more such cases, it is the very fact that people are willing to provide their data for one, distinct purpose makes those data especially attractive as bases for action for quite different purposes.

Measures like these are indisputably *efficient* for the purposes of the institutions concerned. Other things equal, it is always more advantageous for institutions seeking to decide how to deal with large numbers of individuals to know more, rather than less, about the latter. From the individuals' point of view, by contrast, it is almost always preferable to control what personal data becomes available to these same institutions – so as to present one's self in the most favourable light to prospective creditors, tax authorities, driver licensing offices and the like. That is why institutions prefer not to rely solely on such potentially self-censored data from the individuals with whom they deal – but instead to draw data from sources, usually other institutions, with independent means of learning about the individuals concerned. Thus credit-grantors, for example, take it as axiomatic that consumers seeking credit will list on their 'best' past credit accounts on their credit applications, rather than accounts that have gone bad. For this reason, credit grantors rely on credit reporting agencies that, in the US, the UK and much of the rest of the world, can collect and report data on both the accounts credit-seekers prefer to have known, and those they would prefer to be forgotten. Such tensions between data-users and those with whom they deal define privacy struggles everywhere. Practices like unauthorised sharing of data sources across institutions clearly ease the pursuit of institutional interest – but equally inevitably mean loss of individual control over personal data. In other words, they erode privacy.

Finally and most crucially – in this catalogue of shortcomings in practice of the privacy protection principles – is a question that they simply ignore: when should systems of mass surveillance exist? How much of personal life should we expect to be subjected to systematic monitoring by large institutions? Who has the right to create personal data systems like the ones I've been describing in the first place? What 'needs' of institutions, what forms of control or regulation over human affairs are sufficiently pressing to warrant the accumulation and use of massive stores of personal information? Or to put matters the other way: when do institutional powers to record, analyse, share and act upon personal information simply become too intrusive, too invasive of privacy, too threatening in any of a number of ways to be permitted?

9

The most casual look at the evolution of these practices over recent decades reveals a steady stream of new and more enticing forms of personal data becoming available to government and private institutions. Data generated by cell-phone use, e-mail, website visits, supermarket choices, or use of GPS technologies are just some of the salient cases in point. As night follows day, emergence of such new forms of personal data attracts institutional planners. These resourceful state officials and private-sector entrepreneurs constantly seek new ways of exploiting the data for purposes ranging from law enforcement to the pursuit of terrorists to pinpointing advertising targets and consumer credit reporting. The data thus become the 'raw material' for new systems of personal monitoring – systems of *mass surveillance*, I call them (Rule 1973) – that track new areas of a once private life, and thus furnish new bases for institutions to deal with the individuals so tracked.

One may always hope that these new and more extensive forms of surveillance will be guided by principles like those cited in the list above. Data systems based on internet users' website visits; or cell-phone users' logs of communication patterns and whereabouts; or travellers' movements as monitored by airport security, toll road use, or GPS monitoring – these and other forms of data may at best be subject to due process guarantees. That is, they may operate with assurances of legality, of access and correction by the individuals concerned, of limitation of data collection to what is necessary for system purposes. But even on the optimistic assumption that the operators of such systems seek to follow accepted privacy principles in their treatment of personal data, the net extent of life subject to mass surveillance is growing.

The resulting picture of evolving developments since the emergence of privacy as a public issue, a sceptic might observe, is ironic: 40 years later, we have more and more privacy codes – but less privacy.

How are we to account for such a turn of events – an incremental but sustained movement into a less private world, even as pundits decry the loss of privacy, and policy-makers frame codes to protect it?

I've already noted one excessively facile answer to this question. The culprit, in this view, is 'Technology' – as though Technology (with a capital 'T') were some sort of independent agency forcing itself on human beings, regardless of their will in the matter.

Certainly the rise of computing and related information technologies has made privacy invasion far more efficient, cheaper and more attractive to institutions over the last decades. And certainly, too, many emerging pressures on privacy seem to begin with innovations in the technologies of creating, transmitting and interpreting personal information.

But in fact, the press toward institutional collection of information on 'private' citizens, and use of such information to shape institutional action toward the latter, date to well before the rise of computing. Early forms of mass surveillance arose in welfare-state systems for administering social benefits, and in business systems for tracking consumers' use of credit – to take two such examples – as early as the first half of the twentieth century. These systems played pivotal roles in the dealings of institutions with ordinary individuals; in so doing they sparked social controversy, even without the added impetus of computerisation. The early public debates over credit reporting in the United States provide a case in point – an instance where large-scale management of personal data bore on vital public interests, well before anyone had thought to rely on computing to sharpen the extent and efficiency of such reporting. As I've noted, principles developed to regulate consumer credit reporting in the United States provided a template for many later privacy codes, in that country and elsewhere (Rule 2007: 28–30).

Such manifestations of mass surveillance, whether based on written or computerised data, represent a distinctive and highly consequential social innovation of the twentieth century. Since the 1950s, throughout the world's rich democracies, they have become crucial links between institutions and publics in nearly every domain of life.

Surveillance in this precise sense is not necessarily malevolent. Rather, it is an ever-more-pervasive institutional form that may take on widely varying contents. The systems that track eligibility for social security benefits or medical insurance, after all, aim at administering things that most people want. At the other extreme, systems for tracking suspected terrorists, tax evaders or ordinary criminals are no less authentic examples of mass surveillance. And in between, we have personal record-keeping systems governing the administration of consumer credit, insurance, vehicle and driver registration, access to air travel and countless other junctures between institutions and ordinary citizens. Whenever institutions face the task of dealing precisely and 'correctly' with each one of millions of individuals, in light of the exact risks, opportunities and deserts associated with each one, systems of mass surveillance are apt to arise.

Relationships like these are a basic fact of life in the world's 'advanced' societies – so much so, that we forget how particular mass surveillance is to our own times, and how intricate its mechanisms actually are. Seeking credit, boarding an airplane, obtaining telephone service, accessing medical care – these and countless other ordinary and unavoidable life-activities require recourse to major institutions that inevitably want to consult our 'records' as to our relevant actions in the past, as bases for the treatment that they are to mete out to us in the present.

It would be wrong to imagine that the attentions of surveillance systems are only imposed unilaterally on unwilling members of the public. Often, we members of the public demand performances that only they can afford.

Thus, when we are dissatisfied with the treatment we receive from government or private institutions, we often reflexively demand fuller consideration of 'our records'. If the tax authorities make excessive claims on us, we appeal to the documented record of our circumstances, means and obligations. If we feel that we have been wrongly blocked from boarding an air flight because our name appears on a terrorist 'watch list', we demand justice – in the form of closer attention to our past histories and fuller consideration of the evidence of our *bona fides*. Even while deploring the 'invasion of privacy', public opinion is apt to support measures to track down illegal aliens; or to deny welfare payments to those not 'deserving' them; or to ensure that bad drivers pay the costs of their infractions through higher insurance charges. All such measures, obviously, require aggressive forms of surveillance, to identify who deserves what forms of action from the institutions involved.

Whether driven by popular demand or institutional will – or more likely, by some combination of the two – mass surveillance continues to spread. It grows, one might say, both *vertically* and *horizontally*. Vertically, in the sheer amount of relevant information surveillance systems maintain on any one individual; and horizontally, in the extent to which these systems draw upon and support one another. The net result, again, is that more and more areas of an ordinary person's life are subject to institutional monitoring – and that institutions can take more actions toward people, based on such intelligence.

The steady stream of innovation that fuels this trend is not solely or strictly technological. Often it stems from the imagination of people one might term 'surveillance entrepreneurs' in both government and private-sector institutions.

A salient case in point is the breakthrough in marketing consumer credit information that took shape less than twenty years ago. In countries following the US model of credit reporting, every consumer is assigned a credit score – a three-digit number encapsulating his or her desirability as a credit customer. Credit reporting agencies report consumers' credit scores in real time to prospective creditors – credit card issuers, or banks or consumer loan companies – enabling the latter to determine whether to allocate credit to the consumer involved, and if so on what terms.

Around 1990, some ingenious figures in the credit reporting industry got the idea that these scores might also be sold to insurance companies, for use in screening applicants for insurance. Perhaps, they suggested to their counterparts in the insurance industry, people's credit scores would also predict their likelihood of filing insurance claims. Over a period of years, insurers became persuaded of the proposition: applicants with lower credit scores (i.e. worse credit risks) were believed less profitable individuals to insure. The response of the insurance industry? Raise the rates charged to applicants with low credit scores (who also happen to be poorer), or decline to offer them coverage altogether. For the credit reporting industry, of course, this result was a boon: a vast new market for a product that credit reporters already had, so to speak, 'on the shelf'. For the insurance industry, this new use of personal data supposedly made it possible to spot in advance their less desirable customers, and concentrate on doing business with consumers who generate mostly premiums, and not claims.[3]

This sequence can stand as a paradigm for a basic process in the extension of mass surveillance. First, an institution finds a way of collecting, interpreting and using some form of personal data that proves profitable or otherwise efficient for guiding its own dealings with people. Then, another institution discovers (or becomes convinced) that the information so compiled can be used to support some discriminating treatment of persons vital to *that* organisation. Thus a symbiosis is formed: organisation A provides organisation B with crucial data to give the latter an advantage in dealing with people crossing the radar screens of both institutions. Sometimes the recompense from B to A comes in the form of payment; in other cases, it involves sharing some crucial form of personal data needed by the first organization. We see such symbiotic relationships in countless settings – the use of passenger flight information by anti-terrorist agencies, for example, or the use of information on French citizens' addresses generated by the use of that country's welfare state services for use by its tax authorities.

This knitting-together and symbiosis among surveillance systems obviously provides many efficiencies. More intense compilation of personal data by institutions, and the more seamless sharing of such data among them, multiplies their powers to achieve the ends assigned to them. American-style consumer credit reporting – where agencies can monitor virtually all consumers' use of credit in real time, regardless of consumers' preferences in the matter – undoubtedly does help credit grantors choose more profitably to whom they wish to extend credit, and to whom they do not. Tax authorities, by the same token, would certainly benefit from fuller access to data on taxpayers' consumption habits – e.g. their travel bookings or their supermarket choices. Such data would make it much easier to identify those taxpayers whose lifestyles are more lavish than the income they report for tax purposes would support. And certainly, law enforcement and anti-terrorist agencies of the state would benefit from complete access to all citizens' phone calls, e-mail correspondence, and website visits. It would be absurd to deny that such intense scrutiny could, under certain conditions, lead to the capture of terrorists or other law-breakers.

One can extend this list of benefits from existing and potential surveillance measures at length. Indeed, the possibilities are in fact endless. If I have any special contribution to make to debates about surveillance, perhaps it is the insistence that *there is no natural limit* to the realms of life susceptible to monitoring by large-scale institutions. There is no form of personal information, no domain of life that is so private, that it could not provide an attractive basis for decision-making by government or private organisations.

Mass surveillance, in the special sense I've ascribed to this term, manifests itself virtually wherever large institutions, governmental or private, seek to allocate discriminating treatment to very large numbers of otherwise anonymous individuals – giving each one just the right amount of credit; or allocating just the right degree of attention from anti-terrorist forces; or providing just the correct amount of social service benefits; or holding taxpayers responsible for precisely the tax obligations owing from them – in light of their unique circumstances. As new forms of data become available about individuals, and new ways are imagined for using existing data to achieve such discriminating institutional treatments, new areas of life fall under the sway of mass surveillance.

There is absolutely no reason to believe that innovation has run its course in these respects. On the contrary, I hold that institutions will continue to identify new forms of personal data, new areas of life, which when monitored will yield new and more attractive ways to shape treatment of the people concerned. If there is indeed no natural limit to the proliferation of surveillance, the only possible limits are those of human device. By this I mean legislation and policy that simply declare certain forms of monitoring of people's lives *off limits* to surveillance – even when the ultimate aims of the effort have the widest support. This is a stand that legislators and policy-makers have had great difficulty in taking.

True, sometimes they rise to the challenge. Recently the CNIL, France's national privacy protection agency, considered an intriguing request from an insurance company to exploit a new form of personal data. The company wanted to offer insurance at special rates to drivers who would agree to have their cars fitted with GPS devices. These devices would transmit the speed and whereabouts of the car – making it immediately apparent how much the car was being used, and, most importantly, the speeds at which it was being driven. Preferential rates were to be offered to drivers who kept within speed limits – while speeders would be penalised with higher insurance charges (Devillard 2005).

The aims of this ingenious extension of surveillance could hardly be more worthy: to encourage safe, law-abiding driving habits by rewarding good drivers. And there is no reason why the proposed scheme could not have been administered in perfect conformity with the consensus privacy protection principles noted above – collecting no personal data without the subject's consent, for example; or, respecting rights of participants to see and challenge their files; or observing due process rules for decision-making based on the records, etc. It would constitute, in short, yet another example of extension of mass surveillance to new realms of once-private life – accomplished with all the standard privacy guarantees.

Yet the CNIL refused to approve the scheme. It characterised the proposed monitoring as 'trafficking in people's liberty of movement'. 'Consent does not suffice', the CNIL noted, 'to make any use of personal information legitimate'. Some forms of surveillance, the CNIL was saying, are simply excessive, even when carried out for the best of purposes. The gains in efficiency were held not warrant the loss to privacy.

This stance by the CNIL represents a significant stand for privacy values in their pure form – and a rare one, I think, in global comparison. It is hard to imagine the UK Information Commissioner challenging such an obviously privacy-invading imposition, if it were indeed carried out with consent from all parties. Yet this is just one of a continuing stream of innovations in collection and use of personal data, most of which are not subject to institutional scrutiny like that of the CNIL. The accretion of such innovations clearly is moving us toward a world with ever-smaller areas of life free from monitoring by large institutions.

If we do not wish to inhabit such a world, I've suggested, our only choice is to apply a standard born of our own convictions on the value of privacy considerations – as the CNIL did in this case.[4] That is, we need to reject certain forms of monitoring as excessive in their demands on privacy, even where they meet all the standard criteria of good practice in treatment of personal information. That inevitably means elevating privacy as an abstract good above values of efficiency – in the form of profit, security, public security and a host of other considerations that are difficult to trump in any public arena.

And doing this requires some systematic, and strictly normative, rationale as to the point at which institutional scrutiny of once-private life simply becomes excessive, even in good causes. This is a task that privacy-protection thinkers have hardly begun to engage.

Notes

1 The Directive showed the influence of a number of earlier international agreements of principle on privacy issues, including the OECD Guidelines and the European Convention on Human Rights. See Bygrave (2008).
2 HSBC application form, collected from a London branch bank, May 2004.
3 For more detail on the birth of credit scoring and its application to the screening for insurance, see Rule (2007: 101–2 and 108–9).
4 For more detailed consideration of the essential 'goods' implicated in the defence of privacy, see Rule (2007: 182–9).

References

Bennett, C. and Raab, C. (2003) *The Governance of Privacy: Policy Instruments in Global Perspective*. Burlington, VT: Ashgate.
Bygrave, L.A. (2008) 'International agreements to protect personal data', in J.B. Rule and G. Greenleaf (eds) *Global Privacy Protection: The First Generation*. Cheltenham: Edward Elgar.
Devillard, A. (2005) *Les assureurs interdits de suivre a la trace leurs clients* [Online]. Available at: http://www.01net.com/editorial/298941/les-assureurs-interdits-de-suivre-a-la-trace-leurs-clients/ [accessed 9 December 2008].

Rule, J.B. (1973) *Private Lives and Public Surveillance*. London: Allen Lane.
Rule, J.B. (2007) *Privacy in Peril*. New York: Oxford University Press.
Rule, J.B., McAdam, D., Stearns, L. and Uglow, D. (1980) *The Politics of Privacy*. New York: New American Library.

Chapter 2

Building it in: the role of privacy enhancing technologies (PETs) in the regulation of surveillance and data collection[1]

Benjamin J. Goold

What are the proper limits of state surveillance? This is a question that has been asked repeatedly over the past 50 years by privacy advocates, civil libertarians, and others concerned about the steady expansion in the surveillance powers of the modern state. Although few would suggest that countries like the US and the UK are on the verge of descending into some sort of Orwellian, surveillance-fuelled nightmare, the fact that the means of surveillance available to governments already well outstrip those depicted in *1984* clearly points to the need for careful thinking about whether greater limits should be imposed on electronic communications, public area CCTV, and data sharing. Are there aspects of an individual's private life that should never be made the subject of surveillance? Do we have any expectation to privacy in public spaces? How do we ensure that new surveillance technologies do not fundamentally change the balance of power between the citizenry and the state?

Assuming that we are able to reach some sort of broad agreement about such issues, the question then arises as to how best to police and enforce these limits. In the past, when any sort of consensus has been reached – on matters such as wire-tapping and covert CCTV surveillance[2] – the tendency has been to turn to the law as the primary means of restraining the surveillance activities of the state. In the UK, for example, legislation such as the Data Protection Act 1998 and the Regulation of Investigatory Powers Act 2000 provides a reasonably robust – if perhaps overly complex – framework for the authorisation and scrutiny of various forms of police surveillance, as well as a set of legally enforceable safeguards designed to prevent abuse of power and unlawful intrusions into the lives of private individuals. Yet while such legislation has made certain forms of government surveillance more transparent and accountable, there are good reasons to think that this approach is unlikely to succeed in the future. Instead, as surveillance technologies become more sophisticated and the surveillance capacity of the state expands, it will become increasingly hard for the law to act as a effective brake on the more intrusive instincts of law enforcement agencies such as the police and the security services. As a consequence, there is a pressing need to explore new means of controlling and limiting government-sponsored surveillance, and to incorporate these techniques and technologies into existing regulatory networks.

Following a brief examination of the problems of legal regulation, this chapter focuses on the role that can be played by privacy enhancing technologies (PETs) in the regulation of state surveillance. In particular, it argues that such technologies should be given far greater prominence in our thinking about the regulation of surveillance, and seen not as a technological curiosity but rather as an essential part of any new regulatory strategy. As the technology of surveillance becomes increasingly sophisticated, it will not be enough for lawmakers to impose restrictions on the use of such technologies from the 'outside'. Instead, limits will also need to be 'built' into the technologies themselves, with a view to making certain forms of surveillance not only illegal but also technically impossible.

The inadequacies of legal regulation

Although the enactment of legal rules and regulations is perhaps the most common means by which we try to define and limit the powers of government, there are a number of reasons why the law is ill-equipped to deal with the challenge posed by state surveillance to individual privacy and any commitment to open, accountable government. First and foremost, because the law is largely a reactive institution – that is, new laws and legal regulations are usually passed after long deliberation and in response to significant development or change – it will almost always lag behind technical advances in the field of surveillance. Even if we assume that there is sufficient political will and genuine desire on the part of successive governments to ensure that regulatory frameworks keep pace with technological change, new surveillance technologies continue to emerge at such a rate that it is hard to imagine even the most attentive and diligent lawmakers will be able to keep up.[3] This has been particularly the case in the United States, as Colin Bennet has observed:

> The approach to making privacy policy in the United States is reactive rather than anticipatory, incremental rather than comprehensive, and fragmented rather than coherent. There may be a lot of laws, but there is not much protection.
>
> (Bennett 1997: 113)[4]

While it may be possible to alleviate this problem with broad legislative drafting and the creation of independent regulators with extensive discretion, this is only a partial solution. Passing broadly drafted legislation simply shifts the responsibility of defining the limits of surveillance to the courts, who may – not unreasonably – be unwilling to impose restrictions above and beyond those specifically endorsed by parliaments.[5] Equally, while independent regulators – such as the Information Commissioner in the UK – clearly have a role to play, they typically lack the resources and legal powers necessary to ensure that the use of new surveillance technologies is adequately scrutinised and restricted, a point that has been stressed in a recent independent report into data sharing by the UK Information Commissioner (Thomas and Walpart 2008). Furthermore, the law is also unlikely to be able to respond sufficiently quickly or effectively to new surveillance techniques and technologies that differ radically from those that have come before, and which as a consequence present an entirely novel – and possibly poorly understood – threat to individual privacy and state accountability.

As a case in point, despite the fact that the introduction of CCTV into town and city centres across Britain in the 1990s marked one of the largest expansions in state surveillance in history, CCTV remains largely unregulated to this day (Goold 2004). In part, this is due to the fact that by the time lawmakers realised the potential of this technology and the dangers accompanying it, many CCTV schemes already were up and running and tens of thousands of cameras were in operation. Although in recent years various Parliamentary committees and academic commentators have considered the question of whether CCTV should be subject to greater legislative control (House of Commons Home Affairs Committee 2008; Goold 2006), any proposed legislation would now have to take into account the huge financial and institutional investment that has been made in this technology. Any suggestion that CCTV surveillance be significantly curtailed or severely limited by law is, therefore, unlikely to receive much support, or be seen as a viable option. Instead, the best that can be hoped for is that legislation will be introduced which makes it more difficult for the police and local authorities to expand their existing CCTV networks or enhance them with new features such as parabolic microphones or motion tracking sensors.

Aside from the problems created by its inability to keep up with developments in the field of surveillance, there are many other reasons why the law alone is unlikely to be able to act as an effective constraint on the surveillance powers of the state. These include:

(i) The difficulty of detecting illegal surveillance and invasions of privacy

By its very nature, a great deal of government surveillance is covert. For example, the interception of electronic communications and data mining by the police and other law enforcement agencies are typically undertaken without the knowledge of the individuals placed under surveillance. Furthermore, unless those individuals are eventually prosecuted and given the opportunity to view the evidence against them, they may never discover that they have been the subjects of surveillance. In light of this, it is very difficult for members of the general public to determine whether they are under surveillance and whether this surveillance is being carried out in accordance with the law.[6] Although I may, for whatever reason, believe that my telephone is being tapped or my e-mails monitored by the government, typically there is no easy way for me to determine whether this is in fact the case, or to ensure that my privacy is being properly respected. Without this knowledge, even if the regulatory regime includes a complaints procedure and provides for the imposition of sanctions against the government, without the necessary information I am in no position to make a complaint, seek a legal remedy, or demand that the surveillance is brought to an end. In short, covert surveillance creates a regulatory Catch-22: because much surveillance is covert, I cannot know I am under surveillance; but unless I know that I am under surveillance, I cannot use the law to determine whether that surveillance is lawful.

A similar point to this has been made by Daniel Solove, who has argued that US privacy statutes are particularly hard to enforce by virtue of the fact that it is extremely difficult for individuals to trace the source of any illegal disclosure of personal information:

A person who begins receiving unsolicited marketing mail and email may have a clue that some entity has disclosed her personal information, but that person will often not be able to discover which entity was the culprit. Indeed, the trade in personal information is a clandestine underworld, one that is not exposed sufficiently by federal privacy regulation to enable effective enforcement

(Solove 2004: 71–72)

In many jurisdictions, the response to this problem has been to establish a system of independent supervision that aims to ensure that the police and other agencies are not engaging in overly intrusive or unlawful forms of surveillance. In the UK, for example, the Chief Surveillance Commissioner is responsible for overseeing most forms of covert police surveillance, and for reporting any instances of illegality or malpractice.[7] Although the Commissioner's Annual Report is intended to provide the public with information about the extent of covert police surveillance, it can be argued that this does not provide anything like the level of transparency and openness required to ensure that the government does not abuse its surveillance power. Although the Commissioner is nominally independent, because the government answers to the Prime Minister, it is perhaps unreasonable to expect the public to take his Report or assurances about the effectiveness of the regulatory regime at face value. More crucially, because the Commissioner's Report only provides general information about government surveillance practices, individuals still have no way of knowing whether they themselves have been the subject of unlawful surveillance or monitoring. Without this information, they remain unable to make a complaint about or seek a remedy for any violation of their privacy. Put simply, the law cannot act as a defender of individual privacy or as a brake on the surveillance power of the state if it is impossible for individuals to know how and when that power is being used.

(ii) Imposing legal solutions is costly and time-consuming

In addition to the difficulty of detecting abuses of power and breaches of privacy, the law is also faced with another major problem when it comes to the regulation of state surveillance, namely the cost of imposing legal sanctions. Even if we assume that governments are willing to provide individuals – or independent regulators for that matter – with the information they need to detect breaches of the law and file complaints, the question then arises as to how the legal system should respond to such abuses. Simply providing members of the public with a cause of action – say, for breach of privacy – is unlikely to be particularly effective given that governments typically have both the time and resources to contest individuals challenges to their authority and surveillance activities carried out by agencies such as the police and the security services. As recent cases like *Liberty and Others v UK* have shown, it can sometimes take many years for a case against the government to work its way through the court system, during which time the surveillance in question is likely to continue unabated.[8] Moreover, by the time that a final judgment is handed down, the likelihood is that the government will have already obtained the information it was seeking. Even if the amount of compensation awarded is high, or some evidence obtained through the surveillance in question is rendered inadmissible, the fact that legal sanctions can take so long to be levelled means that they are unlikely to act as a sufficiently strong deterrent. This is especially likely where the government believes that there are issues of national security at play. It would, for example, be a brave politician who refuses to authorise a surveillance operation involving individuals who the police or security service claim are planning to carry out a major terrorist operation. Faced with the prospect of being held accountable by the public for failing to act and the prospect of losing a breach of privacy action at some indeterminate time in the future, the choice is unlikely to be a difficult one.

While it is true, of course, that legal sanctions can have the effect of altering future practice and clarifying under what conditions certain types of surveillance will be considered lawful and permissible, the fact remains that they are unlikely to deter the state from abusing its surveillance power as and when it deems it necessary to do so. This problem is also compounded by the fact that the basis of most legal actions against the state for unlawful surveillance will be grounded in notions of privacy, a notoriously weak right that is particularly susceptible to being 'balanced away' in the face of concerns about crime and national security (Goold 2006; Nissenbaum 2004). Because it is inherently difficult to define privacy and compensate individuals where it has been breached, even in those cases where a court concludes that a particular surveillance operation amounted to an unlawful invasion of privacy, it may still be hard for it to resist arguments from the government based on appeal to the greater good and the interests of public safety. Should, for example, all of the evidence obtained from a mass interception of electronic communications be deemed inadmissible simply because the privacy of some innocent individuals has been violated in the process? Should such practices be stopped or restricted on the basis that they can undermine privacy, even if they provide valuable information and intelligence that makes the majority of citizens safer and more secure? Given that most people would have difficulty defining what exactly has been lost in terms of privacy by having one's telephone conversations tapped (but not necessarily monitored), the courts risk being seen as acting disproportionately if they routinely favour privacy and seek to restrain the surveillance activities of the state.

Building in principled restraint and the role of privacy enhancing technology

In light of the limitations of the law and the difficulties associated with policing and enforcing any statutory regulatory regime, the question then arises as to whether there are other, more effective ways to limit the surveillance power of the state. Can we move, for example, to a regulatory framework that is proactive – rather than reactive – in its approach to surveillance? Is it possible to establish an effective – and efficient – system of checks and safeguards that does rely on the co-operation of governments and law enforcement agencies, or the vigilance of individuals and interested civil liberties groups?

One obvious solution to the problems identified in the previous section is to shift the underlying basis of regulation away from one focused on reactive, legal measures to one that seeks to limit the surveillance powers of the state at source. This could be accomplished in two complementary ways. The first would be through the articulation of a set of general, legally enforceable principles that seek to clearly define the limits of state surveillance and the conditions that must be fulfilled before any such surveillance – regardless of the purpose or technology employed – can be carried out. One example of such a principle would be the idea of data minimisation. Broadly speaking, this principle states that personal information should only be collected if it is directly relevant and necessary to accomplish a specified purpose, and that it should only be retained for as it is necessary to fulfil that purpose (Privacy Office 2007). According to this principle, agencies such as the police and security services would only be empowered to gather as much information as is minimally necessary to achieve their stated surveillance objectives, and no more.[9] By requiring all surveillance operations to conform with this principle – and building it into such things as internal

Codes of Practice and field manuals – this would help ensure that any government surveillance is proportionate to its aims, and that those carrying out the surveillance are forced to at least consider the issue of limits and boundaries.

Equally, requiring that all surveillance operations conform with an additional principle of minimal retention – that is, the idea that surveillance data should be destroyed once the specific investigation is over – may also focus minds and lead to a gradual change in the way in which law enforcement agencies think about their use of surveillance techniques and technologies. Certainly, the adoption of such a principle would mark a significant break with traditional principles of data retention, which typically specify the minimum period data must be held by a given authority. By shifting the emphasis from one focused on penalising organisations for not retaining data long enough to one that requires them to destroy such data after a certain time (or once it is no longer needed), the principle of minimum retention aims to protect privacy – in part at least – by reminding organisations that they do not have a right to retain data indefinitely, and that the individual retains ultimate ownership of that information. To some extent this approach mirrors that suggested by Laurence Lessig in his work on regulation and the law as 'code'. According to Lessig, it is important to recognise that the law is only one of a number of regulatory tools, and that other 'modalities' – such as social norms, markets and architecture – can and should also be deployed in our attempts to regulate such things as information practices and new technological developments. In this regard, it also echoes the approach suggested by Bennett and Raab, who have argued that – within any law-based regulatory framework – we need to be prepared to use and combine (in the sense of creating a mutual dependency between) a range of regulatory tools in order to carry out those regulatory tasks that the law, or any other single tool, is either ill-suited to or simply incapable of carrying out (see Lessig 1999a, 1999b; Bennett and Raab 2006).

What is crucial here is to recognise that the value of these two principles lies not simply in their ability to give rise to legal consequences in the event of breach, but rather in the way in which they seek to challenge the assumptions that underlie and drive organisational surveillance. One of the reasons why existing approaches to the regulation of state surveillance have had little effect on actual surveillance practices is because they focus almost entirely on defining the circumstances under which surveillance will be lawful, without providing practitioners with any overarching guidance as to the basis of these restrictions. It can be argued, for example, that one of the reasons why the police and others are inclined to break or subvert legal rules limiting their surveillance activities is because it is difficult for them to understand why those rules exist or to feel committed to them. By fleshing out some of the dimensions of personal privacy – and linking them to relatively clear ideas such as minimal information gathering and minimal data retention – we hopefully provide a better basis for good practice and self-limitation. Moreover, the articulation of clear principles that are deemed to apply to all forms of surveillance avoids the common problem of government agents having to determine to what extent restrictions placed on certain, established forms of surveillance applies to new techniques. Even if the law is – for the reasons noted above – unable to enforce compliance with these general principles, their simple articulation may, over time at least, work to transform the way in which individual agents and officials think about the exercise of surveillance powers.

Having said all of this, it is essential that the introduction of such principles is also accompanied by a shift in the way in which we think about the very design of surveillance technologies and the architecture of government information systems. From a regulatory standpoint, the objective should be to ensure – via detailed legal and technical requirements – that the tools of surveillance are self-limiting. In simple terms, there are two main ways in which this could be achieved. The first is to limit access to certain technologies as a matter of law, and to make it illegal for organisations to own or use particularly intrusive surveillance and data matching technologies. For example, it could be argued that as there is no obvious need for local government agencies to possess sophisticated, CCTV-based facial recognition software; they should be prohibited from purchasing such products by law. By taking this approach, the possibility of abuse is eliminated altogether, and as a consequence, the spread of surveillance in certain contexts can be effectively constrained.

The problem with this approach, however, is that it is inevitably blunt and unrefined. Although a local agency may not need such software on a daily or even monthly basis, there may be occasions when having that additional surveillance capacity is extremely important. As with any blanket ban, the danger is that we completely eliminate the potential benefits of surveillance as well as the costs. As a consequence, a second or more textured approach is, in the majority of cases, likely to be needed. In effect, mechanisms need to be put in place which limit the amount of human agency and discretion associated with surveillance, and which are capable of being adjusted according to the context in which that surveillance takes place and the legitimate purposes for which it is being used.

Arguably, the most promising means of achieving this type of restraint is through the use of what have come to be known as privacy enhancing technologies or PETs. Although PETs were originally software-based tools aimed at preserving the anonymity of computer users and protecting the confidentiality of information sent over the Internet, the term has now come to refer to any technology that is used to protect an individual's privacy.[10] According to a recent European Commission briefing paper prepared for the European Parliament and Council, common examples of PETs include:

- Technologies that automatically anonymise personal data and make it difficult for third parties to determine the origin of that information;

- Encryption tools, which aim to prevent hacking of information transmitted over the Internet;

- Cookie-cutters, which prevent third parties from placing cookies on an individual's computer in order to make it perform certain tasks without the user being aware of them; and

- Platform for Privacy Preferences (P3P) services, which allow Internet users to analyse the privacy policies of websites and compare them with the their preferences as to the information they wish to release.[11]

In its paper, the Commission suggests that encouraging the wider use of PETs would 'improve the protection of privacy as well as help fulfil data protection rules', and as a consequence it calls on the European Union to take a more active role in promoting the development and adoption of these forms of technology.[12] While such moves are to be welcomed, they do not go far enough and are indicative of a continued – and misplaced – belief in effectiveness of legal rules as the primary basis of regulation. By treating PETs as a desirable adjunct to the existing legal framework, the Commission fails to appreciate the seriousness of the challenge it faces, or the need to break the reactive cycle of surveillance regulation. It is not enough to simply encourage the greater use of PETs: instead what is needed is a legal model that places them at the very heart of the regulatory project, and which makes their development and adoption mandatory. Manufacturers of existing surveillance systems should, for example, be required by law to 'build in' certain key privacy enhancing features that government agencies would then be required to use and prohibited from disabling. Furthermore, companies developing new technologies should also be required to design in privacy and limiting mechanisms in order for their products to be licensed for sale. In much the same way as motor companies are required to include airbags and other safety features in their new cars, producers of CCTV systems, tracking devices, and data surveillance software should also be required to 'build-in' privacy protections and mechanisms aimed at preventing users from misusing the technology.[13]

This 'technologically-enhanced' approach to surveillance regulation has a number of key advantages over existing systems that rely primarily on the imposition of legal rules and sanctions. Most significantly, it does not focus solely on modifying the behaviour of those carrying out surveillance activities, or requiring those individuals to interpret the legal restrictions that have been placed upon them. Instead, it explicitly recognises that there is a need to restrict what the technology can do and make it more difficult for government agencies and private organisations to engage in unlawful or overly intrusive surveillance. A simple analogy to this approach is that currently taken by some government organisations and private companies to the use of the Internet by their employees. Whereas in the past employees would have been told that it was inappropriate to visit certain websites while at work or while using computers on their employer's network, today many organisations use sophisticated software which simply makes it impossible for individuals to access these sites. Rather than rely on the individual employees to understand and follow the rules, the employer simply makes it extremely difficult or impossible for them to break them. In a similar way, surveillance technologies should be limited in terms of their accessible capabilities, with the result that those using them are forced to respect individual privacy and the requirements of the law.

The second major advantage of this approach is that it is proactive and preventative, rather than reactive and punitive. Because it focuses on preventing unwanted forms of surveillance and on limiting what government agents can do, in principle it should also reduce the number of abuses and the need for costly external oversight and complaints procedures. If, for example, CCTV systems are designed so that it is simply impossible for an operator to train them on residential buildings – by building in context sensitive 'privacy zones'

– then the need for close, independent oversight of the day-to-day use of these systems is reduced.[14] Equally, if we can reduce the number of abuses by 'designing out' bad practices and illegal behaviour, then the number of genuine complaints that need to be dealt with by the courts will be reduced.[15] This in turn has the potential both to substantially reduce both the cost of carrying out surveillance and to ensure that the privacy of individuals is respected.

Finally, the third advantage of this approach is that it forces both producers and users of surveillance technologies to regard surveillance capacity and legality as inseparable, and therefore encourages them to regard privacy-enhancement as a positive aspect of the technology. At present, companies producing interception technologies, CCTV cameras, and data mining software have no incentive to think about matters of privacy, or about the ways in which their products might be used. By making it a legal requirement for any such devices to have privacy enhancing technologies 'built in', however, such companies are forced to confront these issues, and to negotiate them with their potential customers. Here another analogy is instructive. Because car manufacturers are required, for example, to install emissions reducing technologies and certain safety features – such as seat belts and airbags – in their cars, it is now in their interest to regard these technologies as selling points and to convince customers that their implementation is for their benefit. In essence, they have been co-opted into the project of making the public more aware of the environment and the dangers of driving cars. Over time, the hope is that these values become internalised not only into the costs of these products, but also into the decision-making and choices of the individuals who buy them. In a similar fashion, by making privacy enhancement an essential part of any new surveillance technology, the aim is to bring about a fundamental change in the way in which people and organisations understand this technology, and to encourage them to see issues of surveillance and privacy as inseparable.[16] If every time an operator using a CCTV system strays into a residential area he is blocked by privacy zone software and reminded of the relevant law by an on-screen message, eventually attitudes will (perhaps begrudgingly at first) change and the value of personal privacy will be internalised.

Before moving on to a more detailed consideration of what a PETs-based regulatory framework might look like, it is perhaps worth noting that there is a certain irony to suggesting that the state should – as a matter of law – require government agencies and commercial organisations to adopt privacy enhancing technologies. Up until very recently, most PETs were developed and distributed by groups of computer-literate end-users as a way of preserving their privacy and resisting various forms of electronic surveillance, and tended to take the form of defensive techniques – such as email encryption and the use of low latency anonymity networks.[17] As a consequence, the idea that PETs should be built into all surveillance and data processing systems – and form a central part of any regulatory strategy – represents a major departure from the philosophy that has animated much of the PETs movement to date, and which is at its heart hostile to the very idea of surveillance. Taking this approach to the regulation of surveillance would also, in effect, amount to legitimising what many regard as an information technology counterculture, and transform a relatively marginal form of political resistance into a key component of the overall surveillance and data processing infrastructure of the state.[18]

Sketching a model of regulation: basic principles and privacy enhancing measures

If we assume that the future of surveillance regulation lies with a mixed model based on close harmony between legal and technological restrictions on surveillance capacity, then the first step towards developing such a model is to determine what, at a minimum, would be required to make such a system effective. Here, the challenge is to strike a balance between what is desirable and what is achievable, and to ensure that the two pillars of the model – legal rules and technical restrictions – complement rather than undermine each other.

As has already been noted, many existing systems of legal regulation lack any coherent guiding rationale or set of principles that can be used to develop new laws or interpret the scope of existing rules. In the context of the mixed model being proposed here, it is important to adopt principles that are both able to provide this coherence, but also capable of being reflected in technological terms. Clearly, the principles of data minimisation and minimal retention fulfil these two requirements, and as such can provide much of the foundation for this hybrid approach to regulation. It is not difficult, for example, to imagine a regulatory regime that starts from the assumption that, as a matter of law, surveillance activities must be minimal in their scope, particularly given that there is already a well-developed body of law surrounding related principles such as proportionality and necessity in many jurisdictions. Equally, the idea that data retention should be time limited is one that is already incorporated into many data protection regimes.[19] As a starting point, then, the regulatory regime should be founded on laws which make adherence to these principles mandatory, and which prohibit government agencies and private organisations from adopting technologies which have not been designed with these fundamental restraints in mind. Put another way, principles of data minimisation and minimal retention need to be imposed on both the users and the producers of surveillance technologies equally, with substantial resources being developing and enforcing a framework of regulation by design.

There is another basic principle that should also, ideally, underpin any new regulatory approach to state surveillance. Given that one of the dangers posed to individual privacy by surveillance is the sharing of personal information with agencies and organisations working outside the remit of the original surveillance operation or pursuing some other purpose, there is a need to ensure that data sharing is well regulated and accountable. Furthermore, as data processing and matching can radically transform the character and meaning of any information gathered via surveillance, it is important to ensure that such activities are also subject to restraint and have a defined, legally justifiable purpose. To this end, a third principle – that of minimal data sharing and processing – should be adopted and made part of the foundation of any new regulatory structure. Together, these three principles – of data minimisation, retention, and sharing/processing – would work in concert to ensure that each of the major stages of surveillance (collection, use, and storage of information) is subject to clear legal rules and meaningful technical restrictions, and that the overriding goal of any surveillance activity is limited to the acquisition and use of a minimal amount of personal information.

The question then arises as to how – in technical terms – to ensure that these principles are respected, and how to guarantee that they inform decisions about the design of surveillance systems and the adoption of particular privacy enhancing technologies. Clearly, these principles would first need to be articulated and understood in the context of a more general and overarching respect for individual privacy, and the explicit recognition of the fact that rights should not be normally subjected to utilitarian calculations or balancing exercises. More specifically, however, the regulatory regime would also need to specify exactly how producers and users of surveillance technologies might comply with them, and the technical limitations that they are expected to impose upon themselves before they embark on surveillance activities. Put another way, the police would be expected – before purchasing or operating new CCTV cameras or covert listening devices – to have indicated to potential suppliers that the technology in question must be technically capable of providing the sorts of safeguards required, and that it is compliant with data minimisation, sharing, and retention principles. At a practical level, this might mean that a CCTV supplier has to 'build in' privacy zone capabilities into their systems before offering them for sale, and also include automatic data management software that alerts the police as to when the time has come for them to dispose of digital footage. Potentially, the regulations could go further and specify that the technology should simply make it impossible – under normal circumstances – for the police to retain footage beyond a certain point, with files being automatically erased on a given date. Other examples of privacy enhancing technology that could be incorporated into existing surveillance might also include:

- Software that results in the automatic pixilation of faces captured by CCTV cameras, both in real time and in recordings (which could only be overridden by a controller in pre-defined circumstances);

- Software that encodes all surveillance recordings with digital rights management (DRM) restrictions, such that only authorised users could replay them;[20] and

- File management software that automatically deletes personal information once it has been held for a specified length of time.

Moving away from specific examples, we can construct a simple, relatively modest set of technical requirements that might be mandated by law, and which would need to be included in any new surveillance technology or monitoring system. These could include:

(1) A legal requirement that surveillance systems include self-limiting technologies, which can be set prior to the commencement of any surveillance operation to ensure that it does not exceed the purpose for which it was authorised and undertaken.

(2) Regulations specifying that all electronic data acquired via state surveillance must be automatically 'water-marked', and technical restraints be put in place to ensure that this information cannot easily be transferred, shared, or processed without the proper authorisation.

(3) New laws requiring that all communications within government regarding particular surveillance operations be made subject to electronic audit trails, and technical barriers be established to prevent communication across law enforcement and security agencies unless otherwise authorised.

(4) That government databases used for the storage of surveillance data be designed so that such data has a 'shelf life' and that erasure of that data will take place automatically unless there is deliberate, traceable human intervention.

While on their face these requirements may appear to be extreme, taken as a whole what they seek to establish is a fundamental realignment of the way in which governments think about surveillance and the use of personal information acquired without individual consent. Rather than assuming that the state has an absolute right to gather information about citizens, and that the role of the law is to circumscribe that right, instead this system starts from the premise that the state has no such right, and that at every stage surveillance, data sharing, and data processing should seek to minimise its effect on individual privacy. In legal terms, this approach amounts to a shift in the burden of proof – from the individual to establish why surveillance is excessive to the state to show why any action that violates privacy rights and data minimisation principles should be permitted. Furthermore, by requiring government agencies to take concrete steps towards building this new assumption into their surveillance systems, the law aims to change working practices rather than respond to violations once they become known.

More fundamentally, this approach also represents a new way of thinking about the relationship between law and technology in the field of surveillance. Although we are accustomed to the law laying down standards for consumer goods that are designed to protect the health and wellbeing of the general public, the law has been far less receptive to the idea that technology can provide a solution to some of the structural problems associated with attempting to regulate state surveillance activities. There is no obvious difference – in technical terms at least – between requiring car manufacturers to install airbags in all new cars and requiring the producers of CCTV systems to design their systems so that it is impossible to copy images onto memory sticks or keep camera footage indefinitely.

Conclusion

This chapter has sought, in a very general way, both to highlight some of the problems associated with regulating surveillance technologies, and to suggest ways in which the law and technology can work together to alleviate some of these difficulties. Although it does not attempt to provide anything more than a sketch of the way ahead, it nonetheless aims to bring to the fore a number of fundamental problems with the way in which successive governments in the UK and elsewhere have sought to reconcile developments in surveillance and data collection with the need to respect individual privacy and set proper limits on state power.

Of course, any such exercise is always open to the – not unreasonable – criticism that it is always easier to imagine regulatory frameworks than it is to implement them. Certainly, this chapter does present what might be regarded as an ideal model, which aims to ensure individual laws and future reforms are informed and restrained by broad principles, and to marshal technology as a tool for more effective regulation. While even a reasonably sympathetic government would probably find it difficult to accept or implement all of these recommendations, however, hopefully broad adherence to the principles set out in this chapter would at least prevent it from repeating past mistakes. One could also argue that the adoption – even in principle if not in practice – of this or a similar model would represent a major step forward, if only because it would mark a move away from the reactive, piecemeal approach to regulation that has marred much of the law-making in this area to date. Even a badly implemented regulatory framework that at least recognises the need for technical as well as legal restraints on surveillance is preferable to no plan at all.

Finally, it is perhaps worth emphasising that – despite the steady expansion in surveillance that has taken place over the past thirty years – we are still some way from living in an Orwellian state. Aside from the fact that most governments remain publicly committed to individual privacy and restraining the surveillance powers of agencies like the police and security services, the technology required to enable the state to make cheap and effective use of the vast amounts of data it routinely collects remains some way off. As a consequence, there is still time to strengthen our shared commitment to privacy through the law, and to construct the sorts of forward-looking, technologically enhanced regulatory frameworks that will be necessary as surveillance becomes even more ubiquitous. Unless we take this opportunity, however, there is a danger we may find ourselves living in a society that simply lacks the legal and technological tools required to stem the rising tide of surveillance, or to protect what might be left of our privacy in the years to come.

Notes

1 I would like to thank Simon Halliday, Richard Jones, Ian Loader, Daniel Neyland and Charles Raab for their comments on previous drafts of this chapter.

2 In most countries with extensive public area CCTV systems it is, for example, accepted that these cameras should not be trained on private residences or business premises. Equally, in countries such as the UK, US, and most of Western Europe, telecommunications cannot be tapped without some form of executive or judicial warrant.

3 This is a point that was made repeatedly by members of the Surveillance Studies Network in their report for the UK Information Commissioner. See Surveillance Studies Network (2006).

4 This is a point that has also been made by Lapperrière (1999), who argued that 'in the brave new world of global information law may seem to be a solution of the past ... Privacy legislation does not contribute significantly to reducing the collection and flow of personal data ... Law is essentially reactive or curative ... designed to punish abuse, not to restrain initiatives'.

5 This has been particularly true of the European Court of Human Rights, which has consistently shied away from expanding the ambit of the privacy rights contained in Article 8 of the European Convention on Human Rights to include public spaces. See, for example, the decision in *Friedl v Austria* (1996) 21 EHRR 83.

6 This is a point that has recently been acknowledged by the European Court of Human Rights in their decision in *Liberty and Others v UK* (application no. 58243/00, 1 July 2008). For a discussion of this case, see Goold (2009).

7 For the powers and responsibilities of the Chief Surveillance Commissioner, see the Police Act 1997, Part III and the Regulation of Investigatory Powers Act 2000, Section 62.

8 In *Liberty and Others v UK*, for example, it took just under nine years for the complaint to work its way to the Strasbourg court.

9 It is important to note that this principle would go some way beyond the Third Data Protection Principle as set out in Schedule 1 of the Data Protection Act 1998. Which requires that 'data shall be adequate, relevant and not excessive in relation to the purpose or purposes for which they are processed'. Here the shift from 'not excessive' to 'minimal' data collection aims to significantly reduce the ambiguity of the obligation being placed on public and private organisations.

10 Herbert Burket has, for example, defined PETs as 'technical and organisational concepts that aim at protecting personal identity' (Burket 1997).

11 Communication from the Commission to the European Parliament and the Council on Promoting Data Protection by Privacy Enhancing Technologies (PETs), Brussels, 2 May 2007, COM 228, p. 3–4. According to Data Protection Technical Guidance Note on PETs issued by the UK Information Commissioner on 11 April 2006, PETs can also take the form of 'encrypted biometric access systems that allow the use of fingerprint to authenticate and individual's identity, but do not retain the actual fingerprint; secure online access for individuals to their own personal data to check its accuracy and make amendments; software that allows browsers to automatically detect the privacy polity of websites and compares it to the preferences expressed by the user, highlighting any clashes; and "sticky" electronic privacy policies that are attached to the information itself preventing it being used in any way that is not compatible with that policy'.

12 Communication from the Commission to the European Parliament and the Council on Promoting Data Protection by Privacy Enhancing Technologies (PETs), Brussels, 2 May 2007, COM 228, p. 4–6.

13 It is worth noting that this approach differs somewhat from the 'Lex Informatica' model advocated by Joel Reidenberg. While according to the model set out in this chapter the state is responsible for ensuring that manufacturers and end users of surveillance technologies adopt particular privacy enhancing standards and technologies, in Reidenberg's schema 'the primary source of default rule-making is the technology developer and the social process by which customary uses evolve' (Reidenberg 1998).

14 'Privacy zones' are blacked out areas that appear in a CCTV image if the camera focuses on an area that has previously been designated as private by a scheme administrator. Typically, local government CCTV schemes in the UK employ this technology to prevent operators from looking in the windows on private residences or buildings, and to ensure that the scheme does not contravene the provisions of the Data Protection Act 1998 or the Human Rights Act 1998.

15 It is important to note that I am not suggesting here (or elsewhere in this chapter) that technologies such as PETs can eliminate human decision-making, or that it would be desirable to do so. Rather, the importance of PETs is based on the fact that they can be used to substantially reduce the likelihood that surveillance technologies will be accidentally or deliberately misused, and to encourage good practices and a gradual change in organisational culture.

16 In some respects this argument mirrors that made by David J. Smith in the context of situational crime prevention – namely, that we should not undermine the extent to which legal rules and regulations can transform behaviours and dispositions (Smith 2000).

17 A good example of such a group is the Electronic Frontier Foundation, which were instrumental in helping to establish the popular TOR network of anonymity servers.

18 I am particularly grateful to Richard Jones for this insight into the nature of PETs. One possible outcome of this legitimisation and the forced marriage between surveillance and PETs, however, may be an eventual transformation in the way we understand surveillance as a social phenomenon. Whereas in the past discussions of new surveillance technologies have tended to focus on the dangers for privacy and the threat to anonymity, the adoption of legal frameworks that require all new surveillance measures to be accompanied by privacy technologies may lead us to regard surveillance as a means by which privacy can be circumscribed in both positive and negative senses. In essence, the limits of surveillance and the limits of privacy would then converge, and the tension between them would become a more positive one, with each new advance in surveillance forcing us to redefine privacy and reaffirm our commitment to it as both an individual and a public good.

19 It is worth noting, however, that the current trend – at least in Europe as a result of the drive towards implementing the Data Retention (EC Directive) Regulations 2007 no. 2199 – has towards increasing the length of time which agencies and organisations are required to retain personal data. In this chapter, the principle of data minimisation proceeds from a different concern, namely with protecting the personal information of individuals (rather than enhancing the surveillance and law enforcement capacity of the state).

20 The use of DRM technologies as a means of privacy protection has been advocated by the Royal Academy of Engineering (2007), which argued in a recent report on surveillance that 'if personal data were protected by DRM technology, an individual could set controls over who was able to access data about them and could take steps to ensure that data are not shared with organisations who they would not wish to access their data. Moreover, an individuals' data would be protected from illicit use and copying by employees of companies using that data for fraud – or selling it to other individuals who would use it for fraud'.

References

Bennett, C.J. (1997) 'Convergence revisited: towards a global policy of the protection of personal data?' in P.E. Agree and M. Rotenberg (eds) *Technology and Privacy: The New Landscape.* Cambridge, MA: MIT Press, p. 99.

Bennett, C. and Raab, C. (2006) *The Governance of Privacy: Policy Instruments in Global Perspective* (2nd edn). Cambridge, MA: MIT Press.

Burket H. (1997) 'Privacy-enhancing technologies: typology, critique, vision' in P.E. Agre and M. Rotenberg (eds) *Technology and Privacy: The New Landscape.* Cambridge, MA: MIT Press, p. 123.

Goold, B.J. (2004) *CCTV and Policing: Public Area Surveillance and Policing Practices in England and Wales.* Oxford: Clarendon.

Goold, B.J. (2006) 'Open to all? Regulating open street CCTV and the case for "symmetrical surveillance"', *Criminal Justice Ethics*, 25(1): 3–17.

Goold, B.J. (2009) *'Liberty and Others v UK*: a new chance for another missed opportunity', *Public Law.*

House of Commons Home Affairs Committee (2008) *A Surveillance Society? Fifth Report of Session 2007–08* [Online]. Available at: http://www.publications.parliament.uk/pa/cm200708/cmselect/cmhaff/58/58i.pdf [accessed 28 November 2008].

Lapperrière, R. (1999) 'The "Quebec Model" of data protection: a compromise between laissez-faire and public control in a technological era' in C. Bennett and R. Grant (eds) *Visions of Privacy: Policy Choices for the Digital Age.* Toronto, ON: University of Toronto Press, p. 190.

Lessig, L. (1999a) *Code and Other Laws of Cyberspace.* New York: Basic Books.

Lessig, L. (1999b) 'The law of the horse: what cyber law might teach', *Harvard Law Review*, 113: 501–46.

Nissenbaum, H. (2004) 'Privacy as contextual integrity', *Washington Law Review*, 79(1): 101–39.

Privacy Office (2007) *Privacy Technology Implementation Guide.* Washington, DC: US Department of Homeland Security.

Reidenberg, J. (1998) 'Lex Informatica: the formulation of information policy rules through technology', *Texas Law Review*, 76: 553–84.

Royal Academy of Engineering (2007) *Dilemmas of Privacy and Surveillance: Challenges of Technological Change.* London: Royal Academy of Engineering.

Smith, D.J. (2000) 'Changing situations and changing people' in A. von Hirsch, D. Garland and A. Wakefield (eds) *Ethical and Social Perspectives on Situational Crime Prevention.* Oxford: Hart Publishing, pp. 147–74.

Solove, D. (2004) *The Digital Person: Technology and Privacy in the Information Age.* New York: New York University Press.

Surveillance Studies Network (2006) *A Report on the Surveillance Society* [Online]. Available at: http://www.ico.gov.uk/upload/documents/library/data_protection/practical_application/surveillance_society_full_report_2006.pdf [accessed 28 November 2008].

Thomas, R. and Walport, M. (2008) *Data Sharing Review* [Online]. Available at: http://www.justice.gov.uk/reviews/datasharing-intro.htm [accessed 28 November 2008].

Chapter 3

Regulation of converged communications surveillance

Ian Brown

Telecommunications and computing technologies have seen radical change over the last decade. The mainstream adoption of e-mail, mobile telephones and the Web and the growing use of peer-to-peer Voice over IP telephony have significantly altered the way we communicate.

Massive increases in computing and data storage capability have given states new tools for eavesdropping on these communications. The legal frameworks controlling such invasions of privacy have struggled to keep up. Using the extensive legislative framework recently developed in the UK as a case study, along with examples from other common law and European jurisdictions, this chapter will describe legal and technical measures that can be put in place to prevent the abuse of these powerful new surveillance technologies by governments.

Background

Communications have been surveilled for as long as long-distance communications have taken place. Julius Caesar famously encrypted messages in case they were physically intercepted (Kahn 1973). Queen Elizabeth I used messages intercepted and decrypted by her Secretary of State to convict and execute her cousin Queen Mary (Kahn 1973). From the earliest days of international telegraphy and telephony, governments reserved the right to intercept communications that were a threat to national security or public order (Drake 2000).

While the twentieth century saw revolutionary new communications technologies such as widespread radio and satellite communications, states were generally able to maintain this interception capability – initially through state operation of or influence over national monopoly telecommunications companies, and then through licensing and regulation of privatised providers such as British Telecom.

The last three decades however have seen technical and legal challenges to the ability of governments to intercept communications. The emergence of packet-switched networks (especially the Internet), offshore servers and peer-to-peer systems makes the acquisition of entire communications by wiretapping a small number of points in the network much more difficult. The civilian development of military-strength encryption makes it much harder to understand the contents of intercepted messages. And the vast quantities of data carried by fibre-optic cables makes it much trickier to pick out individual communications of interest.[1] Voice, video and data are all now carried by these 'converged' networks.

The move to digital communications networks has however made it easier for telephone companies to record 'communications data' about the source and destination of calls, and similarly for Internet Service Providers to log web site visits and e-mail details of their customers. Mobile telephony providers are also able to track the physical location of their customers' telephones. The explosion in digital storage capacity and computing power over the last 40 years has made it easier for large volumes of communications and communications data to be sifted and analysed (Brown and Korff 2004) – capabilities that have been fully exploited by intelligence agencies, especially those of the Second World War allies that have continued to co-operate under the UKUSA agreement (Campbell 1999).

At the same time, courts and legislatures have placed strict controls on the intrusion upon privacy caused by communications surveillance. From a situation of almost *carte blanche* to intrude on telephone calls and cable messages until the late 1960s (Diffie and Landau 1999), the US Supreme Court and Congress placed strict limits on federal and state government action through the *Katz v United States* decision,[2] the Omnibus Crime Control and Safe Streets Act of 1968 and the Foreign Intelligence Surveillance Act of 1978 (Solove 2006). In that same year the European Court of Human Rights found in *Klass and others v the Federal Republic of Germany*[3] that: 'Powers of secret surveillance of citizens, characterising as they do the police state, are tolerable under the Convention only in so far as strictly necessary for safeguarding the democratic institutions.'

Twenty years later the UK was forced to catch up by the European Court in *Halford v UK*,[4] and then by the incorporation of the European Convention on Human Rights into domestic law.[5] Most democratic states now limit government communications surveillance to certain purposes specified by law and overseen by judicial or other types of independent regulator.

Communications surveillance normally takes place under conditions of strict secrecy to avoid tipping off those targeted. The existence and activities of communications intelligence agencies such as the UK's Government Communications Headquarters (GCHQ) and the US National Security Agency (NSA) were denied for decades (Kahn 1973: 380). The product of communications intercepts is still excluded from UK court proceedings. How can the surveillance of modern communications networks using powerful computing facilities be kept under democratic control in order to guarantee the protection of citizens' human rights? How can states maintain public confidence against accusations such as those of ex-MI5 officer Peter Wright, who claimed that his colleagues had 'bugged and burgled their way across London' in an attempt to undermine the government of Harold Wilson? (Wright 1987).

This chapter discusses these questions within the law and technology framework first developed by Joel Reidenberg (1998) and Lawrence Lessig, in the particular context of the UK and other key jurisdictions. Lessig described four regulatory mechanisms that are applicable to highly technologised systems: Law, Norms, Market and Architecture (Lessig 1999). While law is widely considered in discussions of privacy and surveillance, these other three mechanisms have so far had a lower profile. How far can social norms, market procurement decisions and the architecture of communications networks and surveillance equipment complement law in restraining government power?

Access to communications and communications data

Surveillance of communications (the use of the post, telephone systems, the Internet, mobile phones etc.) comes under two separate regimes in UK law. Interception of content (what is said in a letter, phone call or e-mail) is authorised for three or six months (depending on the purpose) by the Secretary of State or Scottish Executive under Part I, Chapter 1 of the Regulation of Investigatory Powers Act 2000 (RIPA). Access to data related to the use of communications services may be self-authorised by a wide range of government bodies under Part I, Chapter 2 RIPA.

Interception of communications

Interception of the communications of a specific individual or premises may be requested by the heads of the Security Service (MI5), Secret Intelligence Service (MI6), GCHQ, Serious Organised Crime Agency (SOCA), certain police forces, HM Revenue and Customs, Defence Intelligence or other national government bodies under a treaty obligation (section 6(2) RIPA). It must be undertaken for one of the following purposes (section 6(3)):

(a) in the interests of national security;
(b) for the purpose of preventing or detecting serious crime;
(c) for the purpose of safeguarding the economic wellbeing of the United Kingdom; or
(d) for the purpose, in circumstances appearing to the Secretary of State to be equivalent to those in which he would issue a warrant by virtue of paragraph (b), of giving effect to the provisions of any international mutual assistance agreement.

Between 1 January and 31 December 2007, 2,026 warrants were signed by the Home Secretary and the Scottish Ministers. The number of warrants signed by the Foreign Secretary and the Northern Ireland Secretary is kept confidential, as even the level of surveillance undertaken against overseas targets is considered valuable intelligence.

Section 4(1) further provides that a UK operator of an overseas public telecommunications system may intercept such communications when required by the law of that state. Interception must be carried out for the purposes of a criminal investigation in a state party to a mutual assistance agreement designated under section 1(4) RIPA[6] – such as the European Union's Convention on Mutual Assistance in Criminal Matters of 2000.[7]

A warrant need not specify an individual or premises if it relates to the interception of communications external to the UK under section 8(4), which is the mechanism by which the government authorises intelligence agencies to undertake mass-surveillance of communications sent or received outside the UK, Channel Islands and Isle of Man.[8] Such warrants are wide-ranging and cover classes of traffic such as 'all commercial submarine cables having one terminal in the UK and carrying external commercial communications to Europe'. The Secretary of State must issue a certificate describing in general terms which information should be extracted from the resulting intercepted communications. Intelligence officials then undertake automated searches through this information looking for specific keywords. The resulting intelligence reports have identifying details of citizens or organisations that are incidental to the interception removed. Finally, these reports may only be disseminated to recipients who have a proportionate and necessary purpose to receive the information.[9]

Section 12 RIPA gives the Secretary of State the power to require that public postal services and telecommunications providers facilitate lawful interception of their network. This would include requirements to install interception devices that provide specific capabilities such as those mandated by the European Telecommunications Standards Institute Lawful Intercept standards[10] (e.g. the ability to intercept communications in real-time and to hide the existence of simultaneous wiretaps from each intercepting agency). Communications Service Providers may appeal these requirements to a Technical Advisory Board, constituted by representatives of intercepting agencies and CSPs, who will report to the Secretary of State on the technical and financial consequences of the order. The order may then be withdrawn or renewed. This procedure has yet to be used. Similar powers are contained in the US Communications Assistance to Law Enforcement Act of 1994.

As public telecommunications services, some Voice over Internet Protocol (VoIP) systems such as Skype would be subject to these requirements if provided by a UK company. These services commonly enable users to make calls wherever they are currently accessing the Internet. In some cases they allow users to bypass firewalls by connecting via a well-provisioned 'supernode'. In both cases, users under surveillance could have their communications routed via an interception point rather than directly to their recipient – although this might provide some indication that interception was taking place. In particular, calls between VoIP users and telephone systems could be intercepted at the bridge point between the networks, and by using standard telephony intercept techniques. Skype and other such VoIP software can also be automatically updated whenever a new version becomes available, which would allow 'bugged' versions to be installed remotely. Austrian Internet Service Providers have allegedly already installed equipment that allows Skype calls to be intercepted (Sokolov 2008). However, the programmers of peer-to-peer VoIP software that avoided providing such services would not be required to facilitate interception.

Intercepted information is expressly excluded from legal proceedings (section 17 RIPA) and can only be used for intelligence-gathering. This is because intelligence agencies do not want their operational methods revealed in court under defence questioning. However, the UK Government recently accepted the recommendations of the Chilcot Review (Chilcot 2008), which included removal of this exclusion. While the review suggests that few additional convictions will result, this will bring the UK into line with most other democracies – including both common law jurisdictions such as the US, Canada and Australia, and signatories to the European Convention on Human Rights such as France and Spain.

Bugging

When access to a telecommunications system is complex, another way to intercept a communication is to eavesdrop at one of its endpoints. Physical interference with property to plant a bug must be authorised by the Secretary of State under section 5 of the Intelligence Services Act 1994 (for MI5, MI6 and GCHQ) or senior police or HM Revenue and Customs officers under Part III of the Police Act 1997. When material of a legally privileged, confidential or journalistic nature could be acquired, a Surveillance Commissioner must approve police authorisations under section 97.

Intrusive surveillance of residential premises and private vehicles may be authorised by the Secretary of State, senior HM Revenue and Customs officials and chief constables under RIPA section 32. Except in urgent cases approval is also required from a Surveillance Commissioner. Police Act authorisation will also be needed if entry to or interference with property is required (Home Office 2002).

Agencies are also able to remotely break into computer systems to access communications and other types of data on those systems.[11] Section 10 of the Computer Misuse Act 1990 exempts law enforcement powers of inspection, search and seizure from its prohibitions on unauthorised access to computer material. Such access would require a combined RIPA s.32 intrusive surveillance and Police Act Part III/ Intelligence Services Act section 5 authorisation.

The German Constitutional Court recently placed strict limits upon the ability of government agencies to covertly observe the Internet and clandestinely access computers, PDAs and mobile phones. Building upon previous rulings on rights to 'informational self-determination' and 'absolute protection of the core area of the private conduct of life', the Court determined that:

> From the relevance of the use of information-technological systems for the expression of personality (*Persönlichkeitsentfaltung*) and from the dangers for personality that are connected to this use follows a need for protection that is significant for basic rights. The individual is depending upon the state respecting the justifiable expectations for the integrity and confidentiality of such systems with a view to the unrestricted expression of personality.

Such searches may therefore only be undertaken with judicial approval in cases where there are 'factual indications for a concrete danger' to the life, body and freedom of persons or for the foundations of the state – and not in normal criminal investigations or general intelligence work (Bendrath 2008).

Access to communications data

Access to 'communications data' – subscriber information, records of calls made and received, e-mails sent and received, websites accessed, the location of mobile phones – is regulated under Part I Chapter 2 of RIPA since this was brought into force in January 2004. Previously, this data was accessed by a wide variety of agencies using powers from the common law and various pieces of legislation, including national security, crime prevention and taxation exemptions contained in the Data Protection Act 1998 (sections 28 and sections 29).

Telephone companies and Internet Service Providers typically store communications data for business purposes such as billing and fault diagnosis. Voice over IP service operators such as Skype that operate centralised directory services are also able to log users and calls (Leyden 2006). Mobile telephones can be tracked in near real-time using a live stream of location data from operators.

The statutory Acquisition and Disclosure of Communications Data Code of Practice (Home Office 2008a) expands on the vague definitions of communications data given in RIPA. 'Traffic data' (sections 21(4)(a) and 21(6)) is attached to a communication and includes:

- Identity information relating to a person, apparatus or location e.g. calling line identity and mobile phone cell site location details.
- Data identifying or selecting apparatus e.g. routing information.

45

- Signalling information to actuate apparatus. To cover 'dial-through fraud'.
- Packet headers that indicate which communications data attach to which communications.

'Service use' information (section 21(4)(b)) is data held by a telecommunications company about their customers' activities, such as itemised call and connection records and services used.

'Subscriber information' (section 21(4)(c)) relates to the customer receiving a telecommunications service – for example, the owner of a given telephone number or e-mail address, their payment or demographic details, or details of equipment used.

Communications data can be accessed for the following purposes under section 22(2) RIPA:

(a) in the interests of national security;
(b) for the purpose of preventing or detecting crime or of preventing disorder;
(c) in the interests of the economic wellbeing of the United Kingdom;
(d) in the interests of public safety;
(e) for the purpose of protecting public health;
(f) for the purpose of assessing or collecting any tax, duty, levy or other imposition, contribution or charge payable to a government department;
(g) for the purpose, in an emergency, of preventing death or injury or any damage to a person's physical or mental health, or of mitigating any injury or damage to a person's physical or mental health; or
(h) for any purpose (not falling within paragraphs (a) to (g)) which is specified for the purposes of this subsection by an order made by the Secretary of State.

The Regulation of Investigatory Powers (Communications Data) (Additional Functions and Amendment) Order 2006 adds two further purposes:

(a) to assist investigations into alleged miscarriages of justice;
(b) for the purpose of:
(i) assisting in identifying any person who has died otherwise than as a result of crime or who is unable to identify himself

because of a physical or mental condition, other than one resulting from crime, or

(ii) obtaining information about the next of kin or other connected persons of such a person or about the reason for his death or condition.

A very large number of central and local government departments are able to access certain types of communications data simply by having a senior official make a request to a Communications Service Provider.[12]

The Interception of Communications Commissioner commented in his 2004 report that: 'In addition to the agencies covered by Chapter I of Part 1 of RIPA, and the prisons (138 in number) there are 52 police forces in England, Wales, Scotland and Northern Ireland and 510 public authorities who are authorised to obtain communications data, all of whom will have to be inspected. This is clearly a major task which could not be carried out by one person.'[13]

In his report on 2007 the Commissioner noted for the first time the total number of requests for communications data. Public authorities in total made 519,260 requests.[14] The report provided no further breakdown of the types or purposes of requests.

Retention of communications data

The major change in the UK interception regime resulting from the attacks on the US of September 11, 2001 came in the Anti-Terrorism, Crime and Security Act 2001 (ATCSA) Chapter XI. This gives the Home Secretary the power to require the retention of communications data (but not the content of communications) by phone and Internet companies for periods specified by secondary legislation. While this retention takes place for the purposes 'directly and indirectly related' to national security, the Home Office has consistently argued since then that communications data retained under these provisions may be accessed for any of the purposes specified in RIPA. The Home Secretary told the House of Commons that opposition attempts to limit this access showed 'how stupid the Liberal Democrats are'.[15]

Despite the claimed urgency of these powers, they were never brought into force. The House of Lords added a 'sunset' provision to the powers that caused them to expire unless they were used or renewed; the government by order twice renewed the powers, in

December 2003[16] and December 2005,[17] but then allowed them to lapse in anticipation of forthcoming European legislation.

The Home Office has instead come to 'voluntary' agreements with unnamed communications service providers under which they retain agreed communications data. The Code of Practice on Data Retention approved by Parliament in December 2003[18] governed the period for which each type of data was retained.

The UK Government was the main driving force behind the European Union Data Retention Directive[19] that was adopted on 15 March 2006. This directive requires EU member states to introduce data retention legislation requiring the storage of communications data for a period between six and 24 months. However, the directive allows member states to take a further three years to require the retention of data related to Internet usage; sixteen member states including the UK exercised this option.[20] The UK is now consulting on which specific communications data should be retained by public communications providers (Home Office 2008b), and have proposed the following (based closely upon the Directive):

Fixed network and mobile telephony	Internet access, Internet e-mail or Internet telephony
The calling and dialled telephone number and, in cases involving supplementary services such as call forwarding or call transfer, any telephone number to which the call is forwarded or transferred.	The user ID allocated, plus the telephone number allocated to any communication entering the public telephone network.
The name and address of the subscriber or registered user of any such telephone.	In the case of internet telephony, the user ID or telephone number of the intended recipient of the call.
The date and time of the start and end of the call.	The name and address of the subscriber or registered user to whom an Internet Protocol (IP) address, user ID or telephone number was allocated at the time of the communication.
The telephone service used.	
The International Mobile Subscriber Identity (IMSI) and the International Mobile Equipment Identity (IMEI) of the telephone from which a mobile telephone call is made and of the telephone dialled.	The date and time of the log-in to and log-off from the internet access service.
	The IP address, whether dynamic or static, allocated by the internet access service provider to the communication.

In the case of pre-paid anonymous mobile services, the date and time of the initial activation of the service and the cell ID from which the service was activated.

The cell ID at the start of the mobile communication.

Data identifying the geographic location of cells by reference to their cell ID.

The user ID of the subscriber or registered user of the internet access service.

In the case of internet e-mail or internet telephony, the internet service used.

In the case of dial-up access, the calling telephone number in any other case, the digital subscriber line (DSL) or other end point of the originator of the communication.

Under the proposals this data would be retained for twelve months. This period may be varied between six and 24 months by a written notice from the Secretary of State to a communications provider.

The German Constitutional Court recently issued a preliminary decision on the German implementation of the data retention directive. While permitting data to be stored, the Court limited its use by law enforcement agencies to the investigation of serious crimes where evidence is not otherwise accessible or sufficient, and with a judicial warrant (Manolea 2008).

Encryption

The development of cryptography since the late 1970s has been at least as revolutionary as the concurrent advances of the Internet. Encryption was previously an arcane skill limited mostly to diplomacy and combat. The academic invention of public-key cryptography in 1976 (Diffie and Hellman 1976), followed by its implementation in open source software such as Pretty Good Privacy in the early 1990s (Diffie and Landau 1999), meant that Internet users could protect their communications as strongly as the most technically sophisticated governments. Properly encrypted messages will remain impervious even to multi-billion dollar intelligence agencies such as the US National Security Agency.

Many governments tried, and failed, to block the spread of encryption software (Hosein 2003). It is now built in to Web browsers, e-mail clients and Voice over IP software. E-commerce and Internet security rely on the widespread availability of encryption software. More recent developments include the availability of anonymising networks like Tor (Dingledine *et al.* 2007) and Mixminion (Danezis *et al.* 2003), which mask the source and recipient of communications by encrypting and rerouting messages through nodes that can be located anywhere on the Internet.

The UK has ended up with an uneasy compromise in Part III of RIPA, which gives government agencies powers to serve notices requiring that individuals decrypt a given encrypted message, or to provide the secret decryption keys or passwords that will allow access to protected information. These notices are authorised by senior officials, the Secretary of State or circuit judges, and can include a secrecy requirement that precludes their discussion with anyone except a professional legal adviser. Penalties for ignoring these notices are a two-year jail term, rising to five years for national security-related matters under section 15 of the Terrorism Act 2006 and for breaking a secrecy requirement.

Notices may be served on third parties who are providing encryption services. For example, an Internet Service Provider managing a Virtual Private Network or secure IP telephony services for a client could be required to provide access to unencrypted data traffic, or to the keys necessary to decrypt such traffic. When served upon a firm, notices must be given to senior corporate officers rather than technical staff who manage day-to-day security operations.

It is much more common for secure communications systems to leave control of decryption keys with clients. It would be technically possible for centralised systems such as Skype to support a 'man-in-the-middle' attack on encrypted communications, enabling a surveillance officer to masquerade as a surveillance target and relay communications to and from them. It would also be possible for Skype to remotely switch on weak encryption in a surveillance target's software. However, it seems that this type of co-operation – at least with police forces – has so far not been forthcoming (Wolff 2008). RIPA section 49(9) prevents the seizure of secret keys from companies where they are used only to authenticate other parties, rather than directly to encrypt information.

The access to protected information statutory code of practice (Home Office 2007) restricts the exercise of RIPA Part III powers. In particular, public authorities must obtain written permission from the National Technical Assistance Centre, a division of GCHQ, before serving a notice (section 3.10); and take special care when considering imposing a requirement to disclose a decryption key (Chapter 6). When such a notice is to be served on a company authorised by the

Financial Services Authority, the chief executive of the FSA must first be consulted (section 6.8).

These powers were only brought into force on 1 October 2007 and their use has so far been limited. In response to a parliamentary question the Home Secretary recently stated that eight notices had been served, four in terrorism related cases – in which two people have been charged with failing to comply.[21] The Court of Appeal in one of these cases recently dismissed a claim that these notices interfered with the right to a fair trial, in particular the right against self-incrimination, concluding that:

> In these appeals the question which arises, if the privilege is engaged at all, is whether the interference with it is proportionate and permissible. A number of issues are clear and stark. The material which really matters is lawfully in the hands of the police. Without the key it is unreadable. That is all. The process of making it readable should not alter it other than putting it into an unencrypted and intelligible form that it was in prior to encryption; the material in the possession of the police will simply be revealed for what it is. To enable the otherwise unreadable to be read is a legitimate objective which deals with a recognised problem of encryption. The key or password is, as we have explained, a fact. It does not constitute an admission of guilt. Only knowledge of it may be incriminating. The purpose of the statute is to regulate the use of encrypted material, and to impose limitations on the circumstances in which it may be used. The requirement for information is based on the interests of national security and the prevention and detection of crime, and is expressly subject to a proportionality test and judicial oversight. In the end the requirement to disclose extends no further than the provision of the key or password or access to the information. No further questions arise.[22]

The remaining four cases were investigators into conspiracy to murder; withholding information in relation to conspiracy to murder; conspiracy to defraud; and making indecent images of children (Williams 2008).

Oversight

The Interception of Communications Commissioner, a senior judicial figure appointed under RIPA Part IV to oversee the interception regime,[23] gives an annual report to the Prime Minister – who then presents a censored version to Parliament. Figure 1 below shows the number of warrants granted and in force[ay] since the commencement of RIPA.

The Chief Surveillance Commissioner and Intelligence Services Commissioner also have certain oversight responsibilities for the use of RIPA Part III powers on protected information and on Part II intrusive surveillance (alongside their responsibilities under the Police Act 1997 and the Intelligence Services Act 1994). Notices given under RIPA section 51(6) must be notified within seven days by the armed forces to the Intelligence Surveillance Commissioner and in any other case to the Chief Surveillance Commissioner. Under RIPA Part IV the Intelligence Services Commissioner must keep under review warrants for interference with wireless telegraphy, entry and interference with property; the activities of the intelligence services and armed forces outside Northern Ireland. The Investigatory Powers Commissioner for Northern Ireland reviews intrusive surveillance delegated under RIPA section 31.

Complaints about actions under RIPA by the police or HM Revenue and Customs, and more generally proceedings against the intelligence services, are heard under RIPA section 65 by the Investigatory Powers Tribunal. Under RIPA Schedule 3 its members are appointed for five years by the Queen, and must have held high judicial office or

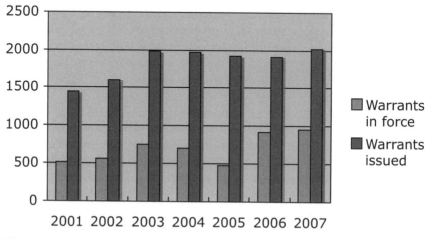

Figure 3.1 Interception warrants

(excepting the Tribunal President) been a barrister or solicitor for at least ten years. There are currently seven members of the tribunal, presided over by Lord Justice Mummery.

The complaints received and resolved by the Tribunal are shown in Figure 2.[25] In 2007 it received 66 new complaints and dealt with 83 cases. However, without requirements to notify after the fact those who have been put under surveillance, there will be little opportunity for those wrongly surveilled to make a complaint. The tribunal must further hear most complaints within one year of challengeable conduct taking place. It cannot consider cases where interception has been carried out without a warrant, and discloses limited information to a complainant (Crossman 2007: 26).

In November 2006 the Tribunal made its only ruling so far in favour of a complainant. It found that the Metropolitan Police had illegally intercepted telephone calls between their own Chief Superintendent, Ali Dizaei and the National Black Police Association, including legal advice to black and Asian colleagues in dispute with their police forces. While the ruling has remained secret, the Metropolitan Police Authority has summarised the judgment as part of its investigation into the legality of intercepts within a covert operation (Metropolitan Police Authority 2007).

The policy, administration and expenditure of MI5, MI6 and GCHQ are reviewed by the Intelligence and Security Committee, established

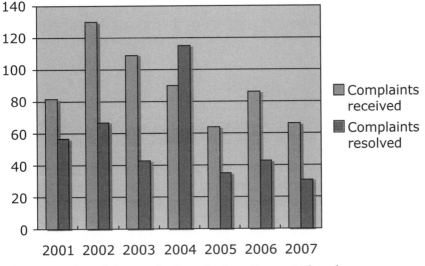

Figure 3.2 Complaints to the Investigatory Powers Tribunal

under section 10 of the Intelligence and Security Act 1994. The Prime Minister appoints for one parliamentary term nine members from the Houses of Commons and Lords, after consultation with the two leading opposition parties. The Committee makes an annual report to the Prime Minister, who lays a copy before Parliament after excluding any matters prejudicial to the continued discharge of the functions of the intelligence agencies.

The heads of the intelligence agencies may refuse to provide information to the committee from a foreign government, or that would identify sources, operational methods or particular operations. According to the Committee the government itself has only once refused to provide copies of papers (Home Office 2008c). In one of its most memorable statements, in 2001 the Committee found that the Investigatory Powers Tribunal was 'dependent on a tiny support structure which is quite incapable of carrying out the job. As we reported, there was not even anybody to open the mail, let alone process it, for many months. That was ludicrous'.[26]

Part II: Improving oversight and regulation

A policy cycle measured in years, combined with a European judicial process that can take over a decade to decide individual cases, will inevitably have difficulty keeping up with the rapid rate of change recently seen in communications technology. The secrecy of intelligence agency operations and the complexity of the *ad hoc* legislative framework that has evolved in response in the UK do not inspire public confidence or adequately protect human rights against the over-mighty executive of the UK parliamentary system (Hailsham 1976).

Under Article 8 of the European Convention on Human Rights, state interference with privacy must be 'in accordance with the law' and 'necessary in a democratic society'. The European Court has repeatedly ruled that 'law' must be detailed, precise and accessible; and that safeguards must be in place to prevent arbitrary interference.[27] A regulatory regime consisting of four acts, over thirty statutory instruments in seven years, multiple codes of practice, four separate Commissioners appointed by and reporting to the Prime Minister, and a pseudo-Parliamentary Committee with no statutory powers might be felt to have limited accessibility and safeguards. Even the distinguished judges of the Court of Appeal and House of Lords Appellate Committee have found the Regulation of Investigatory

Powers Act to be 'a particularly puzzling statute'[28] and 'perplexing'.[29] Only the most optimistic would consider the single case found in favour of the complainant by the Investigatory Powers Tribunal an indication of an adequate safeguard against abuse.

A number of legal measures have been suggested that could improve accessibility and reduce the potential for abuse of communications surveillance. Most significant are enhanced judicial scrutiny; merging and simplifying regimes for intercept, access to communications data and interference with property; and strengthening parliamentary oversight. The technological systems being used to implement surveillance could also be designed in ways that provide significant additional safeguards.

Judicial authorisation and consideration of evidence

The UK is unusual amongst democratic states in allowing politicians to authorise interception. Although the European Court of Human Rights has accepted executive authorisation in cases such as *Klass v Germany* it found at the same time that:

> If the bounds of necessity in a democratic society were not to be exceeded in a field where abuse was potentially so easy in individual cases and could have such harmful consequences for democratic society, it was in principle desirable to entrust supervisory control to a judge, in accordance with the rule of law, since judicial control offered the best guarantee of independence, impartiality and a proper procedure.

These words ring true 30 years later. As is taken for granted in the United States, judicial authorisation and supervision of communications surveillance is the single most important regulatory protection for human rights and safeguard against abuse (Crossman 2007: 24–34).

While the US Sixth Circuit Court of Appeal found that plaintiffs had no standing[30] to challenge an executively authorised surveillance programme instituted by President Bush shortly after the 9/11 attacks,[31] a lower court found that the so-called Terrorist Surveillance Program breached various Bill of Rights protections. District Judge Anna Diggs Taylor concluded that: 'the public interest is clear, in this matter. It is the upholding of our Constitution'.[32] The program was discontinued in January 2007. The FISA Amendments Act of 2008[33] brought the surveillance of Americans' international communications back under the control of the Foreign Intelligence Surveillance Court.

Judicial authorisation is not a theoretical nicety. The Home Secretary was responsible in 2007 for signing 1,881 warrants. If evenly distributed, that would represent more than five warrants every day of the year. It is an awesome responsibility for one individual so frequently to make nuanced decisions of proportionality and necessity at all hours of the day and night – and at all times to separate his political role from his quasi-judicial responsibilities. Former Home Secretary David Blunkett told *The Guardian* in 2006 that:

> At one point, I did really think I was going mad. My whole world was collapsing around me. I was under the most horrendous pressure. I was barely sleeping and yet I was being asked to sign government warrants in the middle of the night.
>
> (Glover and Wintour 2006)

More recently, the Metropolitan Police have been found to have illegally wiretapped one their own staff members and thereby risked damaging 'staff and community confidence' in the force (Metropolitan Police Authority 2007).

The UK Parliament's Joint Committee on Human Rights has also called for judicial oversight:

> We would prefer warrants for the interception of communications to be judicially authorised where the product of the intercept is intended to be used as evidence. In our view this would provide an important independent safeguard against abuse or arbitrariness in the exercise of the power to intercept. The number of interception warrants being issued or modified certainly suggests that it must be difficult for the Home Secretary to give much scrutiny to each request to sign a warrant.
>
> (Joint Committee on Human Rights 2007)

Even within RIPA, circuit judges must give certain Part III authorisations while the quasi-judicial surveillance commissioners must authorise most Part II intrusive surveillance. Part I warrants and notices stand alone in their exclusively executive nature. Judicial authorisation would better protect individuals' rights to a fair trial and to an effective remedy (Articles 6 and 13 ECHR) as well as to privacy. The powers of the Surveillance Commissioners to authorise bugging and burgling should similarly be transferred to the judiciary.

If the government wishes to set up a specific court for the granting of national-security interception warrants applying to external communications sent or received within the UK or concerning UK citizens (similar to the United States' Foreign Intelligence Surveillance Court), members of that court should be judges appointed by the Lord Chief Justice and their judgments should be reviewable by the Supreme Court (as is the case with the FISC). Such warrants would replace the certificates issued by the foreign secretary under RIPA section 8(4) that have recently been declared by the European Court to be incompatible with the foreseeability requirements of the Convention.[34]

As intelligence and law enforcement agencies build up large collections of communications data, consideration should also be given to judicial authorisation of the analysis of such data for patterns that might lead to suspicion against individuals. Germany is one of the few countries to have such procedures in place, in the specific context of the 'mining' of international communications that are indiscriminately collected by their signals intelligence agency. Under German law the so-called 'G10 Commission' must approve monitoring orders that include search terms appropriate to use in the investigation of those dangers described in the orders. The European Court of Human Rights has strongly approved of this procedure and described it as a model that shows up the flaws in the UK approach.[35]

Those undertaking this type of data mining must also keep in mind that its efficacy in identifying suspects continues to be highly controversial, with a recent report from the US National Research Council concluding that:

> Although laboratory research and development of techniques for automated, remote detection and assessment of anomalous behavior, for example deceptive behavior, may be justified, there is not a consensus within the relevant scientific community nor on the committee regarding whether any behavioural surveillance or physiological monitoring techniques are ready for use at all in the counterterrorist context given the present state of the science.
>
> (National Research Council 2008)

The government's recent acceptance that intercept evidence should be allowed to be introduced as evidence in criminal cases[36] will add a safeguard to the use of intercept powers. While the intercepting agency will retain the ability to block prosecutions from going ahead if they feel their operational methods might be compromised, the ability of courts to scrutinise the use of intercepts will allow the case law that is so far largely lacking in this area to better map out the circumstances in which interception is considered proportionate and necessary. Expert witnesses have long been sceptical of the reasons previously given to prevent the production of intercepted evidence in court (Sommer 2006).

If the government wishes to retain a specialist Investigatory Powers Tribunal to consider wrongdoing by intelligence agencies, members should again be judges appointed by the Lord Chief Justice and their judgments be reviewable by the Supreme Court. To further promote public trust the Draconian restrictions on disclosure of information to complainants under RIPA and The Investigatory Powers Tribunal Rules 2000 should be relaxed, and the use of security-cleared Special Advocates appointed by the Law Officers strictly limited. These actions were both recommended by Parliament's Joint Committee on Human Rights, which found that 'the Special Advocate system, as currently conducted, does not afford the individual the fair hearing, or the substantial measure of procedural justice, to which he or she is entitled under both the common law and human rights law' (Joint Committee on Human Rights 2007).

Merging and simplifying regimes for intercept, access to communications data and interference with property

As data mining technology has developed (Soar 2008) it is becoming ever clearer that the intrusiveness of state access to communications data is much closer to that of interception than to past police access to telephone bills. Monitoring an individual's lists of contacts, mobile phone location and websites visited impacts on rights to freedom of thought, expression, assembly and association (Articles 9–11 of the European Convention) as well as the right to privacy. The European Court has recognised the latter in judgments such as *Malone v United Kingdom*:

> The records of metering contain information, in particular the numbers dialled, which is an integral element in the communications made by telephone. Consequently, release of that information to the police without the consent of the subscriber also amounts, in the opinion of the Court, to an interference with a right guaranteed by Article 8[37]

It is also clear that as communications as well as documents are increasingly accessible via computer systems, it makes less sense for two separate regimes to exist in law to regulate searches and interception – especially where they are already forced to interact, as in Police Act authorisations for interference with property to install bugging devices.

A converged regulatory regime would be more accessible and a better match to modern converged communications systems. Combined with the judicial authorisation requirements common to searches, it would also provide better safeguards against abuse and more widely applicable guidance to intelligence and law enforcement agencies through case law.

Statutes and case law regulating physical searches are unsurprisingly better developed than those passed much more recently to regulate interception:

- The Bankers' Books Evidence Act 1879 allows a High Court Judge to order the inspection of bankers' books (including computerised accounts).

- The Police and Criminal Evidence Act 1984 (PACE) allows police investigating a serious arrestable offence to apply to a circuit judge for an order compelling a third party to produce confidential information in their possession.

- The Proceeds of Crime Act 2002 gives powers to police, customs and Asset Recovery Agency staff to apply to a court for a production order. The Director of the Asset Recovery Agency may apply to a judge for an order requiring a person to provide specified information related to an investigation. Investigators may also apply to a judge for a customer information order and account monitoring order, which requires a financial institution to supply information about customers and allow real-time monitoring of financial transactions.

- The Drug Trafficking Act 1994 allows production orders similar to those of PACE to be granted in relation to material that is likely to be of substantial value to the investigation of an individual suspected of producing, supplying, transporting, importing or exporting a controlled drug.

- The Terrorism Act 2000 and Anti-Terrorism Crime and Security Act 2001 provide police similar powers to PACE obtain materials relevant to a terrorist investigation. They also allow for production orders to apply to material which does not yet exist or is not yet in possession of the individual to whom the order is addressed, but will do so within 28 days.

A combined surveillance regime could simply update PACE orders to allow the High Court to authorise interception and related interference with property, intrusive surveillance and access to protected information (replacing ISSA 1994 section 5, the Police Act 1997 Part III and RIPA 2000 Part I Chapter 1, section 32 and Part III) and circuit judges to authorise access to communications data, directed surveillance and the use of covert human intelligence sources (replacing RIPA Part I Chapter 2 and most of Part II). Unauthorised access should be an offence (as it is under RIPA for interception but not access to communications data).

The sensitivity of traffic data and service usage information about individuals' locations, associates and websites visited justify a requirement for judicial authorisation. Rather than the many hundreds of public authorities given access to this data by RIPA, it should be limited to intelligence and law enforcement agencies. While the Interception Commissioner said in his most recent report that 'the local authorities could make much more use of communications data as a powerful tool to investigate crime,'[38] there has been intense public disquiet at rather disproportionate council use of related surveillance powers to undertake investigations into school admissions (Alleyne 2008) and a tax discount given to those living alone (Kirkup 2008).

An argument might be made that subscriber information – especially the name and address of the owner of a specific telephone number or e-mail address – is less sensitive than traffic data and service usage information. The sheer number of accesses to this type of data (estimated to be the vast majority of the 519,260 requests made in 2007) would also in practice make judicial authorisation extremely resource-intensive. It might therefore be acceptable to retain a self-authorisation procedure for this access – although it is not unknown for such 'reverse look-ups' to be misused (Reed Ward and Fuoco 2003).

In all cases, however, subjects should be notified of surveillance once that information would no longer prejudice an ongoing investigation. As stated in §36 of *Klass v Germany*: 'The Court finds it unacceptable that the assurance of the enjoyment of a right guaranteed by the Convention could be thus removed by the simple fact that the person concerned is kept unaware of its violation'. The Court also held that while notification could not take place in every circumstance, its default occurrence in Germany was a strong protection for individuals' right to an effective remedy where a violation of rights has taken place.

Strengthened Parliamentary oversight

In its recent Green paper on constitutional reform, the UK government has recognised that current parliamentary oversight of the intelligence agencies is lacking. It states: 'To ensure that these Agencies command full public support for, and confidence in, the work they do it is important that the representatives of the people hold them to account' (HMSO 2007).

Even before the government has consulted on reforms they suggest that the Intelligence and Security Committee could be moved closer in its procedures to a parliamentary select committee. This would include using standard select committee appointment procedures; allowing the Committee to meet in the Houses of Parliament; having the chair of the Committee lead a debate in the House of Commons on its reports; and strengthening the committee secretariat through the appointment of an independent investigator.

While these would be welcome steps, true parliamentary accountability would require the government to go further. In particular, the various surveillance and interception commissioners should be appointed by and responsible to the Committee rather than the prime minister. The commissioners' annual reports should be made directly to the Committee, whose members already hold the highest security clearance; the Committee should then decide which operationally sensitive parts of these reports should be withheld from publication. The commissioners might also refrain from beginning each report with genuflections toward those they are supposedly regulating, and be slightly less enthusiastic in explaining away errors. It cannot encourage public confidence to witness such gushing displays of regulatory capture as this:

> I have been impressed by the quality, dedication and enthusiasm of the personnel carrying out this work. They possess a detailed understanding of the legislation and are always anxious to ensure that they comply both with the legislation and the appropriate safeguards ... They are all skilled in their work and there is very little danger of any defective application being placed before the

Secretary of State ... The Agencies always make available to me personnel and documents that I have requested. They seem to welcome my oversight, as ensuring that they are acting lawfully and appropriately, and they seek my advice ... I am left in no doubt at all as to the Agencies' commitment to comply with the law. In case of doubt or difficulty, they do not hesitate to contact me and to seek advice.[39]

The commissioners' reports also need to contain far more detailed statistics on the circumstances and results of the use of surveillance powers if the Committee is to be able to come to a decision over their proportionality, as happens in the US.

Restrictions on the Committee's ability to investigate specific operational matters should also be swept away. Even if the Supreme Court were able to review decisions of the Investigatory Powers Tribunal, judges traditionally give wide discretion to the executive on matters of national security. Parliament must have the ability to investigate and take action if serious allegations of abuse are made.

This operational oversight is a key function of the intelligence committees of the US Congress, who even play a role in authorising covert operations and budgetary programmes (Surtevant 1992). The US Senate established its Select Committee on Intelligence to 'provide vigilant legislative oversight over the intelligence activities of the United States to assure that such activities are in conformity with the Constitution and laws of the United States'. A similar fundamental requirement should underpin activities of the Intelligence and Security Committee.

The ability of Parliament to effectively control statutory surveillance powers has been reduced as their details have been increasingly left to secondary legislation that cannot be amended or even in practice rejected. Parliament could regain this control with a more sceptical attitude to 'skeleton' legislative clauses that delegate key aspects to SIs. They could also insist on greater use of 'amendable' SIs,[40] which would allow Parliament for example to prevent specific agencies from accessing communications data under RIPA where a case had not been made that such access would be necessary or proportionate (Crossman 2007).

Parliament also needs much better data on the potential use of surveillance powers before it can make a proper assessment of their proportionality. During the debate over data retention statutory instruments, the Home Office relied on a 'business case' for the powers drafted by the Association of Chief Police Officers. The Foundation for Information Policy Research complained at the time that:

> The examples given by the Home Office concerning the use of communications data are entirely unconvincing. They largely concern time periods that are longer than those proposed for retention in existing plans. They do not attempt any cost/benefit analysis based on cases lost due to missing communications data. They certainly do not justify the very high cost that larger ISPs have estimated for retention mechanisms.
>
> (FIPR 2003)

This type of data should be routinely supplied to Parliament whenever proposals for new surveillance powers are made.

Technological checks and balances

It is a well-established principle of democratic polities that power should be separated and constrained by checks and balances within the architecture of government (de Secondat 1752) – such as the separation of executive, legislative and judicial functions; constitutional and human rights restrictions on majoritarian actions; and the division between federal, state and local government.

As technological systems enable ever-greater potential for government to control and micromanage day-to-day life, similar constraints must be applied to their architecture if human rights are not 'to a large extent be reduced to a nullity'.[41] In particular, systems should be designed to gather the minimum amount of personal data collected to that required[42] by government purposes that have received full democratic and human rights assent. There is otherwise a wearily inevitable process of 'function creep' whereby surplus data becomes used in new surveillance programmes with little or no democratic legitimacy (Whitley and Hosein 2005). In this sense architecture does not just shape policy (Reidenberg 1998) (or code shape law, Lessig 1999); it is more akin to constitutional law. Amendments to that 'law' have similarly long-lasting effect and should face correspondingly high hurdles of considered legislative consent and bipartisan approval.

In the UK we have seen the opposite, with sweeping surveillance powers left to statutory instruments that cannot be amended or even by convention rejected by Parliament. In the extraordinary 2003 parliamentary debate on various statutory instruments made under RIPA, a government peer told the House of Lords:

> When I was leading the Opposition, there were many occasions on which I took the view that what the then government were doing was absolutely appalling and that they had done it without sufficient consultation and discussion. I felt strongly that they should not do it. However, if a proposal came in front of the House as a statutory instrument, I did what all in opposition have done up until now; that is, I held my nose and did not vote against it ... If the Opposition choose now to go down that road, they should know where they are going. At the moment, we are the Government; one day, no doubt, we will be the Opposition. We have long memories.[43]

Legislators should also take care to prevent the deployment of technology that treats all citizens as suspects without any cause. On this fundamental human rights principle alone, requirements for data retention, restrictions on encryption, data mining of communications data and intercept-friendly communications networks should be firmly rejected. In its opinion on the Data Retention Directive, the Article 29 Working Party of European Data Protection Commissioners stated that: 'The decision to retain communication data for the purpose of combating serious crime is an unprecedented one with a historical dimension. It encroaches into the daily life of every citizen and may endanger the fundamental values and freedoms all European citizens enjoy and cherish'.[44] Explaining his decision to release his Pretty Good Privacy encryption software, programmer Phil Zimmerman told the US Senate: 'When making public policy decisions about new technologies for the government, I think one should ask oneself which technologies would best strengthen the hand of a police state. Then, do not allow the government to deploy those technologies. This is simply a matter of good civic hygiene.'[45]

A further case in point is the Communications Data Bill included in the UK government's forthcoming legislative programme (Office of the Leader of the House of Commons 2008). The government is considering including powers to centralise communications data in a government database, where it would be much more amenable to data mining and 'fishing expeditions' for unusual patterns of behaviour (Kablenet 2008). The current federation of communications data in separate locations under the control of telephone companies and Internet Service Providers, and hence the requirement for government agencies to serve notices on those companies to retrieve specific data (and cover the costs of doing so), are strong practical safeguards against abuse.[46] They are also a practical reason for officials to consider the proportionality of requests. The Information Commissioner's Office has commented that the plans are 'step too far for the British way of life' and that:

[B]efore major new databases are launched careful consideration must be given to the impact on individuals' liberties and on society as a whole. Sadly, there have been too many developments where there has not been sufficient openness, transparency or public debate.

(Information Commissioner's Office 2008)

Where surveillance systems are deployed it would also be possible for them to generate more detailed audit trails of communications intercepts and access to communications data. This would for example allow the Interception Commissioner to use automated tools to select unusual cases for further inspection. Systems could also check that warrants had been appropriately issued (by verifying digital signatures made by the courts on those instructions), reducing the possibility of errors and giving the public further confidence that unauthorised surveillance is not taking place.

Part III: Conclusions

While it took nearly a century for American and European con-stitutional and human rights law to catch up with the invention of the telephone, the clear parallels with postal interception were noticed much earlier:

The mail is a public service furnished by the government. The telephone is a public service furnished by its authority. There is, in essence, no difference between the sealed letter and the private telephone message ... The evil incident to invasion of privacy of the telephone is far greater than that involved in tampering with the mails. Wherever a telephone line is tapped, the privacy of the persons at both ends of the line is invaded and all conversations between them upon any subject, and although proper, confidential, and privileged, may be overheard. Moreover, the tapping of one man's telephone line involves the tapping of the telephone of every other person whom he may call, or who may call him. As a means of espionage, writs of assistance and general warrants are but puny instruments of tyranny and oppression when compared with wire-tapping.[47]

This 'greater evil' is still partially recognised by the UK and other countries, where communications surveillance must only take place as a 'last resort' (Australia) or when other means of investigation are not 'reasonable' (Canada, US) (Chilcot 2008). Curiously however, this recognition is not carried through to the introduction of controls equivalent to those instituted on searches centuries earlier in response to executive overreach.[48] A regulatory regime based on executive authorisations that allowed over half a million accesses to communications data in 2007 by 600+ government agencies is perhaps entirely appropriate in the country that used the writ of assistance and general warrant to such disastrous effect in its American colonies.

Even the United States, with perhaps the strongest constitutional and legislative controls on the 'evil incident' of communications surveillance, saw very serious government abuses during the twentieth century. While declaring wiretapping 'unethical', FBI Director J. Edgar Hoover wiretapped a range of political opponents (using the result in an attempt to blackmail civil rights leader Martin Luther King Jr. into committing suicide) (Solove 2006). Between 1940 and 1973 the FBI and CIA illegally read the private mail of thousands of citizens, including congressmen and one presidential candidate, while the National Security Agency received copies of all overseas telegrams sent via RCA and ITT World Communications. The FBI engaged in a particular vendetta against King, bugging and wiretapping his conversations and using the resulting product in an attempt to discredit him based upon his private life and to provide political intelligence for President Lyndon Johnson. President Kennedy also received FBI intercepts on opponents of his legislation and on several journalists. None of these wiretaps were judicially authorised.

Abuse spiralled out of control under President Nixon, with journalists and political opponents placed under surveillance (Diffie and Landau 1999). When the *New York Times* revealed massive domestic surveillance by the CIA, President Ford and then Congress established investigations (Haines 1998) that led to the strict controls of the Foreign Intelligence Surveillance Act of 1978. In a case of history repeating itself, the *New York Times* revealed in 2005 that President George W. Bush had authorised a massive programme of warrantless wiretapping by the National Security Agency (Risen and

Lichtblau 2005), which has since been criticised by a lower court as unconstitutional[49] and shut down. Whistleblowers recently revealed that NSA staff intercepted 'personal phone calls of American officers, mostly in the Green Zone, calling home to the United States, talking to their spouses, sometimes their girlfriends' and 'personal, private things with Americans who are not in any way, shape or form associated with anything to do with terrorism' (Shane 2008).

Clearly, safeguards against government abuse of communications surveillance include tenacious journalists as well as strong independent authorisation procedures and legislative oversight. The secrecy and deliberate obscurity surrounding intelligence operations reduces the impact of social norms and countervailing controls that exist elsewhere within and without government (Caparini 2002). Lawful intercept requirements in the US Communications Assistance to Law Enforcement Act and UK Regulation of Investigatory Powers Act shape the market procurement decisions of Internet Services Providers and hence the architectural decisions of Internet communications equipment manufacturers to enhance governments' surveillance capabilities.

It is difficult to know whether the abuses of various US administrations would have been uncovered in the UK, where an unsatisfactory regulatory framework is combined with an Official Secrets Act[50] that removes a public interest defence from government staff and journalists. In one recent example, GCHQ whistleblower Katharine Gun lost her job after revealing alleged dirty tricks by the National Security Agency. She avoided trial only after it became clear that the case might cause the government immense political embarrassment related to the war in Iraq (Bright 2008).

If governments in future wish to protect human rights and ensure public confidence in surveillance activities that by their nature cannot take place in the full glare of press scrutiny, they must ensure that communications travelling over new converged infrastructures receive comparable protection to that developed since 1776 for homes and correspondence. In addition to legal constraints, effective protection requires a technical Internet surveillance architecture that reflects the separation of powers present in most democracies' constitutions – and market incentives for private infrastructure providers to build such networks, rather than to facilitate interception. Social norms appear to have little utility in the secretive world of intelligence agencies and against politicians who have directed a 'war on terror' that breaches international law (Sands 2008) and their own constitutional systems of government (Goldsmith 2007).

Tony Blair may have considered human rights a rather quaint nineteenth century notion (BBC 2005). George Bush might have been convinced by his lawyers that he has 'inherent authority' as commander-in-chief to bypass the laws and constitution of the United States (Carey Sims 2007). Those more concerned with checks on government abuse of power would not dismiss such constraints so lightly.

Acknowledgements

Many thanks to Nicholas Bohm, Caspar Bowden, Richard Clayton, Duncan Campbell, Clive Feather and Peter Sommer for their comments on drafts of this chapter.

Notes

1 Although very high-speed datastream inspection equipment is now becoming available to Internet Service Providers – for example, Procera's 80Gb/s Deep Packet Inspection PacketLogic PL10000 platform, described at http://www.proceranetworks.com/pl10000 [accessed 8 December 2008].
2 *Katz v United States*, 389 US 347 (1967).
3 2 EHRR 214 (6 September 1978).
4 *Halford v United Kingdom*, ECHR 73/1996/692/884 (1997)
5 The Human Rights Act 1998, c.42.
6 The Regulation of Investigatory Powers (Conditions for the Lawful Interception of Persons outside the United Kingdom) Regulations 2004.
7 2000/C197/01.
8 The British Islands, as defined by the Interpretation Act 1978 s.5.
9 *Liberty and others v United Kingdom*, ECHR Application no. 58243/00, pp. 16–17.
10 See for example ETSI ES 201 671 V2.1.1 (September 2001) at http:// cryptome.sabotage.org/espy/ES201-671-v211.pdf [accessed 8 December 2008].
11 See Encase Enterprise at http://www.encase.com/products/ee_works. aspx for an example of the type of surveillance software that might be surreptitiously installed on a target machine.
12 See the Regulation of Investigatory Powers (Communication Data) Order 2003, updated by the Regulation of Investigatory Powers (Amendment) Order 2005 and the Regulation of Investigatory Powers (Communication Data) (Additional Functions and Amendment) Order 2006.
13 HC 549 printed 3 November 2005, p. 5.
14 HC 947 printed 22 July 2008, p. 8.

15 Hansard 376 Column 1111 (13 December 2001).
16 The Retention of Communications Data (Extension of Initial Period) Order 2003.
17 The Retention of Communications Data (Further Extension of Initial Period) Order 2005.
18 The Retention of Communications Data (Code of Practice) Order 2003.
19 *Directive 2006/24/EC of the European Parliament and of the Council of 15 March 2006 on the Retention of Data Generated or Processed in Connection with the Provision of Publicly Available Electronic Communications Services or of Public Communications Networks and Amending Directive 2002/58/EC* (OJ L, 13 April 2006).
20 Official Journal of the European Union L 105 (13 April 2006) pp. 61–3.
21 Hansard Column 361W (29 April 2008).
22 *R. v S. and A.* [2008] EWCA Crim 2177.
23 Sections 1–11, Parts I, Chapter 2 and III of RIPA.
24 See Reports of the Interception of Communications Commissioner for 2001 (HC 1243 printed 31 October 2002), 2003, (HC 833 printed 22 July 2004), 2004 (HC 549 printed 3 November 2005), 2005–6 (HC 315 printed 19 February 2007), 2006 (HC 252 printed 28 January 2008) and 2007 (HC 947 printed 22 July 2008). Figures for 2005 and 2006 have been linearly smoothed to reflect different reporting periods.
25 See Reports of the Interception of Communications Commissioner for 2001 (HC 1243 printed 31 October 2002), 2003, (HC 833 printed 22 July 2004), 2004 (HC 549 printed 3 November 2005), 2005–6 (HC 315 printed 19 February 2007), 2006 (HC 252 printed 28 January 2008) and 2007 (HC 947 printed 22 July 2008). Figures for 2001 and 2005 have been proportionately adjusted to reflect different reporting periods.
26 The Rt Hon. Alan Beith MP, Hansard 365(62) Column 1150 (29 March 2001).
27 *Liberty and others v United Kingdom*, 56–63
28 *R. v W.*, 2003 EWCA Crim 1632 (12 June 2003) p. 98.
29 [2004] 4 All ER 901, [2005] 1 AC 167, [2004] 3 WLR 957, [2004] UKHL 40.
30 The difficulty of proving that secret surveillance has taken place, especially when the US state secrets privilege prevents discovery being ordered by a court, proved an insurmountable hurdle in this case. However in *Klass v Germany* the European Court of Human Rights resolved this dilemma by giving standing to those who were possible victims of surveillance.
31 *American Civil Liberties Union et al. v United States National Security et al.*, 493 F.3d 644 (6th Cir. 2007).
32 *ACLU v NSA*, 438 F. Supp. 2d 754, 773–78 (E.D. Mich. 2006).
33 H.R. 6304 enacted 10 July 2008.
34 Liberty v United Kingdom, 69.
35 Liberty v United Kingdom, 68–70.
36 The Prime Minister, Hansard Column 958 (6 February 2008).

37 79 ECHR 10 (2 August 1984) 84.
38 See Reports of the Interception of Communications Commissioner for 2007, s.3.26.
39 See Annual Report of the Interception of Communications Commissioner for 2007, s.2.2.
40 See for example s.27 of the Civil Contingencies Act 2004 (c.36).
41 *Klass v Germany*, 36.
42 As they should be within the European Union under Article 6 of *Directive 95/46/EC of the European Parliament and of the Council of 24 October 1995 on the protection of individuals with regard to the processing of personal data and on the free movement of such data*, OJ L 281 (23 November 1995) pp. 31–50.
43 Lord Carter, Lords Hansard 654(169) Col. 1595 (13 November 2003).
44 Opinion 3/2006 (24 March 2006).
45 Testimony of Philip R. Zimmermann to the Subcommittee on Science, Technology and Space of the US Senate Committee on Commerce, Science and Transportation (26 June 1996).
46 These safeguards need legal backing to prevent the 'voluntary' disclosure of communications data without a legal requirement to do so, as happened in the individual cases in the UK pre-RIPA and on a massive scale between AT&T and other telecommunications companies and the US National Security Agency according to the New York Times article 'Bush lets US spy on callers without courts'.
47 Justice Louis Brandeis dissenting in *Olmstead v United States*, 277 US 438 (1928) p. 475–6.
48 Such as the Fourth Amendment to the US Constitution, held by the Supreme Court in *Smith v Maryland* (442 US 735, 1979) not to apply to lists of telephone numbers dialled.
49 *ACLU v NSA*.
50 1989 c.6.

References

Alleyne, R. (2008) 'Poole council spies on family over school claim', *The Daily Telegraph*, 18 April.
BBC (2005) *Full Text of Tony Blair's Speech* [Online]. Available at: http://news.bbc.co.uk/1/hi/uk_politics/4287370.stm [accessed 9 December 2008].
Bendrath, B. (2008) *Germany: New Basic Right to Privacy of Computer Systems* [Online]. Available at: http://www.edri.org/edrigram/number6.4/germany-constitutional-searches [accessed 8 December 2008].
Bright, M. (2008) 'The woman who nearly stopped the war', *New Statesman*, 19 March.
Brown, I. and Korff, D. (2004) *Privacy and Law Enforcement*. London: Information Commissioner's Office.

Campbell, D. (1999) 'The state of the art in Communications Intelligence (COMINT) of automated processing for intelligence purposes of intercepted broadband multi-language leased or common carrier systems, and its applicability to COMINT targeting and selection, including speech recognition', *European Parliament Scientific and Technological Options Assessment Report PE 168.186/Int.St/part4/4*.

Caparini, M. (2002) 'Challenges of control and oversight of intelligence services in a liberal democracy', workshop in Geneva, October 2002.

Carey Sims, J. (2007) 'How the Bush administration's warrantless surveillance program took the constitution on an illegal, unnecessary and unrepentant joyride', *UCLA Journal of International Law and Foreign Affairs*, 12(1).

Chilcot, Sir J. (2008) *Privy Council Review of Intercept as Evidence* [Online]. Available at: http://www.official-documents.gov.uk/document/cm73/7324/7324.pdf [accessed 8 December 2008].

Crossman, G. (2007) *Overlooked: Surveillance and Personal Privacy in Modern Britain*. London: Liberty.

Danezis, G., Dingledine, R. and Mathewson, N. (2003) 'Mixminion: design of a type III anonymous remailer protocol', *IEEE Symposium on Security & Privacy*, pp. 2–15.

de Secondat, C. (1752) *The Spirit of Laws Book XI: Of the Laws Which Establish Political Liberty, with Regard to the Constitution*. London: G. Bell & Sons.

Diffie, W. and Hellman, M. (1976) 'New directions in cryptography', *IEEE Transactions on Information Theory*, 22(6): 644–54.

Diffie, W. and Landau, S. (1999) *Privacy on the Line: The Politics of Wiretapping and Encryption*. Cambridge, MA: MIT Press.

Dingledine, R., Mathewson, N. and Syverson, P. (2007) 'Deploying low-latency anonymity: design challenges and social factors', *IEEE Security & Privacy*, 5(5).

Drake, W. (2000) 'The international telecoms regime', in C. Marsden (ed.) *Regulating the Global Information Society*. London: Routledge.

FIPR (2003) *Communications Surveillance Briefing* [Online]. Available at: http://www.fipr.org/030818ripa.html [accessed 9 December 2008].

Glover, J. and Wintour, P. (2006) 'My world was collapsing', *The Guardian*, 7 October [Online]. Available at: http://www.guardian.co.uk/commentisfree/2006/oct/07/comment.politics4 [accessed 9 December 2008].

Goldsmith, J. (2007) *The Terror Presidency: Law and Judgment Inside the Bush Administration*. New York: W.W. Norton.

Hailsham, Lord (1976) 'Elective dictatorship', *The Listener*, 21 October: 496–500.

Haines, G.K. (1998) 'Looking for a rogue elephant: the Pike Committee investigations and the CIA', *Studies in Intelligence*, Winter.

HMSO (2007) *The Governance of Britain*. London: HMSO.

Home Office (2002) *Covert Surveillance Code of Practice*. London: HMSO.

Home Office (2007) Investigation of Protected Electronic Information Code of Practice [Online]. Available at: http://security.homeoffice.gov.uk/ripa/publication-search/ripa-cop/electronic-information?view=Binary [accessed 8 December 2008].

Home Office (2008a) Acquisitions and Disclosure of Communications Data Code of Practice [Online]. Available at: http://security.homeoffice.gov.uk/ripa/publication-search/ripa-cop/acquisition-disclosure-cop.pdf [accessed 8 December 2008].

Home Office (2008b) A Consultation Paper: Transposition of Directive 2006/24/EC [Online]. Available at: http://www.statewatch.org/news/2008/aug/uk-ho-consult-mand-ret-internet.pdf [accessed 8 December 2008].

Home Office (2008c) Intelligence and Security Committee Annual Report 2006–2007. London: HMSO.

Hosein, I. (2003) 'Regulating the technological actor: how governments tried to transform the technology and the market for cryptography and the implications for the regulation of information and communications technologies', PhD thesis, London School of Economics.

Information Commissioner's Office (2008) A Communications Database Would be a 'Step Too Far' [Online]. Available at: http://www.ico.gov.uk/upload/documents/pressreleases/2008/annual_report_web_version.pdf [accessed 9 December 2008].

Joint Committee on Human Rights (2007) Counter-terrorism Policy and Human Rights: 28 Days, Intercept and Post-charge Questioning. London: HMSO.

Kablenet (2008) Think Tank Slams Communications Data Warehouse [Online]. Available at: http://www.kablenet.com/kd.nsf/Frontpage/518F89E0BBF1CC82802574570048E73D?OpenDocument [accessed 9 December 2008].

Kahn, D. (1973) The Codebreakers. London: Sphere Books.

Kirkup, J. (2008) 'Local councils accused of spying on residents' sex lives', The Daily Telegraph, 25 August.

Lessig, L. (1999) Code and Other Laws of Cyberspace. New York: Basic Books.

Leyden, J. (2006) Fugitive CEO Tracked Down to Sri Lanka After Skype Call [Online]. Available at: http://www.theregister.co.uk/2006/08/25/fugitive_ceo_cuffed/ [accessed 8 December 2008].

Manolea, B. (2008) German Constitutional Court Limits Data Retention Law [Online]. Available at: http://www.edri.org/edrigram/number6.6/germany-data-retention-decision-cc [accessed 8 December 2008].

Metropolitan Police Authority (2007) Metropolitan Police Authority Co-ordination and Policing Committee Report 12: Legality of Telephone Intercepts – Operation Helios. London: Metropolitan Police Authority.

National Research Council (2008) Protecting Individual Privacy in the Struggle Against Terrorists: A Framework for Program Assessment. Washington, DC: National Academies Press.

Office of the Leader of the House of Commons (2008) Preparing Britain for the Future: The Government's Draft Legislative Programme 2008/2009. London: HMSO.

Reed Ward, P. and Fuoco, M.A. (2003) 'Job loss tied to fatal shooting in Shaler', *Pittsburgh Post-Gazette*, 31 October.

Reidenberg, J. (1998) 'Lex Informatica: the formulation of information policy rules through technology', *Texas Law Review*, 76(3): 553–84.

Risen, J. and Lichtblau, E. (2005) 'Bush lets US spy on callers without courts', *New York Times*, 16 December.

Sands, P. (2008) *Torture Team: Rumsfeld's Memo and the Betrayal of American Values*. London: Palgrave Macmillan.

Shane, S. (2008) 'Panel to study military eavesdropping', *New York Times*, 9 October.

Soar, D. (2008) 'Short cuts', *London Review of Books*, 30(16).

Sokolov, D. (2008) *Speculation Over Back Door in Skype* [Online]. Available at: http://www.heise-online.co.uk/security/Speculation-over-back-door-in-Skype--/news/111170 [accessed 8 December 2008].

Solove, D. (2006) 'A brief history of information privacy law' in C. Wolf (ed.) *Proskauer on Privacy*. New York: Practising Law Institute.

Sommer, P. (2006) 'Written evidence submitted to the Select Committee on Home Affairs', *Fourth Report of Session 2005–2006, HC 910-II*. London: HMSO.

Surtevant, M. (1992) 'Congressional oversight of intelligence', *American Intelligence Journal*, Summer.

Whitley, E. and Hosein, I. (2005) 'Policy discourse and data retention: the technology politics of surveillance in the United Kingdom', *Telecommunications Policy*, 29: 857–74.

Williams, C. (2008) *Police Go Slow with Encryption Key Terror Powers* [Online]. Available at: http://www.theregister.co.uk/2008/05/05/ripa_encryption_section_49_figures/ [accessed 8 December 2008].

Wolff. P. (2008) *The Bavarian Intercept Proves Skype is Secure* [Online]. Available at: http://skypejournal.com/blog/2008/01/the_bavarian_intercept_proves.html [accessed 8 December 2008].

Wright, P. (1987) *Spycatcher*. London: Viking.

Chapter 4

From targeted to mass surveillance: is the EU Data Retention Directive a necessary measure or an unjustified threat to privacy?

Marie-Helen Maras[1]

The Madrid and London bombings brought about a significant change both in European conceptions of the threat posed by al-Qaeda and concerning the appropriateness of measures with which to respond to these attacks (Maras 2008). In response to this threat, one of the measures introduced by the EU and its Member States in order to facilitate the tracking and prosecution of terrorists was the Data Retention Directive (Directive 2006/24/EC), which calls for an unprecedented mass collection and storage of information on all European citizens for a significant period of time. This measure represents a new direction for surveillance: a shift from a more targeted mode of surveillance to one of mass surveillance.

This chapter begins by exploring this shift from targeted to mass surveillance. The next section considers whether the Directive, a mass surveillance measure, respects particular substantive commitments to human rights. Specifically, it examines which human rights this measure interferes with, while primarily focusing on the right to privacy. The legal protection of this right is established by Article 8 of the European Convention on Human Rights (1950). The final section analyses the jurisprudence of the European Court of Human Rights[2] in order to determine whether or not the Directive meets the criteria for a justified interference with the right to privacy. This analysis is motivated by the following questions: Is this measure in accordance with the law? Is it a necessary and proportionate response to the threat? The task of this chapter is to critically assess whether in fact it could be said that the Data Retention Directive is a justified measure, understood in respect of its adherence to the rule of law and respect for human rights (predominantly, the right to privacy).

A climate ripe for mass surveillance: introducing the Data Retention Directive

Consider a society where every website you visited, every phone call you made (and to whom the call was made), and your precise location when the call was made, were recorded and stored for two years by communications service providers. In this society, access to this information would be given to a wide range of authorities without requiring them to obtain prior authorisation, by search warrant or court order. Imagining just this, Heymann (2003: 135–138) predicted that by 2010, the fear of terrorism could have changed societies by creating an 'intelligence state', where intelligence agencies were not limited in gathering private information, had no burden of establishing the need for such information beyond a reasonable doubt, and could engage in illegal activities secretly, and thus without political accountability. A characteristic of such a state would be that vast quantities of information, concerning citizens' private data and wholly innocent activities, would be collected by intelligence agencies in order to increase the stock of analysable information; in the hope that such information 'may' tie into something else in the future (Lyon 2003: 37).

Heymann was wrong; not in terms of his assertion about the creation of an 'intelligence state', but in terms of the date that this state would be realised. The society described above is not a fictitious scenario but an imminent reality within the European Union. In 2004, the following measures were introduced in the EU: 'passenger name record' (PNR) checks on all flights in and out of the European Union (whereby the personal information of passengers is recorded, stored and transferred to authorities in the United States upon request), IDs, visas, and passports with biometric identifiers (e.g. digital fingerprints and retinal scans), whose information is stored on a central database, and the Data Retention Directive (Directive 2006/24/EC), which was originally proposed in 2004 (yet passed in 2006) and permits the wide retention of communications data. These measures illustrate how such technologies of surveillance are being used to significantly increase the quantity of analysable information for subsequent use by authorities. The incorporation of the Data Retention Directive into Member States' laws will result in the creation of the society described above because it mandates the blanket retention of data on all EU citizens (for a period of no greater than two years), which reveals 'who everyone talks to (by email and phone), where everyone goes (mobile phone location co-ordinates), and what everyone reads online (websites browsed)' (Bowden 2002: 21). The introduction of these measures in the European Union suggests that the 'intelligence state' envisioned by Heymann is being realised sooner than expected. The question that follows is: is terrorism, as Heymann claims, the driving force behind the forthcoming 'intelligence state' and measures such as the Directive?

The primary aim of the Directive is to retain data in order to ensure its availability for the investigation, detection, and prosecution of serious crimes such as terrorism and organised crime (Recital 21). In terms of terrorism, al-Qaeda and related Islamic terrorist groups pose the greatest security threat to Europe. The investigations of the attacks on 9/11 revealed that not only were there al-Qaeda operational cells in Europe but also a significant number of al-Qaeda support cells, which make up terrorist networks that are both affiliated and unaffiliated with al-Qaeda. The attacks on Madrid and London brought home the lesson that attention needed to be paid to these support networks, which had received relatively less consideration than operational networks after 9/11.

The Madrid and London bombings, which together resulted in more than 250 deaths, revealed that Europe's counter terrorism strategy was far from adequate. Intelligence and law enforcement agencies were unable to detect the perpetrators of these attacks because they were unaffiliated terrorists, with no direct ties to al-Qaeda. This demonstrated how Europe faces a threat beyond al-Qaeda and related Islamic terrorists groups. As Vidino (2006: 359) stated 'Europe is growing its own terrorists, through the radicalisation of the Muslim community within Europe, thus creating the "new face of al-Qaeda in Europe"'. The attacks on Madrid and London illustrated this point by revealing home-grown terrorists, who were inspired by al-Qaeda's cause, rather than directed by (or directly linked with) them. Whilst there is no doubting that terrorism is a motivating force behind the implementation of these measures and the move towards Heymann's 'intelligence state', it is possible that other factors equally contributed to this occurrence. For example, it may be that the European Union's bid to tackle serious and organised crime also played a major role in the implementation of these measures.

Organised crime is prevalent in all EU Member States: 3,000 active organised crime groups with approximately 30,000 members have been identified by authorities within the European Union.[3] Indeed, indigenous organised crime groups were reported as representing a major threat to Europe (Council of the European Union 2005: 5). Technological advances and the erosion of borders (which allowed the free movement of persons and goods), and lax border control and security not only created a set of opportunities for organised crime groups to engage in serious criminal activity (e.g. drugs trafficking and illegal immigration) but also made such activity difficult to detect. In terms of technology, the internet provided organised crime groups and their members with a means of communication (e.g. instant messaging, internet chat rooms and email), which not only provided them with swift communications but also, when combined with encryption tools, afforded them with an unprecedented level of security (Europol 2006: 18–19). Consequently, measures aimed at detecting members of organised crime groups through communications (e.g. the Data Retention Directive) and measures aimed at strengthening the security of borders and monitoring the movements of persons and goods (e.g. biometric passports, IDs, and visas) were considered necessary to fight organised crime. Therefore, it could be argued that the bid to tackle organised crime is part of what motivates the introduction of these measures and the move towards the 'intelligence state'. It could also be argued that it occurred because the lines between serious crime, organised crime and terrorism are increasingly becoming blurred. For instance, terrorist groups, like organised crime groups, engage in serious criminal activity such as illicit firearms trafficking, in pursuit of accomplishing their goals and funding their operations (Makarenko 2004: 130). The investigation of the Madrid bombings revealed that the perpetrators of the attacks supported themselves by engaging in criminal activities.

Nevertheless, while it could be argued that the need to investigate, detect, and prosecute serious and organised crime is part of what is motivating the introduction of these measures and move towards the 'intelligence state', what justified the implementation of these measures politically, was terrorism. Prior to the Madrid bombings measures such as national IDs with biometric identifiers and the Directive mentioned above, were severely criticised as being unjustified. Previously, the European Parliament (2004: 4) had stated on 9 March 2004 that any form of mass surveillance was unjustified and that only targeted measures were justifiable. Targeted surveillance refers to the surveillance of a specific individual (or individuals) on a case-by-case basis, based on reasonable suspicion (or probable cause). This type of surveillance was only authorised if it included appropriate safeguards such as the requirement of search warrants or court orders. Any measure that did not meet these requirements of surveillance is – and in the case of the European Parliament was – considered unjustified.

In the wake of the Madrid bombings (which occurred on 11 March 2004), however, this view changed. The European Council's statement, in the *Declaration on Combating Terrorism* (adopted on 25 March 2004), on the urgency and necessity to adopt measures such as biometric IDs and wide retention of communications data attests to this. The implementation of these measures reveal, in contrast to the claims made by many authors (Cole 2002/2003; Sunstein 2005; Whitaker 2006, to name a few) that counter terrorism measures are inherently selective, a new, emerging trend: one that does not focus on the targeting of suspected terrorists. These measures illustrate a shift both in European conceptions of their appropriateness and the measures themselves, which went from the surveillance of allegedly threatening individuals and groups to measures aimed at the population as a whole.

Dworkin (2002) asserts that 'the trade-off is not between *our* liberty and *our* security in times of threat, but between *our* security and *their* liberty'; by 'their' Dworkin means 'the freedoms of small suspect groups, like adult male Muslims' (Ignatieff 2005: 32). By implementing a mass surveillance measure, the Data Retention Directive, a different trade-off is observed. The trade-off is, in contrast to what Dworkin and others (e.g. Cole 2002; Gross 2002/2003; Tribe 2002/2003) say, between *our* civil liberties and *our* security in the face of the current threat of terrorism. The question that follows is: which of *our* civil liberties is the Directive sacrificing?

Which civil liberties?

While recognising that improving intelligence is crucial in preventing future terrorist attacks, the indiscriminate collection of large quantities of information, without particular suspicion of wrongdoing, intrudes on due process, inhibits political activity, and erodes privacy (Cole and Dempsey 2006: 245–246). In terms of due process, the Directive cedes to agencies largely unchecked powers to 'conduct surveillance even when it has no basis for suspecting criminal activity' (Chang 2003: 33) because it requires the retention of data on all citizens prior to any investigation and access to this data can occur without the requirement of court orders (or search warrants). In terms of protected political activity, surveillance can threaten political freedoms, such as the freedom of expression and freedom of association (Davis 2003: 126). Specifically, data retention can have a chilling effect[4] on an individual's conduct and speech. For example, if an individual suspects (or even knows) that the web sites they browsed (such as those advocating against the war on terrorism) were recorded and stored and that this might put the individual at risk, they might give up the right to exercise their political freedoms.

With data retention, one obvious concern with 'such data warehousing is that it leads to the creation of immense searchable databases of personal information, and more broadly, the privacy of the individuals whose information is retained' (Austin 2001: 255). Privacy is a multivalent social and legal concept, where the definitions of privacy have ranged from the right to be let alone (Cooley 1907; Wong 2005: 148), to the capacity to keep certain things secret (Janis, Kay and Bradley 2000: 30), to the right to control other individuals' access to oneself and information about oneself (Fried 1970; Wong 2005: 141). Despite its complexity and ambiguity, 'privacy is closely connected with the emergence of a modern sense of self' (Galison and Minow 2005: 258). The emergence of the modern self, however, depends on individuals' ability to achieve self-determination and develop their personality free from coercion. That is, they must be free to makes choices about who they are, who they associate with, and with whom they want to share information.

The right to personal autonomy and human dignity demands that an individual should be 'allowed to make these choices without undue interference by the state or other individuals' (Foster 2003: 359). As Raz (1977: 204–205) noted, 'respecting human dignity entails treating humans as persons capable of planning and plotting their future. Thus, respecting people's dignity includes respecting their autonomy, their right to control their future'. The reason why privacy has a special status as a human right is its close connection to human dignity and personal autonomy (Feldman 2002: 515; Goold 2002: 22). It is for this reason that privacy is such an important human right and as such, while states may interfere with this right (because it is a qualified right), they 'must rigorously justify doing so' (Feldman 2002). The following analysis will focus on the impact of the Data Retention Directive on the right to privacy. This right was chosen not only because of its close connection to human dignity and personal autonomy, but also because the shift from targeted to mass surveillance, resulting from the blanket retention of data, threatens privacy to the point that it extinguishes the very essence of the right.

A justified measure?

According to Article 8(1) of the European Convention on Human Rights, 'everyone has the right to respect for his private and family life, his home and his correspondence'. The jurisprudence of the Strasbourg Court reveals that telecommunications fall within the scope of 'private life' and 'correspondence' and are protected whether they originate in or are sent to an individual's home or business premise.[5] In terms of data retention, the Strasbourg Court protects the individual against the gathering of his/her private information (Krieger 2004: 65). Specifically, in *Malone v United Kingdom*,[6] the Strasbourg Court held that metering information, which includes information on numbers dialled (an integral element in the communications made by telephone) and the duration of the calls made, falls within the scope of 'private life' under Article 8(1). It follows that information on, for example, a caller's location (retrieved from mobile phones) would, by analogy, also be protected. The same could be said about internet data (e.g. sender and receiver information, time and date of message, etc.). In fact, in *Copland v United Kingdom*,[7] the Strasbourg Court held that the collection and storage of personal information relating to the applicant's e-mail and Internet usage is protected under Article 8.

The jurisprudence of the Strasbourg Court reveals that the right to privacy is continuously engaged when authorities seek, collect, store, process, compare, or disseminate personal information about a data subject (Feldman 2002: 530). Since the retention of data falls within the scope of Article 8(1), what needs to be determined is whether this Directive constitutes a justified interference with privacy.

Article 8 is a qualified right because it is subject to the limitations set out in Article 8(2). According to Article 8(2), interference with this right by public authorities can occur when it:

> Is in accordance with the law and is necessary in a democratic society via the interests of national security, public safety or the economic well being of the country, for the prevention of disorder or crime, for the protection of health or morals, or for the protection of the rights and freedom of others.

Interferences with this right are justified so long as the grounds for qualification of this right are satisfied. The analysis below explores whether this Directive meets the criteria of Article 8(2) and as such, whether or not it constitutes a justified interference with the right to privacy.

In accordance with the law

According to Article 8(2), one of the criteria that must be met is that the interference must be 'in accordance with the law'. The Strasbourg Court ruled, in a trilogy of cases, that the phrase 'in accordance with the law', creates three requirements: 'the interference must have some basis in domestic law', it must be adequately accessible, and 'must be formulated so that it is sufficiently foreseeable'.[8] This phrase is thus not limited to whether the measure in question was permitted under domestic law (Emmerson and Ashworth 2001: 205). The Strasbourg Court 'has always understood the term "law" in its "substantive" sense, not its "formal" one'.[9] As such, in *Malone*, this phrase was identified as relating 'to the quality of the law, requiring it to be compatible with the rule of law'.[10] Here, the quality of the law, which pertains to written as well as unwritten law, is determined by the conditions of foreseeability and accessibility.[11]

The jurisprudence of the Strasbourg Court[12] reveals that the law in question must be adequately accessible to those individuals who are likely to be affected by the interference, in order to allow them to reasonably foresee the potential consequences of this measure, and plan their behaviour accordingly (Feldman 2002: 665). When laws are foreseeable in this way, citizens 'can regulate their conduct accordingly, so as to avoid invoking unwelcome intrusions by the state' (Privacy International 2003: 4). Mechanisms which facilitate surveillance (e.g. the Internet, and cell-phone networks) are increasingly being built into societies' infrastructures. It is becoming increasingly difficult for individuals to avoid the use of these technologies in their daily lives. It is worth noting that the activities of everyday life generate digital records of the activities of its citizens. Individuals are subjecting themselves to surveillance by default, because the records of their activities are being retained indiscriminately (Whitley and Hosein 2005: 869). This blanket data retention offers individuals no reasonable means to avoid surveillance. Such an occurrence, however, is contrary to the rule of law.

The rule of law requires that the power of the state is circumscribed by law, which specifies the limit of the scope of the executive's activity. As indicated in *Malone*, blanket powers of the executive are contrary to the rule of law (Warbrick 2002: 290). Similarly, in *Maestri v Italy*,[13] the Strasbourg Court stated:

> It would be contrary to the rule of law ... for a legal discretion granted to the executive to be expressed in terms of unfettered

power. Consequently, the law must indicate with sufficient clarity the scope of any such discretion and the manner of its exercise.

Therefore, it could be argued that the blanket retention of traffic data offends the core principle of the rule of law because it fails to provide citizens with sufficient clarity on the scope of this discretion and the manner of its exercise. In fact, one of the reasons why the Directive provides agencies with wide and uncertain scope of powers is because data may be accessed by a wide range of authorities. According to Recital 17 of the Directive, retained data should be provided to 'competent national authorities'. It does not limit the access to this data to designated authorities. As a result, Member States' interpretation of 'competent national authorities' may not only differ significantly but may also extend well beyond the appropriate judicial and law enforcement authorities, which access should be limited to.

These differences in interpretation are evident in Member States' data retention laws. For example, in France, the relative legislation on data retention[14] allows only judicial authorities and police forces to access retained data; whereas access to this data in the Netherlands and the United Kingdom is not limited to law enforcement authorities. In the Netherlands, two decisions, one from the Dutch Supreme Court (*Lycos Netherlands v Pessers*)[15] and the other from the District Court of The Hague (*Stichting Brein v KPN Telecom*),[16] ruled that retained subscriber data by Internet service providers can be disclosed to third parties (in this case, they were several parties in the music and video industry represented by the Dutch organisation Brein) (De Vries and Van Tol 2006). Furthermore, in the United Kingdom, the Regulation of Investigatory Powers (Communications Data) Order 2003 allowed a significant number of different agencies to have access to retained data (Kosta 2006: 5).[17] Indeed, this Order includes a long list of public authorities who can access all types of communications data (such as Emergency Ambulance Services, Fire Authorities, and Financial Services Authority) and an even longer list of those who can only access certain types of communications data such as subscriber data (Environment Agency, Health and Safety Executive, and the Food Standards Agency) (Munir and Yasin 2004: 198).

The Directive also requires Member States to 'adopt legislative measures concerning the right of access to, and use of, data by national authorities, as designated by them' (Recital 25). The fact that access to the data is determined by Member States may result in governments affording agencies powers to access this information arbitrarily. This is contrary to the rule of law because the powers of authorities are not limited and regulated by requirements such as warrants or reasonable suspicion. By contrast, targeted surveillance is not only applied to named individuals and is highly specific, but also requires law enforcement agencies to have reasonable suspicion when conducting surveillance and requires warrants for the surveillance of these individuals. The opposite is true for mass surveillance. In France, security services have the technical platforms in place to know who has contacted whom, when and where; by a simple click, they can obtain all the information they need from telecommunications and internet service providers (Privacy International 2007). In 2006, a new anti-terrorism law was passed in France,[18] which allowed for direct police access to logged communications data by providers (Privacy International 2007).

Consider as another example the Regulation of Investigatory Powers Act (RIPA) 2000 in the UK. In particular, section 22 notices of RIPA (where police officers serve notices to service providers in order to give police access to the data retained), are not authorised by the courts but by police officers holding the rank of inspector or superintendent (depending on the type of data that is requested) (Danby 2002: 10). Access to this data does not require a search warrant. A search warrant is necessary only if law enforcement authorities want to access communications in 'real time' or want to access 'content data'.[19] In Ireland, access to this information is the same in sections 64(2) and 64(3) of the Criminal Justice (Terrorist Offences) Act 2005 as it is in the Interception of Postal Packets and Telecommunications Act 1993; namely, an army officer or a member of the police force of sufficient rank can access this data without any need for external approval (McIntyre 2008: 331). These powers, therefore, extend well beyond measures based on the rule of law, where states' surveillance is limited and regulated by requirements such as warrants and court orders.

Similarly, the proposed mass surveillance resulting from the implementation of the Directive also extends well beyond the rule of law. Data will be retained on all citizens regardless of their links with terrorism and access to this data will not require warrants, thus raising concerns of the privacy rights of individuals whose data is being retained and accessed. Thus, the implementation of the Data Retention Directive, which will result in the creation of an immense traffic data warehouse, may put the entire 'population at the inadmissible peril that daily life can be monitored without authorisation' (Goemans and Dumortier 2003: 8). This places the legality of the Directive in question. In *Silver v United Kingdom*,[20] the Strasbourg Court 'made it clear that a law which "allows the exercise of unrestrained discretion in individual cases will not possess the essential characteristics of foreseeability and thus will not be a law"' (De Hert 2005: 79). Accordingly, 'any exploratory or general surveillance not carried out on a case-by-case basis in the event of reasonable suspicion' and without a search warrant (or court order) is prohibited (Allitsch 2002: 167; Breyer 2005: 368).

In *Kopp v Switzerland*,[21] the Strasbourg Court asserted that the law must protect individuals against arbitrary use of powers and was careful to ensure that lawyer–client communications were protected. Indeed, concerns have been raised as to whether the proposed Directive adequately protects the confidentiality of protected communications because it mandates the retention of data of both legal entities and natural persons (Article 1.2). On this matter, the European Parliament (2004: 6) declared in a resolution that the Member States' data retention laws constituted an interference with the right to privacy because they were not in full conformity with the Convention. This resolution held that these laws 'fell short of the requirement of respecting confidentiality of protected communications', such as lawyer–client communications. In 2005, however, the same Parliament supported a proposal for the Data Retention Directive, which mandated the retention of all 'traffic and location data of both legal entities and natural persons' (Article 29, Data Protection Working Party 2004: 4). Applying the reasoning of the European Parliament mentioned above, the Directive would also constitute an unjustified interference with the right to privacy because it does not 'adequately protect the confidentiality of protected communications' and as such, is not in full conformity with the Convention.

In contrast, it could be argued that 'if a statute permits indiscriminate interference, the problem does not lie in the precision of the law' (Breyer 2005: 367). That is, if the Directive 'allows everyone to foresee that all traffic data will be recorded and retained for a certain period of time', then it does not violate the requirement of foreseeability (Breyer 2005). However, as indicated in the Parliament's resolution, one of the reasons why the laws of Member States on data retention were not in full conformity with the Convention was because they 'fell short of the requirements of being authorised by the judiciary on a case-by-case basis' (European Parliament 2004: 6). This demonstrates that while targeted surveillance of individuals which is authorised and reviewed on a case-by-case basis is in accordance with the law, the mass surveillance resulting from the blanket retention of data proposed by the Directive is not. According to the reasoning of the European Parliament, the Directive constitutes an unjustified interference with the right to privacy.

The analysis above sought to show how the blanket retention of data fails to provide individuals with a reasonable means to avoid the surveillance of their personal data, provides wide scope of powers to authorities, may result in the arbitrary use of powers by authorities, and fails to protect confidential communications because of the fact that data is retained on everybody. As such, it is clear that this Directive does not satisfy the requirements of 'in accordance with the law'. Nevertheless, since this Directive has not been transposed into national law by the majority of EU Member States,[22] an analysis of 'necessary in a democratic society' is required in order to determine the compatibility of the Directive with Article 8.

Necessary in a democratic society

The second condition that must be met, is that the interference with the right must be 'necessary in a democratic society' in pursuit of one or more of the legitimate aims prescribed in Article 8(2). First, the Strasbourg Court considers whether or not the measure was in pursuit of one or more of the stated aims listed in Article 8(2). Recital 21 of the Directive reveals that this measure pursues a legitimate aim because its objective is to retain data for the 'purpose of the investigation, detection and prosecution of serious crime', where serious crime such as terrorism falls within the categories of the legitimate aims mentioned in Article 8(2). Generally, the Strasbourg Court does not dispute the aim for which a particular measure was taken. The debate, therefore, focuses on whether or not the measure was 'necessary in a democratic society' (Warbrick 2002: 307).

While states enjoy a margin of appreciation in implementing measures in pursuit of a legitimate aim, the margin goes hand in hand with supervision by the Strasbourg Court.[23] The scope of this margin depends both on the nature and seriousness of the legitimate aim pursued (and the interests at stake) and on the particular nature and severity of the interference involved.[24] In cases concerning the disclosure of 'personal data',[25] the Strasbourg Court 'has recognised that a "margin of appreciation" should be left to the competent national authorities in striking a fair balance between the relative conflicting public and private interests'.[26] As the Strasbourg Court stated in *Leander v. Sweden*,[27] there is 'no doubt as to the necessity, for the purpose of protecting national security, for the ... states to have laws granting the competent domestic authorities power'. Where the aim of the interference with the right is to maintain national security or to combat terrorism, the Strasbourg Court 'tends to allow states a wide margin of appreciation'.[28] In light of the importance of combating terrorism and the problems presented to intelligence and law enforcement agencies by home-grown terrorists, Member States believe that they should have a wide margin of appreciation for implementing counter terrorism measures.

At the core of the Strasbourg Court's review of the margin of appreciation lies the requirement that there must be an appropriate relationship between the legitimate aim and the means used to achieve it. Therefore, when determining whether a measure is 'necessary in a democratic society', the Strasbourg Court examines whether the state has shown that the interference with the right corresponds to a 'pressing social need', whether the measure employed is proportionate to the legitimate aim pursued, and whether the reasons given to justify this measure are 'relevant and sufficient'.[29] Any curtailment of rights as a result of counter terrorism measures 'should be proportionate to the dimension of the terrorist threat' (von Schorlemer 2003: 276).

While the word 'proportionality' is not found within the Convention or in its various additional protocols, it has become a dominant theme within the jurisprudence of the Strasbourg Court (Eissen 1993: 125; McBride 1999: 24). The context in which this doctrine is most frequently used is when the Court assesses whether or not an interference with a qualified right is justified as being 'necessary in a democratic society' (Clayton and Tomlinson 2000: 279). In assessing the proportionality of a measure, the Strasbourg Court determines 'whether a fair balance was struck between the demands of the general interest of the community and the requirements of the protection of the individual's fundamental rights'.[30] This need for balancing necessitated resort to the concept of proportionality; without it, 'the formulation of the Convention provisions would be open to restrictions depriving the rights ... of all content' so long as they were 'in accordance with the law' and for a legitimate purpose (McBride 1999: 24).

A measure will be considered disproportionate if the limitations introduced 'restrict or reduce the right in such a way or to such an extent that the very essence of the right is impaired'.[31] Accordingly, states must demonstrate that the measures they implemented do not go beyond what was necessary to achieve their objectives (Emmerson and Ashworth 2001: 93). Therefore, proportionality requires further scrutiny as to what type of information is required, for what particular purposes is it required, and how long the period of retention should be to in order to ensure minimal interference with the right (Taylor 2003: 98). As Emmerson and Ashworth (2001: 91) argue 'it is on the issue of proportionality that most alleged violations of Article 8 ultimately turn'.

Proportionality tests

Proportionality requires that there is a rational connection between the objective a particular measure pursues and the means the State has employed to achieve that objective (Emmerson and Ashworth 2001: 93). Proportionality also requires that, in relation to crime, surveillance should only be used 'against serious, properly defined offences, that it should be based on well founded suspicion and not be merely exploratory, and should be used in the absence of the likely success of other measures' (Starmer 1999; Davis 2003: 142). The analysis of 'in accordance with the law' demonstrated that the proposed surveillance of the Directive was not based on well founded suspicion, thus failing this test of proportionality. In order to determine whether the Directive meets the remaining requirements of proportionality, the type of information retained, the purposes of retention, the existence of less intrusive measures and their ability to achieve the Directive's objectives, and the period of retention are examined.

First, as a means of evaluating proportionality, the Strasbourg Court examines the type of information that is required. The Directive mandates the blanket retention of personal data, which concerns 'any information relating to an identified or identifiable natural person' (Article 2(a) Directive 2002/58/EC). It consists of 'those facts, communications, or opinions which relate to the individual and which it would be reasonable to expect him to regard as intimate or sensitive and therefore to want to withhold or at least restrict their collection, use, or circulation' (Wacks 1989: 26; Feldman 2002: 618). The Directive explicitly calls for the retention of the following categories of data concerning fixed network telephony, mobile telephony, internet access, internet e-mail and internet telephony (Article 5): data necessary to trace and identify the source of a communication (e.g. name and address of the subscriber or registered user); data necessary to identify the destination of a communication (e.g. numbers dialled, user ID or telephone number of the intended recipient or recipients); data necessary to identify the date, time, and duration of a communication (e.g. date and time of start and end of communication or the data and time of log-in and log-off of the Internet e-mail service); data necessary to identify the type of communication (e.g. telephone or Internet service used); data necessary to identify users' communication equipment or what purports to be their equipment (e.g. called telephone numbers or telephone number called for dial up access); and data necessary to identify the location of mobile communication equipment (e.g. data identifying geographic location).

The databases created by the retention of such data, will create a near complete map of the private lives of all EU citizens using communications (whether phone or Internet), by revealing their contacts (by phone or e-mail), movements (mobile phone location data), and interests, political views, sexual preferences and religious affiliations (through websites they browsed) (Bowden 2002: 21; Breyer 2005: 365). Article 8 of Directive 95/46/EC, however, explicitly 'prohibits the processing of personal data revealing racial or ethnic origin, political opinions, religious … beliefs … and the processing of data concerning … sex life'. Since Directive 95/46/EC is applicable to the data retained in accordance with the Data Retention Directive, the retention of this type of information is prohibited (Recital 15, Data Retention Directive). While acknowledging that the retention of data in respect of those who may be guilty of offences or responsible for violations of state security might be necessary and proportionate to the threat of terrorism, the retention of data on all EU citizens 'goes beyond the bounds of what is required to protect democratic institutions and amounts to a perverse inquisition'.[32]

Despite claims to the contrary, communications data is not retained because it is less intrusive than the content. As Walden (2004: 11) argues:

> While the volume and value of communications data has expanded considerably; conversely, obtaining access to the content of a communication is increasingly hampered through the use of cryptographic techniques, either built into the technology or applied by the user.

The value of communications data has expanded considerably because, as the analysis above illustrates, the retention of this data can reveal an individual's contacts, activities, locations, habits, and 'restricted personal data'. In so doing, it provides a detailed account of an individual's private life. Also, as a result of technological advances in communications, devices such as third generation mobile phones can pinpoint a user's location to a few meters, requiring only that the phone is switched on. Moreover, traffic and location data are easier to obtain than content data as a result of new technologies, which inhibit access to the content of communications data. For example, the use of Pretty Good Privacy (PGP) software (a technique for encrypting messages; often used to protect messages on the Internet) provides cryptographic privacy and authentication for users, thus hampering law enforcement agencies' access to the content of the communication. Consequently, 'law enforcement agencies are increasingly reliant on evidence derived from communications data rather than content' (Walden 2001: 11).

Proportionality tests also determine whether this measure results in powers which overreach themselves unnecessarily. One way this is determined is by examining the purposes of retention. According to Article 1(1) of the Data Retention Directive, data is retained 'in order to ensure that the data are available for the purpose of the investigation, detection and prosecution of serious crime, as defined by each Member State in its national law'. The Directive, therefore, does not define 'serious crime', leaving it instead to the interpretation of Member States. The Council of the European Union (2006: 2) did, however, declare in a separate statement that Member States should have due regard to the crimes listed in Article 2(2) of the Framework Decision on the European Arrest Warrant (2002/584/JHA) and crimes involving telecommunications when defining 'serious crime'. Nevertheless, Article 2(2) of the Framework Decision on the European Arrest Warrant consists of an exhaustive list of crimes, which includes crimes such as counterfeiting, piracy of products, and computer-related crime.

The lack of definition of 'serious crime', therefore, indicates that there is no expressed limit to the scope of the powers conferred by the Data Retention Directive. For instance, in Germany, the relative legislation[33] concerning access to traffic, location and internet data states that data can be accessed for 'any serious offence or offence made with the use of a telephone or computer' (Schwartz 2002–2003: 786). As one German treatise pointed out, the latter can encompass an offence such as making insulting telephone calls (Pfeiffer 2002: 224; Schwartz 2002–2003: 786). In similar fashion, the approved Data Retention Bill[34] in Germany included a list of crimes – not limited to serious crimes – for which data can be accessed, such as offences committed via telecommunications networks (including the sharing of copyrighted content) (EDRI 2007). However, a recent case[35] in the German Constitutional Court held, in an interim ruling, that Germany's data retention law was problematic and as such, retained data could only be accessed for serious crimes and with a judicial warrant (DRI 2008). Other countries, such as Ireland and the United Kingdom, have not followed suit. In Ireland, section 64(1) of the Criminal Justice (Terrorist Offences) Act 2005 allows access to retained data 'for the purpose of civil proceedings in court'. Even in the UK, where serious crime is defined in domestic law in the Serious Crime Act 2007, the list of offences included in this Act 'is nothing if not comic. Murder, rape, arson, manslaughter, kidnapping ... are not thought to constitute serious crimes. Fishing for salmon in breach of the Salmon and Freshwater Fisheries Act 1975 is' (Campbell 2007: 23).

Retained personal data could be used for investigating minor offences or even monitoring individual's communications without any grounds for suspecting them of an offence (Joint Committee on Human Rights 2001; Danby 2002: 33). It is argued that the need for the inclusion of criminal offences other than terrorism was based on the belief that because of the way terrorists operate, drawing a distinction between terrorists' activities and other crimes would be extremely difficult.[36] However, as Lord Peyton of Yeovil argued, while the arming of the government with the necessary powers to combat terrorism is not being questioned, giving them powers 'just for good measure' to perform a significantly wider function is unjustified.[37] Therefore, while it was initially introduced for a legitimate reason (national security in the face of the current threat of terrorism), this measure is no longer legitimate if it is used for a wider set of applications such as ordinary criminal justice purposes. Indeed, when data retention was debated by the House of Lords in the United Kingdom concerning the Anti-Terrorism, Crime and Security Bill (2001–2002), the Earl of Northesk and Lord Goodhart, among several others, argued that unless data retention was limited to terrorists it should not be included in the Bill.[38] Similarly, the argument goes that the inclusion of offences other than terrorism within the scope of the application of the Data Retention Directive would clearly be disproportionate because what is justifying this measure is the uncertainty of the current threat of terrorism.

Proportionality also requires further scrutiny as to the purposes for which the data is retained. As previously mentioned, data is officially retained for law enforcement purposes. The jurisprudence of the

Strasbourg Court reveals that even the simple storage of data for law enforcement purposes represents an attack on our civil liberties.[39] If the Strasbourg Court has declared that the storage of data even through means of targeted surveillance (on a case-by-case basis) constitutes an unjustified threat to privacy, then logically the blanket retention of data would clearly be disproportionate. Indeed, the jurisprudence of the Strasbourg Court reveals that states are required to minimise interference with rights, as far as possible, by 'seeking to achieve their aims in the least onerous way as regards to human rights'.[40] An illustration of this can be seen in *Campbell v United Kingdom*,[41] where the Strasbourg Court rejected the government's claim that the interference was necessary in order to 'ensure that prohibited material was not contained in the mail', on the grounds that the same objective could have been achieved by other less harmful means to the individual's rights such as 'by opening the mail in the presence of the prisoner without actually reading it' (Taylor 2003: 90). Thus, in *Campbell*, a blanket rule permitting the opening of prisoners' mail violated the right to privacy (Emmerson and Ashworth 2001: 95). This judgment demonstrates that even in respect of prisoners, whose rights can legitimately be subjected to greater limitation (Cameron 1998: 91–92), the Strasbourg Court has declared blanket measures to be disproportionate.

As a means of testing proportionality, the Strasbourg Court also often examines whether or not the state could have achieved the same objective by using other means, which are less harmful and less intrusive to the rights of individuals. Privacy infringements, therefore, would only be possible if there were no other means available to safeguard the interests 'at stake in a less invasive-to-privacy way, or less violating of the data subject's rights' (Pérez Asinari and Poullet 2004: 105). Two things need to be determined here: whether or not another less invasive measure exists and whether or not it can safeguard the interests at stake. Data preservation has been suggested as a less intrusive alternative to data retention. Data preservation is based on targeted surveillance, where 'it affects only a limited number of individuals during specific periods rather than the entire population all of the time' (Rauhofer 2006: 340). It provides 'authorities with the power to order the logging and disclosure of traffic data in regards to … communications' on a case-by-case basis (Breyer 2005: 373). This differs significantly from data retention, which consists of the blanket, routine storage of data for a prolonged period of time in case of a subsequent need for access (UK Home Office 2003: 15). Since data preservation is directed at a particular person or persons, it does not pose the same threats to privacy as data retention. Likewise, the Council of Europe's Convention on Cybercrime allows law enforcement agencies to request data to be preserved upon notice for certain periods of time (the 'fast-freeze–quick thaw' model). Under this model, service providers are to store the data quickly, upon request by law enforcement authorities. This model provides for only individual secure storage of data, which is subsequently quickly released to authorities upon receipt, for example, of a court order. Accordingly, data preservation and the 'fast-freeze–quick thaw' model constitute less intrusive alternatives to data retention.

Since a less intrusive measure exists, what needs to be determined is whether or not this measure can safeguard the interests at stake. The European Commission conducted an impact assessment, which explains why the data preservation option is not satisfactory in terms of meeting the policy objectives of the Directive, which includes the need to ensure data remains available for a reasonable period in order to contribute to the efforts to prevent and combat terrorism (Commission 2005: 12). Here, an examination is required as to whether or not data preservation would create (or had created) a situation in which data was no longer available.

After 9/11, the efforts of communications service providers in the EU to assist criminal and terrorism investigations were lauded for their efficiency and effectiveness (APIG 2003: 28). For example, a letter sent to communications service providers in the UK from the National Hi-Tech Crime Unit, thanked service providers on the behalf of authorities for their excellent co-operation in providing assistance (by preserving data) to authorities in their investigations (which began after 9/11 and ended in February 2002). Moreover, while traffic data was used to secure the convictions of the perpetrators of the Omagh bombing and murder of Veronica Guerin, this information 'was gathered within the six-month window previously mandated by European data protection laws' (Lillington 2007). Thus far, the lack of data availability does not appear to have been an issue. Was this the case after the attacks on Madrid?

As the Commission stated 'the investigation into the Madrid bombings relied heavily on obtaining and analysing traffic data going back three to six months' (Commission 2005: 12). Nevertheless, it was shown that the 'ongoing co-operation and recent cases (including Madrid) prove that there is a good and sufficient co-operation between law enforcement and industry' (Office of the US Trade Representative 2004: 1–2). In fact, the perpetrators of the Madrid bombings were tracked via already existing data (Retzner and Schu 2006: 9). Furthermore, the efforts undertaken by communications service providers to support law enforcement and intelligence agencies preservation requests in the aftermath of the London bombings were unprecedented since 9/11 (ITAA 2005: 4–5). Therefore, the co-operative experience of service providers and authorities have affirmed that data storage according to present industry practices (no longer than necessary for business purposes; except if data preservation requests are made by authorities) is sufficient to advance the desired result: the availability of data for law enforcement purposes (ITAA 2005).

If current co-operation between law enforcement and industry has been and is effective, then why is mandatory data retention required? The Article 29 Data Protection Working Party (2005: 6), established by Directive 95/46/EC, stated that the 'circumstances justifying data retention, even though they are said to be based on the requests coming from the competent authorities in Member States, do not appear to be grounded on crystal-clear evidence'. In fact, Member States and members of the European Parliament, Council and Commission have not, thus far, 'provided any persuasive arguments that retention of traffic data to such a large-scale extent is the *only* (emphasis added) feasible option for combating crime or protecting national security' (Article 29 Data Protection Working Party 2004: 4). The terrorists responsible for the Madrid and London bombings were tracked via communications data available through data preservation requests, as opposed to mandatory data retention. Additionally, in 2006, mandatory data retention was not used to foil terrorists' plots in Germany ('German Trolley Bomb Case') and Denmark (Danish 'Homegrown' Vollsmose Group).[42] Indeed, data retention laws were not even in effect in those countries at the time. Since data retention is not the least intrusive measure and a less intrusive alternative is available which can safeguard the interests at stake, it is unlikely that this measure will be considered proportionate.

The final test of proportionality examines the length of time for which surveillance occurs. Member States argued that mandatory data retention was required because 'in investigations, it may not be possible to identify the data required or the individual involved until many months or years after the original communication' (Council of the European Union 2004: 5). According to the Directive, data should be retained for a period of no less than six months and a period of no greater than two years (Article 6). During the European Parliament (2005) debate on the proposal for a directive on data retention, MEP Jean-Marie Cavada stated that generally the minimum six-month retention period is applied by telecommunications service providers and is sufficient for managing their contracts and marketing. An analysis of data requests for law enforcement purposes carried out by telecommunication companies in Europe also revealed that the majority of data requested by agencies was not older than six months (Article 29 Data Protection Working Party 2004: 4). Additionally, a recent study on the disclosure of data made by the police in the United Kingdom revealed that the majority of data required by law enforcement agencies (85%) were less than six months old (UK Presidency Paper 2005). Nevertheless, this study also revealed that where data between seven and twelve months was required, this data was subsequently used in complex investigations into more serious crimes, such as murder (UK Presidency Paper 2005). The European Commission, as well as the Presidency of the European Council, attached importance to the results of this study, which demonstrated, overall, that traffic data of up to one year was required by law enforcement agencies. Retention of data for one year would be less intrusive and could safeguard the interests at stake. Yet, the Directive calls for *two* years maximum and not one. Thus, the evidence presented suggests that the period of retention is disproportionate to the aims pursued.

The analysis of 'necessary in a democratic society' revealed that this Directive failed the tests of proportionality, provided by the jurisprudence of the Strasbourg Court, to justify its implementation. While this measure was introduced for a legitimate reason, the application of this Directive to offences other than terrorism was clearly disproportionate. By providing for the blanket retention of data, this Directive fails the test of proportionality because it does not seek to achieve its objectives in the least onerous way possible. Moreover, given the success of the co-operation between service providers and law enforcement, the noted availability of data, and lack of clear evidence of the failure of existing preservation schemes to safeguard the interests at stake, less intrusive measures cannot be ruled out as meeting the objectives of the Directive. Furthermore, the length of time proposed for data retention was clearly disproportionate to the need of such data by law enforcement agencies. Consequently, this Directive does not satisfy the criteria for a justified interference with the right as specified in Article 8(2) and therefore, is incompatible with Article 8 of the European Convention on Human Rights. As such, this measure is an unjustified threat to privacy.

It is worth noting that the negative consequences of the Directive are not limited to the legal sphere.[43] The debate on the costs of data retention and mass surveillance should not stop there. Stimulating a debate on the appropriateness and the costs and consequences of mass data retention makes possible the identification of more effective and less intrusive counter terrorism policy. In the aftermath of the Madrid and London bombings, the EU introduced measures in the *Declaration on Combating Terrorism* that call for the mass surveillance of citizens, their communications, and movements without probable cause. Access to this personal information is permitted without the need of a search warrant or court order. These measures seek to create an environment where information on every citizen can be stored, analysed, monitored, made available, and shared with law enforcement and intelligence agencies. Viewed together, these measures illustrate how governments are increasingly seeking universal surveillance of their citizens. And yet, the implications of this have not been fully explored. It is time to consider what is really at stake – economically, legally, socially, politically, and even in terms of security – when all citizens become the subjects of surveillance.

Despite the severity of the threat, the European Union should not implement measures that go against its very founding principles, not least respect for the rule of law and human rights (Article 6(1), Treaty on European Union). Whilst affording terrorists the liberty to plot attacks and avoid detection can threaten security, it does not follow that in order to deal with terrorism human rights must be sacrificed. If the European Union's measures do not take place within the framework of the rule of law, they allow terrorists to destroy the very foundations of a democratic society. In sum, it is simply wrong to conclude that the EU and its Member States *must* abandon their commitments to the rule of law and human rights in order to deal with the current threat of terrorism. The Data Retention Directive is just such an abandonment.

Notes

1 I would like to sincerely thank Dr Lucia Zedner, my DPhil thesis supervisor (University of Oxford), for her guidance, advice, and comments on my research, of which this chapter is a part of (see Maras 2008). Special thanks to Dr Ben Goold and Dan Neyland for this opportunity and for their criticisms of earlier drafts.
2 Hereafter Strasbourg Court.
3 Since these numbers only reflect known groups, the actual number of organised crime groups and their members is likely to be significantly higher (Bruggeman 2002: 5–6).

4 This term is used to describe 'when individuals otherwise interested in engaging in a lawful activity are deterred from doing so in light of perceived or actual government regulation of that activity' (Horn 2005: 749).

5 *Klass and Others v Federal Republic of Germany* (1979–80) 2 EHRR 214, para. 41.

6 (1985) 7 EHRR 14, para. 84.

7 (2007) 45 EHRR 37, para. 44.

8 *Sunday Times v United Kingdom* (No. 1) (1979–80) 2 EHRR 245, para. 49; *Silver v United Kingdom* (1983) 5 EHRR 347, para. 87–88; and *Malone v United Kingdom* (1985) 7 EHRR 14, para 66 (Clayton and Tomlinson 2000: 322–323).

9 *Huvig v France* (1990) 12 EHRR 528, para. 28.

10 *Malone*, para. 67; *Kruslin v France* (1990) 12 EHRR 547, para. 30.

11 *Sunday Times*, para. 47 and 49.

12 See, for example, *Malone*, para. 66; *Sunday Times*, para. 49; *Silver*, para. 87 and 88.

13 (2004) 39 EHRR 38, para. 30.

14 Décret no 2006-358 du 24 mars 2006 relatif à la conservation des données des communications électroniques.

15 Supreme Court ('Hoge Raad') judgment of 25 November 2005, *LJN*: AU4019.

16 District Court of The Hague judgment of 5 January 2007, *LJN*: AZ5678.

17 The 2003 Order was amended by the Regulation Investigatory Powers (Communication Data) (Amendment) Order 2005.

18 See Article 6, Loi no 2006–64 du 23 janvier 2006 relative à la lutte contre le terrorisme et portant dispositions diverses relatives à la sécurité et aux contrôles frontaliers.

19 In these cases, the Home Office and not the courts authorise these warrants (Statewatch Observatory 2005).

20 (1983) 5 EHRR 347. See also *Malone*, para. 68.

21 (1999) 27 EHRR 91.

22 The proposed deadline for Member States to enact relevant laws and regulations that comply with the provisions of this Directive is no later than 15 September 2007. Sixteen Member States have requested to postpone the application of this Directive (as per Article 15(3) of the Directive). As of 30 November 2007, only seven Member States have notified the Commission of their transposition measures (Commission 2007).

23 *Barthold v Germany* (1985) 7 EHRR 383, para 55; *Funke v France* (1993) 16 EHRR 297, para. 55.

24 *Leander v Sweden* (1987) 9 EHRR 433, para. 59.

25 'Personal data' is defined by Article 2 of the Council of Europe Convention for the Protection of Individuals with regard to Automatic Processing of Personal Data as 'any information relating to an identified or identifiable individual'.

26 *Peck v United Kingdom* (2003) 36 EHRR 41, para. 77.

27 (1987) 9 EHRR 433, para. 59.

28 See, for example, *Leander* para. 59 and 67 in Opinion of AG Leger on 22 November 2005 on Joined Cases C-317/04 and C-318/04 *European Parliament v. Council of the European Union and European Parliament v Commission of the European Communities* (2006) ECR I-4721, para. 230.

29 *Handyside v United Kingdom* (1976) 1 EHRR 737, para. 50; *Gillow v United Kingdom* (1989) 11 EHRR 335, para. 55 (Warbrick 2002: 307–308).

30 *Sporrong and Lönnroth v Sweden* (1983) 5 EHRR 35, para. 69; *Belgian Linguistic Case* (1968) 1 EHRR 252, para. 5.

31 *Rees v United Kingdom* (1987) 9 EHRR 56, para. 50.

32 Concurring Opinion of Judge Pettiti in *Kopp*, p. 120.

33 German Code of Criminal Procedure (*Strafprozeßordnung*) § 100g.

34 German Data Retention Bill, Regierungsentwurf für eine Gesetz zur Neuregelung der Telekommunikationsüberwachung und anderer verdeckter Ermittlungsmaßnahmen sowie zur Umsetzung der Richtlinie 2006/24/EG.

35 BVerfG 1 BvR 256/08.

36 Hansard HL vol 629 col 772 (4 December 2001) (Danby 2002: 44).

37 Hansard HL vol 629 col 769 (4 December 2001) (Danby 2002: 43–44).

38 Hansard HL vol 629 col 252 (27 November 2001); Hansard HL vol 629 col 954 (4 December 2001) (Danby 2002: 39 and 47).

39 See, for example, *Klass*, *Rotaru*, and *Amann v Switzerland* (2000) 30 EHRR 843 and *Rotaru*.

40 *Hatton and Others v United Kingdom* (2002) 34 EHRR 1, para 97.

41 (1993) 15 EHRR 137.

42 In Germany, on 31 July 2006, bombs were placed on two regional trains near Cologne in an attempted coordinated terrorist attack. On 5 September 2006, in Denmark, individuals of a home-grown terrorist group, who had allegedly planned several terrorist attacks on undisclosed targets in Denmark, were arrested for their procurement of materials to make explosives (Europol 2007: 18–19).

43 A comprehensive evaluation of the Directive, which includes its legal, economic, social, and political consequences, efficacy, and impact on EU security, has been conducted elsewhere (Maras 2008).

References

All Party Parliamentary Internet Group (APIG) (2003) 'Communications Data: Report of an Inquiry by the All Party Internet Group' [Online]. Available at: http://www.apcomms.org.uk/apig/archive/activities-2002/data-retention-inquiry/APIGreport.pdf [accessed 18 March 2008].

Allitsch, R. (2002) 'Data retention on the Internet', *Computer Law Review International*, 3(6): 161–68.

Article 29 Data Protection Working Party (2004) 'Opinion 9/2004 on a draft Framework Decision on the storage of data processed and retained for the purpose of providing electronic public communications services or data available in public communications networks with a view to the prevention, investigation, detection and prosecution of criminal acts, including terrorism. [Proposal presented by France, Ireland, Sweden and Great Britain (Document of the Council 8958/04 of 28 April 2004)' (1885/04/EN) [Online]. Available at: http://www.privacyinternational. org/issues/terrorism/library/article29pm20041115b.pdf [accessed 28 April 2007].

Article 29 Data Protection Working Party (2005) 'Opinion 4/2005 on the Proposal for a Directive of the European Parliament and of the Council on the Retention of Data Processed in Connection with the Provision of Public Electronic Communication Services and Amending Directive 2002/58/EC (COM(2005)438 final of 21.09.2005)' (1868/05/EN) [Online]. Available at: http://ec.europa.eu/justice_home/fsj/privacy/docs/wpdocs/2005/wp113_en.pdf [accessed 21 February 2007].

Austin, L. (2001) 'Is privacy a casualty of the war on terrorism?' in R.J. Daniels, P. Macklem and K. Roach (eds) *The Security of Freedom: Essay's on Canada's Anti-Terrorism Bill*. Toronto: University of Toronto Press.

Bowden, C. (2002) 'Closed circuit television for inside your head: blanket traffic data retention and the emergency anti-terrorism legislation', *Computer and Telecommunications Law Review*, 8(2): 21–4.

Breyer, P. (2005) 'Telecommunications data retention and human rights: the compatibility of blanket traffic data retention with the ECHR', *European Law Journal*, 11(3): 365–75.

Bruggeman, W. (2002) 'Security and combating international organised crime and terrorism', *ESCA World 6 Conference* [Online]. Available at: http://www.ecsanet.org/ecsaworld6/contributions/session1/Bruggeman.doc [accessed 29 April 2007].

Cameron, I. (1998) *An Introduction to the European Convention on Human Rights*. (3rd edn). Uppsala, Sweden: Iustus Förlag

Campbell, G. (2007) 'Serious crime prevention orders: unleashed!', *Counsel*: 21–3.

Clayton R. and Tomlinson, H. (2000) *The Law of Human Rights*. Oxford: Oxford University Press.

Chang, N. (2003) 'How democracy dies: the war on our civil liberties', in Brown, C (ed.) *Lost Liberties: Ashcroft and the Assault on Personal Freedom*. New York: The New Press.

Cole, D. (2002) 'Enemy aliens', *Stanford Law Review*, 54(5): 953–1004.

Cole, D. (2002/2003) 'Their liberties, our security', *Boston Review*, 27(6) [Online]. Available at: http://bostonreview.net/BR27.6/colereply.html [accessed 12 March 2007].

Cole, D. and Dempsey, J.X. (2006) *Terrorism and the Constitution: Sacrificing Civil Liberties in the Name of National Security*. New York: The New Press.

Commission (EC) (2005) 'Annex to the: Proposal for a Directive of the European Parliament and of the Council on the retention of data processed in connection with the provision of public electronic communication services and amending Directive 2002/58/EC', *Staff Working Document Extended Impact Assessment* COM(2005) 438 final [Online]. Available at: http://ec.europa.eu/justice_home/doc_centre/police/doc/sec_2005_1131_ en.pdf [accessed 2 October 2006].

Commission (EC) (2007) *Transposition of Data Retention Directive 2006/24/EC: Summary Report* [Online]. Available at: http://ec.europa.eu/justice_home/ news/events/data_retention/meeting_report_30_11_07.pdf [accessed 17 March 2008].

Cooley, T. (1907) *A Treatise on the Law of Torts*. Chicago: Callaghan and Company.

Council of the European Union (2004) 'Draft Framework Decision on the retention of data processed and stored in connection with the provision of publicly available electronic communications services or data on public communications networks for the purpose of prevention, investigation, detection and prosecution of crime and criminal offences including terrorism' [Online]. Available at: http://www.statewatch.org/news/2004/ apr/8958-04-dataret.pdf [accessed 27 April 2007].

Council of the European Union (2005) '2005 EU Organised Crime Report – Public Version' [Online]. Available at: http://www.europol.europa.eu/ publications/Organised_Crime_Reports-in_2006_replaced_by_OCTA/EU_ OrganisedCrimeReport2005.pdf [accessed 29 April 2007].

Council of the European Union (2006) 'Proposal for a Directive of the European Parliament and of the Council on the retention of data processed in connection with the provision of public electronic communication services and amending Directive 2002/58/EC [first reading]–Statements' [Online]. Available at: http://register.consilium.eu.int/pdf/en/06/st05/ st05777-ad01.en06.pdf [accessed 29 April 2007].

Danby, G. (2002) 'Communications data: access and retention', *House of Commons (HC) Library Research Paper 02/63* [Online]. Available at: http://www.parliament.uk/commons/lib/research/rp2002/rp02-063.pdf [accessed 14 February 2007].

Davis, H. (2003) *Human Rights and Civil Liberties*. Cullompton: Willan Publishing.

De Hert, P. (2005) 'Balancing security and liberty within the European human rights framework: A critical reading of the Court's case law in the light of surveillance and criminal law enforcement strategies after 9/11', *Utrecht Law Review*, 1(1): 68–96.

De Vries, H. and Van Tol, M. (2006) 'ISP disclosure: Dutch courts rule on ISP disclosure', *Data Protection Law and Policy*, 3(2).

Digital Rights Ireland (DRI) (2008) 'German Constitutional Court restricts data retention' [Online]. Available at: http://www.digitalrights.ie/2008/03/20/ german-constitutional-court-restricts-data-retention/ [accessed 7 April 2008].

Dworkin, R. (2002) 'The threat to patriotism', in C. Calhoun, P. Price and A. Timmer (eds) *Understanding September 11*. New York: The New Press.

Eissen, M-A. (1993) 'The principle of proportionality in the case-law of the European Court of Human Rights', in R.St.J. MacDonald, F. Matscher and H. Petzold (eds) *The European System for the Protection of Human Rights*. London: Martinus Nijhoff.

Emmerson B. and Ashworth, A. (2001) *Human Rights and Criminal Justice* (1st edn). London: Sweet and Maxwell.

European Council (2004) 'Declaration on combating terrorism' [Online]. Available at: http://www.consilium.europa.eu/uedocs/cmsUpload/DECL-25.3.pdf [accessed 3 November 2006].

European Digital Rights (EDRI) (2007) 'Data retention and increased surveillance in Germany' [Online]. Available at: http://www.edri.org/edrigram/number5.8/germany-data-retention [accessed 7 April 2008].

European Parliament (2004) 'European Parliament resolution on the first report on the implementation of the Data Protection Directive (95/46/EC)' COM(2003) 265 [Online]. Available at: http://www.europarl.europa.eu/omk/sipade3?SAME_LEVEL=1&LEVEL=5&NAV=S&LSTDOC=Y&DETAIL=&PUBREF=-//EP//TEXT+TA+P5-TA-2004-0141+0+DOC+XML+V0//EN [accessed 20 November 2006].

European Parliament (2005) 'Data retention', *Debate*, 13 December.

Europol (2006) *EU Organised Crime Threat Assessment 2006* [Online]. Available at:. http://www.europol.europa.eu/publications/OCTA/OCTA2006.pdf [accessed 29 April 2007].

Europol (2007) *EU Terrorism Situation and Trend Report 2007* [Online]. Available at: http://www.europol.europa.eu/publications/EU_Terrorism_Situation_and_Trend_Report_TE-SAT/TESAT2007.pdf [accessed 17 March 2008].

Feldman, D. (2002) *Civil Liberties and Human Rights in England and Wales* (2nd edn). Oxford: Oxford University Press.

Foster, S. (2003) *Human Rights and Civil Liberties*. London: Longman.

Fried, C. (1970) *An Anatomy of Values*. Cambridge, MA: Harvard University Press.

Galison, P. and Minow, M. (2005) 'Our privacy, ourselves in the age of technological intrusions', in R.A. Wilson (ed.) *Human Rights in the 'War on Terror'*. Cambridge: Cambridge University Press.

Goemans, C. and Dumortier, J. (2003) 'Mandatory retention of traffic data in the EU: possible impact on privacy and on-line anonymity' [Online]. Available at: http://www.law.kuleuven.ac.be/icri/publications/440Retention_of_traffic_data_Dumortier_Goemans.pdf?where=&temp=b8b0461b67e73df2e73c67fb9900738b [accessed 10 February 2007].

Goold, B. (2002) 'Privacy rights and public spaces: CCTV and the problem of the "unobservable observer"', *Criminal Justice Ethics*, 21(1): 21–27.

Gross, O. (2002/2003) 'Misguided response', *Boston Review*, 27(6) [Online]. Available at: http://bostonreview.net/BR27.6/gross.html [accessed 12 March 2007].

Hansard HL, vol. 629 col. 252 (27 November 2001).

Hansard HL, vol. 629 col. 769 (4 December 2001).

Hansard HL, vol. 629 col. 772 (4 December 2001).

Hansard HL, vol. 629 col. 954 (4 December 2001).

Heymann, P.B. (2003) *Terrorism, Freedom and Security: Winning Without a War.* Cambridge, MA: MIT Press.

Horn, G. (2005) 'Online searches and offline challenges: the chilling effect, anonymity, and the new FBI guidelines', *New York University Annual Survey of American Law,* 60: 735–78.

Ignatieff, M. (2005) *The Lesser Evil: Political Ethics in the Age of Terror.* Edinburgh: Edinburgh University Press.

Information Technology Association of America (ITAA) (2006) *Data Retention Advisory* [Online]. Available at: http://www.itaa.org/global/docs/ITAA_ DataRetentionAdvisory.doc [accessed 15 September 2007].

Janis, M., Kay, R. and Bradley, A. (2000) *European Human Rights Law: Text and Materials* (2nd edn). Oxford: Oxford University Press.

Joint Committee on Human Rights (2001) 'Second Report: Anti-terrorism, Crime and Security Bill', *Session 2001–2002,* HL 37/HC 372.

Krieger, H. (2004) 'Limitations on privacy, freedom of press, opinion and assembly as a means of fighting terrorism', in C. Walter, S. Voneky, V. Roben and F. Schorkopf (eds) *Terrorism as a Challenge for National and International Law: Security versus Liberty?* Heidelberg, Germany: Springer.

Kosta, E. (2006) 'Data Retention Directive: What the Council Cherishes, the Privacy Advocates Reject and the Industry Fears …'. Proceedings 45th FITCE Congress – 'Telecom Wars: The return of the profit' (Athens, 30 August – 2 September 2006).

Lillington, K. (2007) 'Retention of Mobile Data a Threat to Everyone's Privacy', *The Irish Times* (2 March).

Lyon, D. (2003) *Surveillance after September 11.* Malden, MA: Polity.

Makarenko, T. (2004) 'The crime–terror continuum: tracing the interplay between transnational organised crime and terrorism', *Global Crime,* 6(1): 129–45.

Maras, M-H. (2008) *From Targeted to Mass Surveillance: The Consequences and Costs of the Data Retention Directive.* Thesis for DPhil in Law. Oxford: University of Oxford [publication forthcoming, with different title].

McBride, J. (1999) 'Proportionality and the European Convention on Human Rights', in E. Ellis (ed.) *The Principle of Proportionality in the Laws of Europe.* Oxford: Hart Publishing.

McIntyre, T.J. (2008) 'Data retention in Ireland: privacy, policy and proportionality', *Computer Law and Security Report,* 24(4): 326–34.

Munir, A.B. and Yasin, S. (2004) 'Access to communications data by public authorities', *Computer Law and Security Report,* 20(3): 194–99.

Office of the United States Trade Representative (2004) 'Public Comments on Enhancing the Transatlantic Dialogue between the US and the European

Union: MCI–Attachment of ITAA Comments' [Online]. Available at: http://www.ustr.gov/assets/World_Regions/Europe_Middle_East/Transatlantic_Dialogue/Public_Comments/asset_upload_file557_7049.pdf [accessed 29 April 2007].

Opinion of AG Leger on 22 November 2005 on Joined Cases C-317/04 and C-318/04 *European Parliament v Council of the European Union and European Parliament v Commission of the European Communities* [2006] ECR I-4721.

Pérez Asinari, M.V. and Poullet, Y. (2004) 'The airline passenger data disclosure case and the EU–US debate', *Computer Law and Security Report*, 20(2): 98–116.

Pfeiffer, G. (2002) *Strafprozessordnung § 100a* (4th edn). Munich.

Privacy International (2003) 'EU data retention legislation: a violation of rights guaranteed by the European Convention on Human Rights' [Online]. Available at: http://www.privacyinternational.org/article.shtml?cmd%5B347%5D=x-347-57875 [accessed 10 January 2007].

Privacy International (2007) 'PHR2006–French Republic'. Available at: http://www.privacyinternational.org/article.shtml?cmd[accessed47]=x-347-559537 [accessed 10 January 2008].

Rauhofer, J. (2006) 'Just because you're paranoid, doesn't mean they're not after you: legislative developments in relation to the mandatory retention of communications data in the European Union', *Script-ed*, 3(4): 322–43.

Raz, J. (1977) 'The rule of law and its virtue', *Law Quarterly Review*, 93: 195–211.

Retzner K. and Schu, R. (2006) 'Data retention – a bone of contention', *Electronic Business Law*, 8(1): 6–11.

Schwartz, P.M. (2002–2003) 'German and US telecommunications privacy law: legal regulation of domestic law enforcement surveillance', *Hastings Law Journal*, 54: 751–803.

Starmer, K. (1999) *European Human Rights Law*. London: LAG.

Statewatch Observatory (2005) 'Data retention and police access in the UK – a warning for Europe' [Online]. Available at: http://ics.leedsac.uk/papers/vp01.cfm?outfit=ks&folder=70&paper=91 [accessed 21 November 2006].

Sunstein, C.R. (2005) *Laws of Fear: Beyond the Precautionary Principle*. Cambridge: Cambridge University Press.

Taylor, N. (2003) 'Policing, privacy and proportionality', *European Human Rights Law Review* (Special Issue: Privacy): 86–100.

Tribe, L.H. (2002/2003) 'Liberty for all: a response to David Cole's "Their Liberties, Our Security"', *Boston Review*, 27(6) [Online]. Available at: http://bostonreview.net/BR27.6/tribe.html [accessed 12 March 2007].

UK Home Office (2003) 'Consultation paper on a code of practice for voluntary retention of communications data' [Online]. Available at: http://www.poptel.org.uk/statewatch/news/2003/mar/atcs.pdf [accessed 3 October 2006].

UK Presidency Paper (2005) 'Liberty and security: striking the balance' [Online]. Available at: http://www.edri.org/docs/UKpresidencypaper.pdf [accessed 24 November 2006].

Vidino, L. (2006) *Al-Qaeda in Europe: The New Battleground of International Jihad*. New York: Prometheus.

von Schorlemer, S. (2003) 'Human rights: substantive and institutional implications of the war against terrorism', *European Journal of International Law*, 14: 265–82.

Wacks, R. (1989) *Personal Information: Privacy and the Law*. Oxford: Clarendon.

Walden, I. (2001) 'Balancing rights: surveillance and data protection', *Electronic Business Law*, 3(11): 10–15.

Walden, I. (2004) 'Addressing the data problem: the legal framework governing forensics in an online environment', in C. Jensen, S. Poslad and T. Dimitrakos (eds) 2995 *Lecture Notes in Computer Science: Trust Management* [Online Book Series].

Warbrick, C. (2002) 'The principles of the European Convention on Human Rights and the response of states to terrorism', *European Human Rights Law Review*, 3: 287–314.

Whitaker, R. (2006) 'A Faustian bargain? America and the dream of total information awareness', in Haggerty K.D. and Ericson, R.V. (eds) *New Politics of Surveillance and Visibility*. Toronto: University of Toronto Press.

Whitley, E.A. and Hosein, I. (2005) 'Policy discourse and data retention: the technology politics of surveillance in the United Kingdom', *Telecommunications Policy*, 29: 857–74.

Wong, R. (2005) 'Privacy: charting its developments and prospects', in M. Klang and A. Murray (eds) *Human Rights in the Digital Age*. London: GlassHouse.

Part 2

Technologies and techniques of surveillance

Chapter 5

Surveillance, accountability and organisational failure: the story of Jean Charles de Menezes

Daniel Neyland

Introduction

Surveillance and accountability are increasingly pervasive modes of social and organisational activity. The increasing use of CCTV cameras, border crossing technologies, identity-based assessments, traffic management and lifestyle governance are said to include forms of surveillance. At the same time there are increasingly frequent calls for particular people and organisations to be accountable, to be held to account, to be assessed, audited, made transparent and rendered available for analysis. However, these two areas of activity only provoke occasional questions. For example, there seems to be an absence of detailed scrutiny of what both surveillance and accountability might mean, for whom, carried out in what way and for what purpose. This paper will suggest that surveillance and accountability are frequently closely tied together and by looking at both modes of activity we can begin to address some of these absent questions.

Accountability often involves the reconstruction or replaying of particular kinds of histories in order to render them accountable. When company accounts are audited, the accounts are used to reconstruct and assess some particular aspects of the company's history which went into their production. Surveillance systems are often noted for making available rich histories of visuals, sometimes texts and sometimes audio replays of particular days or events or locations. In this way, CCTV systems, for example, are noted for their accountability. They are said to be able to make available rich histories of times, places and actions through which particular modes of accountability can operate (for example, individuals can be held to account for their actions recorded on tape, or CCTV systems themselves can be held to account through taped activity). Often calls for accountability appear to assume that accountability in and of itself is a clear-cut process characterised by certainty and positive outcomes.

This chapter will argue that many features of accountability are open to question. For example, audited company accounts can be questioned for the extent to which they reflect the position, strength or offer an accurate reflection of company business. The same kinds of ideas are found in surveillance systems; although talk of surveillance systems is frequently characterised by certainty over the kinds of information they make available and there is ever increasing expansion of surveillance systems, these systems are also open to a series of complex questions. This chapter will take one particular surveillance operation – the case of Jean Charles de Menezes – as its focus in order to look at the complex ways in which surveillance and accountability are interwoven in order to make judgements about, in this case, organisational failure. The chapter, first, introduces forms of surveillance and accountability before, second, telling the stories of Jean Charles de Menezes. Third, the chapter presents the complex multitude of accountability processes involved in this case. Fourth, the chapter analyses the ways in which the accountability process produces an assessment of the surveillance operation as an organisational failure.

Surveillance and accountability

In order to understand the complex relationship between surveillance and accountability, we need to take a look in more detail at these two forms of activity. Surveillance has been analysed in broad and narrow terms. The broad version of surveillance typically encapsulates a range of information collection processes. A typical broad version of surveillance can be found in the work of Lyon (2001) who suggests that surveillance can be considered as: 'any collection and processing of personal data, whether identifiable or not, for the purposes of influencing or managing those whose data have been garnered' (2001: 2). A narrow version of surveillance is more closely tied into specific moments of information scrutiny. In place of a focus on broad means of information collection comes a narrow focus on the specific practices of information interrogation. A typical narrow version of surveillance can be found in the work of Bennett (2006). He suggests that greater attention needs to be paid to the details of exactly who has their personal data scrutinised, to what effect. For Bennett most data collected is entirely routine and free from further scrutiny, both for the collectors and subjects of collection. Bennett suggests, however, that this is a highly selective, contingent process and forms the point at which questions should be asked of whose information is selected for greater scrutiny, why and for what end. This selectivity involves issues of identity (who someone is) and claims about likely future action (for example, what threat they might pose).

Although the broader version of surveillance captures more types of activity, it may be too broad for our purposes here. It might prove more useful in this paper to adopt the narrow version of surveillance in order to bracket more clearly the phenomenon which will form the subject of analysis. In this narrow approach surveillance can thus be understood as those moments of data scrutiny, where particular actions, people and things are interrogated in some detail. This narrow version of surveillance does not tell us much about the connections between surveillance and forms of accountability. What different modes of accountability might there be? How can these help us to think about surveillance activities? I will propose two headings under which we can understand modes of accountability and I will try and relate each of these to practices of (narrow) surveillance.

The first mode of accountability is what we might term *constitutive* accountability. This refers to forms of interaction which operate as occasions of accountability. For example, conversations might involve one speaker providing an utterance to be held to account by a second speaker whose subsequent response is then available to be held to account by the first speaker (Garfinkel 1967; Luff and Heath 1993). This approach treats accountability as a pervasive phenomenon, constitutive of everyday forms of interaction (constitutive in that through holding each other to account, more or less mutual intelligibility is accomplished). However, the form of accountability outlined can be characteristic of professional as well as everyday settings (Lynch 1998; Suchman 1993). In professional settings, the ways in which interactions operate as moments of accountability are tied into the operational practices of an organisation (for example, meetings are held as opportunities for parties to hold each other to account and those meetings form part of the structure of the organisation as they are timetabled, minuted and their existence becomes an expectation amongst organisational members). Constitutive forms of accountability can be characterised by more ad hoc, less systematic forms of interaction than other areas of accountability (see below).

In a surveillance system such as a CCTV camera system, constitutive accountability has both mutual and non-mutual aspects. Mutual constitutive accountability occurs in surveillance operations such as CCTV systems between CCTV staff (who work in teams and may hold to account each other's actions) between staff and their managers (who may have an interest in, for example, upholding CCTV code of practice) and between staff and police officers (often connected by a radio system through which they share information and also establish accountability). The accountability is mutual as each gets to hold the other to account and continually make judgements regarding the appropriateness of the others' activity. Interactions between these individuals are often recorded and made available for future occasions of accountability (see demonstrative accountability). There are also non-mutual aspects to this accountability. For example, under the terms of covert surveillance schemes, those under surveillance would be unaware that their actions were being held to account and would be unaware in the short-term of judgements made about them. Furthermore in public area CCTV systems, those appearing on monitors do not get to participate in holding CCTV staff to account in the same way that their images are held to account by the CCTV staff. In these non-mutual forms of interactions, accountability is unevenly distributed.[1]

The second mode can be termed *demonstrative* accountability. This relates to those forms of assessment where an organisation is held to account for past actions. The organisation is called upon to demonstrate that they have acted in certain ways. The demonstrations involve the organisation's past actions being measured, judged or appraised according to certain principles, expectations, standardised measures, benchmarks, laws, codes of conduct or practice, performance indicators and so on (see Power 1997; Baxter and Chua 2003). The principles which form the basis for assessment form the focus for accountability. One suggestion is that these principles also act as a means through which an organisation steers itself and through which its members come to prioritise certain types of activities and organisational goals (Miller 1992; Miller and O'Leary 1994; Rose 1999). These assessments are often tied into further forms of accountability such as external auditing whereby organisations are expected to be able to demonstrate that they have adhered to certain standards and standard practices. The demonstrative aspect of this form of accountability can involve the organisation under assessment being called upon to produce information for an often unspecified mass audience. This includes, for example, company accounts made available for the public good or in the public interest. In effect these 'publics' tend to be fairly narrow and specialised (those who are interested in and have the time and skill to read reports, accounts and other ephemera made available by organisations; that is they are not, in practice, often noted as members of the general public). This form of accountability includes calls for organisations to make certain types of information available and for (sometimes publicly funded) organisations to demonstrate their value for money, responsibility (social, corporate), transparency[2] and ethical standards. Demonstrative accountability is consequential as organisations are actively encouraged to adopt particular principles in their activities (legal, ethical, financial) and specific protocols on making information available for assessment. Indeed, for public organisations their funding can depend on an ability to demonstrate that they have adhered to these protocols.

Calls for more demonstrative accountability through principles and protocols involve two aspects. Suggestions of a need for more accountability around a particular event, for example, often involve questions of what happened during the event (such as who did what to whom). Thus calls for more of this type of accountability are based around the idea that utilising principles and protocols can produce a clear, single, certainty – or a particular kind of truth – for an event. Calls for more demonstrative accountability also involve claims that someone or thing (for example an organisation) needs to be held to account. That is, the person or organisation should have to face the 'consequences' of their actions (already established as the 'truth'). In this way, calls for more 'demonstrative' accountability involve ideas of a 'truth' to be produced and a 'consequence' (or series of consequences) to follow from the truth.[3] These calls for more demonstrative accountability assume both the truth and consequence are more or less straightforward. However, principles to guide actions and protocols for assessment are not straightforward.

The accountability principles can also be consequential for the types of activity that the organisation carries out (see, for example, Strathern 1999; 2002; 2004). The consequences can operate in two ways. First, an organisation and its members can have their activities redefined by the principles on which they will be held to account. A frequently reiterated version of this is the UK research assessment exercise whereby a system to assess academic output through publications is said to have encouraged more and more publication in a narrow range of journals (the measures did not measure, but became targets to aim towards). A second outcome from this mode of accountability can be that lists of things to be held to account can encourage organisations to treat the list as providing detail on the kinds of activities which will not be held to account. For example, if the Information Commissioner asks government departments to provide annual returns on their practices of information storage, but does not mention on the list of things that departments need to report the use of unencrypted CDs of personal information sent by private courier firms, the government department may develop a sense that these non-listed types of activity are unlikely to be scrutinised. Such lists of activities to be held to account are always narrower than the possible range of organisational activities that could be considered and such narrowness can be consequential.

Thus far in this chapter these two modes of accountability have been separated out for ease of presentation. However, in any particular incident of surveillance, these modes of accountability can come together in varied ways. Turning attention now to a specific surveillance incident – the story of Jean Charles de Menezes – can help us to understand how these modes of surveillance and accountability operate in practice, how they come together and how they form the basis for asking questions of 'what is going on' and 'what went wrong?' The next section of the chapter provides the stories told of Jean Charles de Menezes before then proceeding to analyse the modes of surveillance and accountability involved. This case is particularly noteworthy due to the extent of information made available about the surveillance operation and subsequent accountability.[4]

The stories of Jean Charles de Menezes[5]

Story 1: 'Frank' a surveillance officer's story

'Frank' (an operational codename supplied by the police) was carrying out a covert surveillance operation (Operation Theseus 2) on a block of flats at 21 Scotia Road, south London. The block of flats was placed under surveillance at around 5am on the morning of 22 July 2005. The address was found on a gym membership card in a pocket on a bag containing explosives which had failed to detonate at Shepherd's Bush tube station on the previous day (this was one of several bags of explosives which had all failed to detonate on 21 July 2005, two weeks after bombs had exploded on a London bus and several tube trains). The gym card indicated that Hussain Osman lived at the block of flats.

'Frank' was an SAS surveillance expert working with a team of SO12 officers, who were trained in carrying out surveillance operations. The surveillance team had a plan to intercept people leaving the communal exit of the Scotia Road flats some distance from the flats in order to question potential suspects, but also not raise alarm amongst those inside the flats. 'Frank' had been in position since 5.30am at the same time that CO19 officers were also called to the scene. CO19 officers are specialist trained firearms officers. CO19 would carry out the interceptions. SO12 officers carried guns, but only for their own protection, not for armed interceptions. By 9.30am there was still no sign of CO19 trained firearm officers and still no definite plan on where interceptions of suspects should take place.

At precisely the moment a suspect left his flat, 'Frank' – whose job was to operate the video equipment – was using the bathroom. Over the radio 'Frank' suggested to the control room (Room 1600 at New Scotland Yard) that a white male had left 21 Scotia Road, not carrying anything. 'Frank' suggested he had been unable to get a clear identification of the suspect and had not had the chance to video him. 'Frank' suggested 'It might be worth somebody else having a look'.

Story 2: Jean Charles de Menezes' story

Jean Charles de Menezes left his flat to go to work as an electrician at 9.30am. He was running a little late. He got on a bus to take him to Brixton tube to catch a tube train to North London where he was working on a job with a friend. When he reached Brixton tube station he found the station closed (due to previous terror scares). Jean Charles de Menezes then phoned his friend and said he might be late and would get on another bus to Stockwell tube station to catch a tube there. Once de Menezes reached Stockwell tube station he picked up a free Metro newspaper, used his ticket to go through a ticket barrier and, seeing a train waiting, ran onto the train.

Story 3: Cressida Dick's story

Cressida Dick was Gold Commander, the senior police officer in command of Room 1600 in New Scotland Yard. From this room several simultaneous surveillance operations were being carried out, covering different leads generated by the previous day's incidents.

From the control room Dick was kept up to date with the movements of the Scotia Road suspect. By the time the suspect reached Stockwell tube station, Dick had received five positive identifications of the suspect as Hussain Osman from more than one surveillance officer. Although Dick was aware that SO12 surveillance officers did not have specialist firearms training, she ordered them to perform an armed intervention on the suspect outside Stockwell tube station in order to stop him from detonating a bomb on a train. However, several seconds after issuing this order, 'Trojan 80' a senior officer in charge of CO19 firearms officers informed Dick that firearms officers were now in position at the station (this was 4.5 hours after they were initially called to 21 Scotia Road). Aware that CO19 officers had training in armed interventions in suicide bombers and that SO12 officers had no training in this area, Dick stopped the surveillance officers from performing an intervention. So at this point, CO19 officers who were reportedly in position at Stockwell tube station were ordered to carry out an armed intervention and 'stop', 'challenge' and 'arrest' the suspect.

Story 4: Surveillance team's story

Following on from 'Frank's' suggestion that 'It might be worth somebody else having a look' at the suspect, 'Ivor' and 'Ken' (both surveillance officers from SO12) took up pursuit of the suspect. They attempted to get a positive identification of the suspect and tried to understand what he was doing and where he was going. They followed him on a bus to Brixton, where the suspect got off the bus and made a mobile phone call. The surveillance team noted this behaviour as suspect got on a bus, got off a bus, made a phone call and got on another bus – this was reported as classic terrorist activity to shake off a surveillance team. One of the surveillance officers 'Edward' reported over the radio at this stage that the suspect looked North African.

'Ken' and 'Ivor' had followed the suspect and used the radio system to keep Cressida Dick up to date with what was happening and to request instruction on their next actions. Although initially ordered to carry out an armed intervention, they were then told that CO19 trained firearms officers were at the scene. This meant they no longer needed to perform such an intervention. However, under their surveillance at this point the suspect entered Stockwell tube station and there were no firearms officers from CO19 in position. 'Ivor' and 'Ken' entered the station in pursuit of the suspect several seconds ahead of firearms officers who jumped the ticket barrier and pursued the surveillance officers down the escalators. At this point 'Ken' and 'Ivor' and the firearms officers lost contact with Room 1600 as their radios did not work underground.

'Ivor' and his fellow surveillance officers followed the suspect on to the train. One officer used his foot to hold the door open so the train could not leave. Firearms officers from CO19 then entered the train carriage. Several surveillance officers pointed toward the suspect and one said 'He's here' and pointed to the suspect again. At this point, the suspect got to his feet. In court Dick suggested that officers gave the suspect a warning at this point, although no independent witness in the carriage corroborated this. 'Ivor' held the suspect, pinning his arms to his side. 'Ivor' then felt a bullet fly past his ear and was dragged away from the suspect. The suspect was then shot seven times in the head. A firearms officer held a gun against 'Ivor' until he could identify himself as a police officer. In the immediate aftermath of the incident commuters fled in panic and firearms officers gave chase to the tube driver who ran off down a tunnel.

Attempts at accountability

These stories of Jean Charles de Menezes have been made available[6] by the variety of attempts at accountability made in the time since his death. These forms of accountability have involved: two investigations carried out by the Independent Police Complaints Commission (resulting in two reports – Stockwell 1 looking at the shooting itself and Stockwell 2 which investigated complaints from the de Menezes' family about police officers' comments after the event); the Metropolitan Police Authority (the watchdog for the Metropolitan police which passed a vote of confidence in the Commissioner of the Metropolitan Police, Sir Ian Blair); the London Assembly (an elected body connected to the mayor's office which passed a vote of no confidence in Sir Ian Blair following the incident); and a court trial based on the Health and Safety at Work Act. These activities focused on both constitutive accountability (assessing the events of the day itself and who did what to whom, utilising what kinds of judgement) and demonstrative accountability (what systems were in place for holding activities and organisations to account, with what outcomes). These forms of accountability produced a significant number of issues. This chapter will now turn attention to first the focus on who or what would be the appropriate unit of responsibility to be held to account and then, second, the moment to moment detail of the events themselves.

Units of responsibility

An initial complaint brought by the de Menezes family to the IPCC was that the Metropolitan Police had issued misleading statements to the media regarding Jean Charles de Menezes. It was alleged that the statements were misleading in saying that de Menezes failed to respond to a challenge, was wearing a thick or padded jacket and jumped ticket barriers and that police officers already knew these claims were untrue by the time they briefed the media. The IPCC investigated for several months and produced a 140 page report which attempted to figure out the appropriate unit of responsibility to be held to account. The focus narrowed to the conduct of seven individual officers. The report makes recommendations for each individual. These range from the Commissioner Ian Blair who is held not responsible, but merely uninformed, to junior colleagues who are held to have made mistakes, but are not fully responsible and in need of advice and training. Assistant Commissioner Hayman was found responsible:

> Following the shooting of Mr de Menezes he had a responsibility to keep the Commissioner informed and has stated that he used his judgement to decide whether or not that was necessary. He briefed the Commissioner, MPA [Metropolitan Police Authority] and senior colleagues at the 17:00 Management Board sub-meeting on lines which he must have known were not consistent with what he had told the CRA [Crime Reporters Association]. This causes us serious concern. (Stockwell 2: 106)

Following these discussions regarding the appropriate unit of responsibility, were suggestions over appropriate accountability measures. The IPCC recommended that the officer deemed responsible should be held to account by the appropriate authority:

> It is recommended that the MPA as the Appropriate Authority, consider what action they intend to take concerning the conduct issues identified in relation to AC Hayman. (Stockwell 2: 106)

The IPCC acted as the initial organisation to decide on appropriate units of responsibility to be held to account and the appropriate organisation to decide on the consequences of accountability. Hence the modes of accountability are interwoven in complex ways. The constitutive accountability of the day itself (who did what to whom, who made what judgements based on access to what information) is used as a focus for assessing subsequent demonstrative accountability (did these actions and judgements adhere to standard practice, who or what should be the unit of responsibility for those actions and what should follow from demarcations of responsibility).

Other accountability activities in the de Menezes case followed a similar pattern in attempting to establish units of responsibility. The Metropolitan Police Authority and the London Assembly both identified an individual – the Commissioner Ian Blair – as the potential unit of responsibility, however the Metropolitan Police Authority provided a vote of confidence while the London Assembly provided a vote of no confidence. However, this focus on the individual as the unit of responsibility was not consistent across these forms of accountability. The IPCC also carried out an investigation into the activities of the police force (as an aggregate entity) on 22 July 2005. Initially fifteen individual officers were considered as possible individual units of responsibility, however charges against eleven of these officers were dropped. Charges against four senior officers were treated as a single block and the appropriate accountability process was initially deemed to be the forthcoming inquest (although charges were later dropped before the inquest had taken place). The IPCC investigation then reported on the conduct of the Metropolitan Police Service. As a result of the IPCC investigation the Metropolitan Police Service were charged under the Health and Safety at Work Act (1979) of failing to protect the public from a potential terrorist. The IPCC report was presented as part of the evidence at the trial. The trial constituted the potential unit of responsibility to be held to account as the police service. It was the police service that was to be judged as potentially threatening the health and safety of the public. As one of the surveillance officers (codename) 'Alan' said at the start of the trial (from behind a screen) 'We are here to be accountable'. The 'we' part of this statement emphasises the collective unit of responsibility and individual officers' identities (apart from commanders) would remain hidden.

Moment to moment detail

During the Health and Safety trial, the focus of accountability assessment again involved a complex interweaving of constitutive and demonstrative accountability based on interactions of 22 July 2005. These interactions included police communications, command structures, forms of identification, visual images, technology available, training which might or might not have helped during the events of the day, timing, transport, what counts as health and safety, who may have been at what kind of risk and so on. Due to space constraints, this chapter will focus on two areas of accountability activity to highlight the ways in which moment to moment interactions were held to account and decisions made about police responsibility. Although the trial as a whole focused broadly on whether or not the police had adequately protected or failed to protect the health and safety of the public (by allowing a suspected suicide bomber on to two buses and a tube train), we can see how this accountability process operated by focusing on discussions of, first, visual images and, second, use of language in the trial.

Visual images

Much of the trial depended upon reconstructing the events of the day of 22 July 2005 in order to render them available for accountability. This included drawing together logbooks from Room 1600 at New Scotland Yard, CCTV images from street cameras and from public transport, questioning police officers (commanders and surveillance officers) and public witnesses. Visual images became a particular focal point for these discussions. Initially questions were asked of surveillance officers regarding the suspect leaving the communal exit of the flats. The surveillance officers from SO12 suggested during the trial that on visual contact the suspect looked to be from North Africa. Commander Dick's order to stop the suspect at Stockwell tube station was, she said at the trial, based on increasing confidence in their identification and his behaviour: 'nervousness, agitation, sending text messages, [using] the telephone, getting on and off the bus, all added to the picture of someone potentially intent on causing an explosion'. Dick had also been shown footage the day before of a would-be bomber entering Stockwell tube station. She said during the trial that this footage added to her conviction that this was their suspect.[7]

The visual images appeared to play a central role here both on the day of 22 July 2005 (where the visual images became focal points for constitutive accountability relations between, for example, surveillance officers and their seniors) and in the retrospective replaying of events in court (with images forming part of the demonstrative accountability of the Metropolitan Police Service). On 22 July 2005 visual images were used to match the suspect's face to the suspect they were searching for, his physical activities were interpreted as nervous because he was about to commit a terrorist act and he was noted as entering a place (Stockwell tube station) the commanding officer had previously been shown as a location for potential acts of terror. The visual images also played an important role in the retrospective replaying of the events of 22 July, with CCTV footage and pictures of Hussain Osman and Jean Charles de Menezes featuring in the trial.

This suggests that the images enabled the police officers to re-tell the events of the day with a strong and clear certainty. They had made a visual identification, they could replay their pursuit of the suspect through CCTV, they could recall his physical activity (nervousness and agitation) and his location (Stockwell tube station). However, the visual images were not so certain. At different points during the trial the prosecution used the log of events from the control room to argue that officers in Room 1600 were in 'a state of chaos'. Officers were said to have poured into the room and senior officers could not hear what surveillance officers were saying over the radio. At first they thought the surveillance officers were saying it definitely was not Hussain Osman and then they thought they were saying it definitely was him. Control room officers 'were looking for certainty – they did not appear to have a strategy to cope when this certainty was absent'.[8] Thus the strength of the visual images appears less certain. It turns out that the images did not speak for themselves, but rather various parties attempted to get the images to speak for them.[9]

The summing up at the end of the case further emphasised this focus on the suspect, Jean Charles de Menezes' visually available actions. According to Ronald Thwaites QC, defence, de Menezes may have failed to comply with officers who challenged him 'because he thought he had drugs in his pocket, or because he had forged a stamp in his passport' and 'Furthermore he looked like the suspect and he had behaved suspiciously. Not only did he not comply, he moved in an aggressive and threatening manner as interpreted by the police and as would be interpreted by you and me in those circumstances, less than 24 hours after an attempt to bomb on the Underground and a bus had taken place'. This view was contrasted strongly by Clare Montgomery, QC, prosecution, who suggested de Menezes was acting no differently to 'hundreds of others ... His conduct that morning was no different from the conduct of hundreds of other commuters who come into the city'. In this part of the trial the visual aspects of de Menezes' actions form the basis for articulating his identity as potential terrorist or normal commuter. The work required to establish his position on one side of a boundary between normality and terrorism involved using the same visual actions as likely evidence of his position.[10] Initially this episode can be noted as a demonstration of the complexity of constitutive accountability (the visual actions of de Menezes were a source of claim and counter-claim on 22 July) and demonstrative accountability (it is not straightforward to determine whether or not this use of visuals fitted standard practice, could have been improved upon, should be the basis for punishment, and so on).

An episode in the court trial which exemplified this use of visual images to link de Menezes to a suspected terrorist involved a police composite picture of Jean Charles de Menezes and Hussain Osman. The composite picture of de Menezes and Hussain Osman was designed by the defence to demonstrate the difficulties of identifying the suspect.

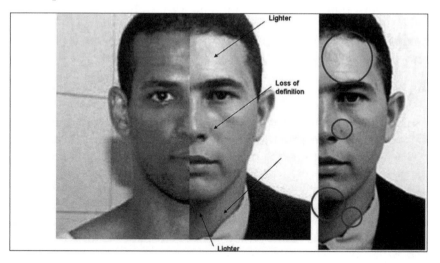

However, the prosecution claimed that the picture had been altered by 'either stretching or resizing, so the face ceases to have the correct proportions'. Michael George a forensic expert called upon by the prosecution tried to recreate the picture using Microsoft Powerpoint, but could not. De Menezes' face appeared to have been brightened and had lost definition compared with the original police photo –

particularly around the left nostril and chin. The defence countered that the attempt to show manipulation was a 'pseudo-scientific exercise'.[11]

The point here is not to prove either way the provenance of the image. Instead the visual images highlight the complexity of the accountability process. Firstly, there is constitutive accountability during the events themselves. The visuals are used and discussed in order to make sense of what is going on, to decide what actions should occur next and who should take responsibility for those actions (for example, should the surveillance officers intervene, should they wait for firearms officers, the commanders give orders and those are logged and they sign the log next to those orders). Through this real-time accountability over the radio and between colleagues face-to-face, sense is constituted of the situation and actions carried out.

Secondly, in the court trial there is demonstrative accountability. The trial becomes the occasion through which the police must demonstrate their actions. This involves attempts to replay the constitutive form of accountability in order to assess whether or not the public were put at risk, why the suspect was mis-identified, why he was allowed to enter forms of public transport, how certain police officers were in their identification and whether or not appropriate decisions were made. Although attempts were made to utilise the visual images as evidence that the police acted correctly, that they were certain in their (mistaken) identification and did as much as any police officers could do, the visual images do not retain this certainty. Arguments in the court were presented between the certainty and uncertainty of the visual identification. For example, the composite picture was used to attempt to demonstrate how difficult identification was and also to question the provenance of the image. Also the CCTV footage of surveillance officers pursuing the suspect was used to confirm their journey and also used to raise questions over why the suspect was allowed on to public transport. These may appear to be peculiar properties of attempts at accountability using visual images. However, if we now turn attention to the use of language on the day of 22 July 2005, we can see similar questions arise.

Language

In the story of Jean Charles de Menezes visual images were used both in the constitutive accountability of the day itself and in the demonstrative accountability that followed in the Health and Safety trial. In the events of 22 July 2005 and in the trial, language occupied a similarly prominent position in accountability assessments. During the trial Commander Dick suggested that they did not want the suspect to enter the tube 'where he might detonate a bomb or where we might lose surveillance'. Dick suggested that her use of the term 'stop' was meant to convey a 'conventional armed challenge'. She did not foresee that the term itself would mean that the suspect would be shot. Dick suggested that through his similar appearance to the intended suspect and 'through his behaviour that day, as I understand it, that behaviour when challenged, he came to be shot'. In this exchange the visual access to the suspect's actions, his movements, the way he looks, are held up as more significant in the outcome (his shooting) than in the use of the word 'stop'. However, during the trial the term 'stop' and its openness to interpretation was a matter of some discussion. Dick did not see this matter of interpretation as significantly different from other areas of police work. She suggested that, for example, although there are numerous guidelines in place for police work, individual officers have to make judgements. Making the decision to shoot involved (for all officers) a 'considerable amount of professional judgement, despite the guidelines and procedures which officers have to abide by'. Given this interpretability, the prosecution asked if Dick thought that other officers in her position might have made different decisions. She replied 'Possibly, yes'.[12]

Here we can find words, guidelines and professional judgements which were each involved in the real-time constitutive accountability of the day and were also each recorded for the possibility of future occasions of demonstrative accountability. This might not appear surprising in that a basic principle introduced under constitutive accountability at the start of this chapter was that accountability involved constituting a sense of what was going on in any particular interaction. In that case, police officers' use of particular terms and interactions which involved making sense of those terms would appear to be a conventional example of constitutive accountability. Commander Dick appeared to pay recognition to this when suggesting that making sense of terms and guidelines was part of what police officers do in their day-to-day jobs. It was nothing unusual. However, the use of firearms by the police has led to attempts to lift certain types of interaction outside these constitutive forms of accountability.

The principal example of these attempts to move away from everyday language terms has been the development of what is known as 'Operation Kratos'. This has been termed by some a 'shoot to kill' policy. However the Metropolitan Police have been keen to argue that 'Operation Kratos' is not such a policy. Assistant Commissioner Steve House, Central Operations Metropolitan Police suggests:

House: 'Well I think you're mixing up two concepts there which is it can end in the person's death, yes, because they are shooting at someone's head. But the instruction is not shoot to kill, the instruction is to immediately incapacitate the person.'

Interviewer: 'And in the case of a suicide bomber, immediate incapacitation means shooting him in the head'

House: 'Shooting in the head, yes'[13]

One principle of 'Operation Kratos' is that it does not use conventional language terms when running. Thus firearms officers on the ground are in direct communication with senior officers, but have a specific set of terms to use regarding 'use of lethal force'. These terms are designed to lift communication out from forms of constitutive accountability whereby officers would ordinarily use everyday language (in principle open to interpretation) and make sense of that language in the interaction. This interpretability appears characteristic of the use of 'stop' in the de Menezes case.

Introducing specific sets of terms appears to shift the basis of communication from the possibility of multiple interpretations to a few definitive terms which determine clear responses. On the face of it, it would appear that in the case of suicide bombers 'Operation Kratos' with its clear commands would mean that senior officers could either order someone to be killed or not. However, a little like the use of visual images in the de Menezes case, this apparent certainty can be misleading. Even if a clear set of terms has been developed to determine action, it is claimed that officers on the ground still need to make sense of the actions they see before them. For example, Inspector Tony Kelly, Specialist Firearms Instructor from the Metropolitan Police suggests that in training: 'We're making them [police officers] aware that it's never going to be a black and white scenario, so the officer has to make that decision in himself'. Officers must use a combination of what they see before them and senior command who may have access to intelligence in deciding to use lethal force.

The decision to shoot or not in the case of suicide bombers is likely to result in the suspect's death. However, the decision to shoot is not necessarily as straightforward as a command from senior officers to kill. The officers on the ground interact with senior officers and their access to intelligence, to constitute a decision to shoot (and in all likelihood kill) or not. The use of non-everyday language terms is designed to play a role within the back and forth communication of 'Operation Kratos' activities. Constituting the decision to kill or not involves the use of non-everyday language terms so that in the immediate situation officers on the ground and in the control room are clear as to what is going on and who will carry out what kind of action and this will remain clear for future occasions of demonstrative accountability as these terms are recorded in log books (and all police shootings are referred to the IPCC for investigation).

Returning to the de Menezes Health and Safety trial, questions were asked of Commander Dick as to whether or not this was an example of 'Operation Kratos' in action. Dick suggested that although she had received training in 'Operation Kratos' and she and Commander McDowell (who helped establish the strategy for 22 July 2005) had used that training to shape their strategy, their activities were not carried out under 'Operation Kratos'. In the trial this was taken to mean that a 'shoot to kill' policy was not in operation. However, it also meant that the exclusive language terms associated with 'Operation Kratos' were not in operation. Instead terms such as 'stop' were used. This use of everyday language terms appears to have resulted in various members of the operation having constituted different senses of what the decision was that had been made. The use of language was thus central to the constitutive accountability of the day. The difficulties of replaying this language use in the demonstrative accountability of the court case further highlighted the pervasiveness of this confusion. It should also be noted that this confusion over use of language was occurring simultaneously with confusion over whether or not the suspect's identity had been confirmed, the strength of that identification, whether or not firearms officers were in position, and so on. In the next section we will turn attention to the ways in which this demonstrative form of accountability was used to designate the Metropolitan Police Service's constitutive forms of accountability as a failure.

Accountability and failure

The Metropolitan Police Service were taken to court under the Health and Safety at Work Act and pleaded not guilty to failing to adequately protect the public from risk. Within the trial it was the Police Service rather than any individual officer which was made the unit of responsibility and called upon to enter into a form of demonstrative accountability. The outcome of the case was that the Metropolitan Police Service were found guilty and fined £175k and ordered to pay costs of £385k. Much of the discussion in the aftermath of the trial focused on ideas of organisational failure.

Firstly, the IPCC's first investigation into the incident was published at the end of the trial (although it had been produced a year earlier, it could not be published as it was to be considered evidence in the Health and Safety trial). The IPCC report produced nineteen failings. These included:

1 There was a failure adequately to communicate Commander McDowell's strategy to the officers who took over the running of the operation on 22 July, the surveillance officers and the firearms officers.

3 The control room officers, the firearms officers and the surveillance officers had a confused and inconsistent understanding of what the strategy was for Scotia Road.

5 There was a failure to ensure that an CO19 firearms team was in attendance at Scotia Road when Mr de Menezes emerged from the communal doorway.

10 Information as to the identification of Mr de Menezes, his clothing and likely level of threat was not properly or accurately assessed or disseminated to officers and in particular the firearms officers.

11 There was a failure to ensure that doubts about the correctness of the identification of Mr de Menezes as the suspect were communicated to relevant officers in the control room at New Scotland Yard.

13 There was a failure to deploy firearms officers at relevant locations in time to prevent Mr de Menezes from getting onto a bus and entering Stockwell Tube Station.

15 There was a failure to take effective steps to stop tubes or buses or take other traffic management steps so as to minimise the risk to the travelling public.

17 There was a failure to give a clear or timely order that Mr de Menezes be stopped or arrested before he entered Stockwell Tube Station.

18 There was a failure to give accurate information to Commander Dick as to the whereabouts of CO19 when she was deciding whether CO19 or SO12 surveillance officers stop Mr de Menezes.

19 There was a failure to minimise the risk inherent in effecting the arrest of Mr de Menezes by armed officers whether in relation to the location, timing or manner of his arrest.

Through these failings we can see many features of constitutive and demonstrative accountability. In terms of constitutive accountability, there is much emphasis on the communicative aspects of the day's events. 'Failure to communicate', 'confused and inconsistent understanding', 'failure to give a clear or timely order', 'failure to give accurate information to Commander Dick', each appear to make the point that making sense of what was going on during the day proved a struggle and constituting appropriate decisions was difficult. Each of these aspects of the struggle to constitute a sense of the actions of the day were held to account in the demonstrative forum of the court and the IPCC's reports. The police notably failed to adequately demonstrate evidence to back their assertion that they were not guilty of a failure to protect public Health and Safety.

Secondly, various public figures and organisations commented on the demonstrative accountability aspects of the trial and its outcome. Comments focused on the twin aspects of truth and consequence in demonstrative accountability. Many of these commentators noted failures of the Metropolitan Police and identified particular individuals who should take responsibility for those failures, even if the trial had not identified them as units of responsibility.

Trial judge Mr Justice Henriques said 'I am deliberately not going to name any individual as having failed. This was a corporate failing with a number of failures contributing to the ultimate tragedy'.

Dr Sandra Bell, Royal United Services Institute 'Continuously throughout this trial we heard it was not an ideal situation – but in this information age, that really isn't an excuse'.

Nick Clegg, Liberal Democrat Home Affairs Spokesman 'I just start from a very simple principle that policing needs to be seen to be accountable'.

Simon Hughes, President Liberal Democrats 'This was a collective failure of responsibility, a collective breach of the law, and both the police service, led by the commissioner, and the police authority, who are politically accountable people, will have some very severe questions to answer, and rightfully so'.

Shami Chakrabati, Director, Liberty 'I think it's very sad that it's taken two-and-a-half years for there to be any semblance of accountability'.

Len Duvall, Chair of the Metropolitan Police Authority 'We must remember an innocent man died during the course of a Met police operation – this is damning enough'.[14]

Thirdly, although it might appear from preceding analysis (of nineteen failures and responses from various public figures focused on failure) that the Metropolitan Police had failed, the Metropolitan Police Commissioner, Sir Ian Blair, reflected on the guilty verdict. He suggested that although the court trial and IPCC were awash with talk of failure, the Metropolitan Police Service were not characterised by systemic failure. Corporate, individual, informational, communicative and temporal failure, were separated off from this other category of 'systemic' failure. The latter was used to imply that the type of failure which characterised 22 July 2005 was not so ingrained into the Metropolitan Police Service that it was likely or guaranteed to reoccur. This category of failure became important for Ian Blair in figuring out the consequences of accountability; he argued that he should not resign as a result of the constitutive and demonstrative accountability failings because these failings were not 'systemic'. According to Ian Blair 22 July, was an 'isolated breach' under 'extraordinary circumstances' and he would only have 'considered his position' if there had been 'systemic failings'. Ian Blair continued: 'This case thus provides no evidence at all of systematic failure by the Metropolitan Police. I am not going to consider my position about the events, as the judge described, of a single day in extraordinary circumstances'.[15] It seems that the variety of accountability activities (IPCC, MPS, Health and Safety Trial) did not establish a clear and unified unit of responsibility, a single means of accountability or a certain outcome in terms of the consequences of being held to account. Thus truth (of failure) and consequences (which might follow from failure) are not so straightforward.

Fourthly, an alternative to questioning the type of failure, was to question the type (or means) of accountability. There was much discussion during and notably after the trial as to whether or not Health and Safety legislation was the appropriate mode of accountability. It was suggested that to be accounted for through (and noted a failure on the terms of) Health and Safety legislation was not necessarily clear-cut. In this sense, it may not be appropriate to think of the police service actions as a failure – it was the form of accountability that was inappropriate. Ken Jones, president of the Association of Chief Police Officers, suggested that the Health and Safety trial would have major (mostly negative) repercussions for the way police officers went about their activity and Ken Livingstone as Mayor of London, said: 'Health and safety legislation was not drawn up for these extreme situations'.[16] This suggests that calls for greater accountability in relation to surveillance activities (such as those that surround the case of Jean Charles de Menezes) need to take account of the complexities, uncertainties and arguments over what counts as 'truth' and what consequences ought to follow.

Conclusion

In sum, although the constitutive and demonstrative forms of account-ability appear to emphasise a series of failings, questions were also asked about types of failure and the appropriateness of types of accountability. This suggests that modes of accountability, although apparently oriented towards creating definitive versions of what went on, who or what should be responsible for what went on and what the consequences ought to be, such definitive outcomes appear out of reach. Although surveillance systems offer rich archives of histories to be replayed, this richness does not necessarily reduce, but could indeed increase, the number of questions of accountability which can be asked.

Broadening this point out, with increasing numbers of activities recorded and made available for future replaying in future occasions of accountability, what are the implications of this uncertain conclusion? With biometrics soon to be recorded and made available as a means of accountability, with numerous countries around the world following the UK's lead in installing CCTV cameras and with more and more information collated, stored and mobilised on the movements of populations across and between borders, will there be an ever increasing array of the kinds of accountability seen around the shooting of Jean Charles de Menezes? This may not necessarily be the case. The narrow version of surveillance is important to remember here: there are only ever a small number of actions which are the subject of constitutive accountability (most CCTV images are never looked at, most forms of information are not scrutinised). Within this small number there are even fewer incidents subject to later, retrospective demonstrative accountability. As the number of ways of recording activities and the number of opportunities for accountability increases, the proportion of incidents of accountability will decrease (there will be ever more information to ignore).

Furthermore, during these moments of accountability, the more information which is made potentially available through surveillance systems to be held to account, the more questions and (possibly) the less certainty there will be; on rare occasions of demonstrative accountability there are likely to be multiple sources of information to be drawn together to form multiple truths. Tied into this, as the case of Jean Charles de Menezes demonstrates, an increase in the use of technology, does not lead to a reduction in the chances of failure (even if the precise nature of failure becomes a matter of dispute). In the future of surveillance, what we may find is an increase in the recording, storing and mobilisation of information, with proportionately fewer actions held to constitutive accountability, with even fewer actions the subject of retrospective demonstrative accountability, and no decrease in the likely 'failure' of surveillance systems. With more technology, there may be an increase in types and decrease in predictably of failure. Thus what we might experience is a larger amount of information which is never scrutinised, a greater number of activities which will never be held to account, continuing uncertainty in accountability outcomes (with ever more information meaning ever more questions can be asked) and no necessary reduction in the possibility of surveillance-based organisational failure.

Notes

1   However, it should be noted that CCTV systems do feature other modes of accountability, such as engagement-based accountability. In this mode of accountability, structures are put in place which actively invite audiences external to an organisation to participate in an aspect of the organisation (for an overview, see Irwin 1995; Kleinman 2000; Kitcher 2001). Like many publicly funded organisations, local government run surveillance activities such as CCTV systems are held to account in this way. CCTV systems are expected to display signs informing the public of the cameras, who is responsible for the cameras and contact details for how to get in touch with system operatives. A problem for these forms of accountability is that it is not always clear that members of

the public are aware of the CCTV cameras, don't necessarily know how CCTV operates, what CCTV does, or that they as members of public can and/or should make a complaint about the system.

2 Transparency has been considered from a number of different perspectives in poetry (Gordon 1969), post-modernism (Vattimo 1992; Baudrillard 1993), philosophy (Westphal 1986), political analysis (Wall 1996), psychology (Tagiuiri *et al*. 1955) and studies of accounting (Humphrey *et al*. 1995; Gray 2002; Zadek and Raynard 1995; Sikka 2001; Canning and O'Dwyer 2001; Drew 2004).

3 On occasions, however, calls for more demonstrative accountability do not involve such detail, but are instead focused on a more basic argument that there is a need for greater accountability without much regard for how an accountability process might operate, who might carry out accountability and what might be the purpose of accountability (see, for example, AccountAbility 2007).

4 This also, of course, makes the case untypical. Most surveillance operations are far less publicly available.

5 The data presented in this section derives from information presented on the IPCC website (http:www.ipcc.gov.uk) and from court discussions (reported in the *Guardian*, 2 October 2007: 6; 18 October 2007: 4; 19 October 2007: 11; 26 October 2007: online).

6 For example on the IPCC website (http://www.ipcc.gov.uk).

7 This paragraph contains excerpts from: *Guardian* 19 October 2007: 11.

8 The log itself and its record of apparent visual identification was also called into question. It was suggested that there was no system in place to prevent officers changing the log after events and it has been alleged that a crucial amendment was made to the log. Originally a log stated that a positive identification had been made. Later the word 'not' was inserted according to the BBC (2006).

9 This paragraph contains excerpts from: *Guardian*, 2 October 2007: 6.

10 This paragraph contains excerpts from: *Guardian*, 26 October 2007: online.

11 This paragraph contains excerpts from: *Guardian*, 18 October 2007: 4.

12 This paragraph contains excerpts from: *Guardian*, 19 October 2007: 11.

13 Excerpt taken from: Panorama: Stockwell, Countdown to killing, broadcast 8 March 2006 on BBC1.

14 These quotes taken from: BBC (2007) available from http://news.bbc.co.uk/1/hi/uk/7073347.stm

15 Excerpts in this paragraph taken from: *Daily Mail*, 2 November 2007. http://www.dailymail.co.uk/pages/live/articles/news/news.html?in_article_id=491123&in_page_id=1770&ct=5

16 Excerpts in this paragraph also taken from: *Daily Mail*, 2 November, 2007.

References

AccountAbility (2007) [Online]. Available at: http://www.accountability21. net/ [accessed 2 December 2008].

BBC (2006) *Panorama: Stockwell, countdown to killing.* Broadcast 8 March.

Baudrillard, J. (1993) *The Transparency of Evil: Essays on Extreme Phenomena.* London: Verso.

Baxter, J. and Chua, W. (2003) 'Alternative management accounting research – whence and whither', *Accounting, Organisation and Society,* 28(2): 97–126.

Bennett, C. (2006) 'What happens when you book an airline ticket (revisited): The collection and processing of passenger data post 9/11' in M. Salter and E. Zureik (eds) *Global Surveillance and Policing.* Cullompton: Willan Publishing.

Canning, M. and O'Dwyer, B. (2001) 'Professional accounting bodies' disciplinary procedures: accountable, transparent and in the public interest?', *European Accounting Review,* 10(4): 72–550.

Drew, C. (2004) 'Transparency of environmental decision making: a case of soil cleanup inside the Hanford 100 area', *Journal of Risk Research,* 7(1): 33–71.

Garfinkel, H. (1967) *Studies in Ethnomethodology.* Cambridge: Polity Press.

Gordon, M. (1969) *Transparent Web – A Book of Poems.* London: Arcadian Press.

Gray, R. (2002) 'The social accounting project and Accountability Organizations and Society privileging engagement, imaginings, new accountings and pragmatism over critique?', *Accounting, Organizations and Society,* 27(7): 687–707.

Humphrey, C., Moizer, P. and Owen, D. (1995) 'Questioning the value of the research selectivity process in British university accounting', *Accounting, Auditing and Accountability,* 8(3): 141–65.

Irwin, A. (1995) *Citizen Science.* London: Routledge.

Kitcher, P. (2001) *Science, Democracy and Truth.* Oxford: Oxford University Press.

Kleinman, D. (2000) *Science, Technology and Democracy.* Albany, NY: New York University Press.

Luff, P. and Heath, C. (1993) 'System use and social organization: observations on human-computer interaction in an architectural practice', in G. Button (ed.) *Technology in Working Order: Studies of Work, Interaction and Technology.* London: Routledge.

Lynch, M. (1998) 'The discursive production of uncertainty: the OJ Simpson "dream team" and the sociology of knowledge machine', *Social Studies Of Science,* 28(5–6): 829–68.

Lyon, D. (2001) *Surveillance Society: Monitoring everyday life.* Buckingham: Open University Press.

Miller, P. (1992) 'Accounting and objectivity: the invention of calculable selves and calculable spaces', *Annals of Scholarship*, 9(1/2): 61–86.

Miller, P. and O'Leary, T. (1994) 'Governing the calculable person', in A.G. Hopwood, and P. Miller (eds) *Accounting as Social and Institutional Practice*. Cambridge: Cambridge University Press.

Neyland, D. (2006) *Privacy, Surveillance and Public Trust*. London: Palgrave-Macmillan.

Power, M. (1997) *The Audit Society*. Oxford: Oxford University Press.

Rose, N. (1999) *Powers of Freedom*. Cambridge: Cambridge University Press.

Sikka, P. (2001) 'Transparency and accountability of the professional accountancy bodies: some observations on the Canning and O'Dwyer paper', *European Accounting Review*, 10(4): 751–62.

Strathern, M. (1999) 'The aesthetics of substance', in M. Strathern (ed.) *Property, Substance and Effect*. London: Athlone.

Strathern, M. (2002) 'Abstraction and decontextualisation: an anthropological comment', in S. Woolgar (ed.) *Virtual Society? Technology, Cyberbole, Reality*. Oxford: Oxford University Press.

Strathern, M. (2004) *Commons and Borderlands: Working Papers on Interdisciplinarity, Accountability and the Flow of Knowledge*. Oxfordshire: Sean Kingston Publishing.

Stockwell 2 Report (2007) 'An investigation into complaints about the Metropolitan Police Service's handling of public statements following the shooting Jean Charles de Menezes on 22 July 2005', *IPCC* [online]. Available at: http://www.ipcc.gov.uk/index/resources/evidence_reports/investigation_reports/stockwell_two.htm [accessed 4 December 2008].

Suchman, L. (1993) 'Technologies of accountability: of lizards and aeroplanes', in G. Button (ed.) *Technology in Working Order: Studies of Work, Interaction and Technology*. London: Routledge.

Tagiuri, R., Kogan, N. and Bruner, J. (1955) 'The transparency of interpersonal choice,' *American Sociological Association*, 18(4): 368–79.

Vattimo, G. (1992) *The Transparent Society*. Cambridge: Polity Press.

Wall, S. (1996) 'Public justification and the transparency argument', *The Philosophical Quarterly*, 46(184): 501–7.

Westphal, J. (1986) 'White', *Mind*, 95: 311–28.

Zadek, S. and Raynar, P. (1995) 'Social auditing, transparency and accountability', *Accounting Forum*, 19(2–3).

Chapter 6

Perceptions of government technology, surveillance and privacy: the UK Identity Cards Scheme

Edgar A. Whitley[1]

Introduction

On 13 June 2008, the opposition home secretary David Davis resigned from his position in the shadow cabinet and as an MP, triggering a by-election in his constituency of Haltemprice and Howden. The reason for this unprecedented event, he stated, was to fight 'against the slow strangulation of fundamental British freedoms by this government' (Davis 2008). Davis resigned the day after the government had pushed proposals through the House of Commons to extend detention without charge up to 42 days. However, he also listed other examples of the 'insidious, surreptitious and relentless erosion of fundamental British freedoms' (Davis 2008) including 'the most intrusive identity card system in the world, a CCTV camera for every fourteen citizens and a DNA database bigger than that of any dictatorship with thousands of innocent children and a million innocent citizens on it' (Davis 2008).

Despite press speculation that his actions were driven, at least in part, by internal party dynamics, Davis's actions appear to have been motivated by an issue of principle which raises the question of why it was this issue in particular (rather than, for example, other politically sensitive issues like Europe or the Iraq war) that triggered his resignation.

In this chapter, I will argue that Davis's actions can be best understood as part of a wider transformation of public perceptions of surveillance and privacy in the UK. Thus, it is increasingly common to find newspaper articles about issues of surveillance and privacy, often featuring prominently on the front pages of national newspapers. Previously, such stories would warrant only a few column inches on an inside page, if at all. In addition many of the 'tabloid' newspapers, more commonly associated with more authoritarian social attitudes, have also adopted a critical tone in their coverage of the surveillance agenda.

As such, the chapter explores a key theme in social science research, namely the nature of our world and the role of social action in shaping the persons, phenomena and entities that inhabit it (Osborne and Rose 1999). In particular, the chapter develops our understanding of what is meant by 'the public', how 'public opinion' may be developed and measured. Are the phenomena discussed in this chapter issues that really affect the majority of UK citizens, and if so what kind of issues are they? Do public attitudes to privacy issues follow a common path, whereby, for example, UK attitudes to identity cards might mirror the experiences of the Australia card in the 1980s (Davies 2004)? Or are they simply the concerns of an informed elite and the editors of the newspapers they read?

The chapter examines these questions in the context of debates about privacy and surveillance where we find ourselves 'thrown' into a world that is increasingly mediated by technological devices with surveillance capabilities (Haggerty and Ericson 2000; RAE 2007). Thus, in addition to methodological issues that the topic itself implies (Haggerty and Gazso 2005) we need to ask whether this is a topic which individuals can meaningfully take a position on? If it is, are they able to act as a result to influence and shape the technological advances that take place (MacKenzie and Wajcman 1999)? If it is not, what does this tell us about the public, its perceptions of surveillance and privacy and the relationship with public policy (Burstein 1998)?

In the United Kingdom, an important recent event in relation to privacy, government technology and surveillance was the government's proposals to introduce biometric identity cards for all UK citizens. Of particular significance was the LSE Identity Project's report into the proposals (LSE Identity Project 2005b) and the government's response to the LSE report. This became a news story in and of itself (Whitley et al. 2007) but also raised awareness about and interest in the scheme, interest that has continued to this day. Indeed, it could be argued that much of the recent increase in media interest in privacy related topics was triggered by the events surrounding the proposals for identity cards.

The chapter therefore begins by reviewing the key events in the life of the Identity Cards Scheme, outlining the key civil liberties concerns with the proposals. Next the chapter explores how public opinion about the scheme has been measured using traditional opinion polls. This is followed by consideration of other surveillance related stories that have been reported in the media and reflects on the role that media coverage may have on public perceptions and opinions. The chapter ends with a discussion of what this suggests for the nature of privacy as a topic and the role of public perceptions in the policy making process.

Key events in the life of the Identity Cards Scheme

The current Identity Cards Scheme has its origins in proposals for 'entitlement cards' that were first proposed by the then Home Secretary David Blunkett in 2002. On 29 November 2004, following a two-and-a-half-year gestation, and following a name change from entitlement cards to identity cards, the government introduced and published its Identity Cards Bill. The Bill passed its Third Reading in the House of Commons on 10 February 2005. The Second Reading debate in the House of Lords took place on 21 March 2005, after which the Bill was suspended pending the general election. The proposal to introduce biometric identity cards was a key element of the 2005 Labour party election manifesto, which stated:

> We will introduce ID cards, including biometric data like fingerprints, backed up by a national register and rolling out initially on a voluntary basis as people renew their passports.
>
> (The Labour Party 2005)

The scheme that the Labour party was proposing was based around a National Identity Register, the use of biometrics, online verification and an audit trail of verifications (LSE Identity Project 2005b). The scheme was intended to address various policy concerns including addressing identity theft and terrorism, benefit fraud and illegal working. It was also required to be in accordance with international obligations and enable e-government and access to government services (Wadham *et al.* 2006).

As the Identity Cards Bill made its first passage through Parliament, there was increasing concern within business, academia and civil liberties groups about the lack of informed public debate about its implications for the United Kingdom. In response to that concern, in

January 2005 a group of individuals based at the London School of Economics and Political Science (LSE) initiated a project to examine in detail the potential impacts and benefits of the Identity Cards Bill (LSE Identity Project 2005b). Many of the concerns arose from the potential effects of the scheme on policing, identity fraud, the legal environment in the UK and public trust.

To oversee its work, the Identity Project had an advisory group of sixteen professors from LSE. These are contributory experts in disciplines ranging information systems and government to law, social policy, economics, media and regulation. In addition, a further 60+ named individuals and numerous unnamed individuals contributed to the report, drafting and reviewing chapters.

The LSE team released an interim report (LSE Identity Project 2005a) in March 2005 to coincide with the Second Reading debate in the House of Lords. The purpose of this report was to review key aspects of the scheme, to begin to inform the debate and to seek feedback on the analysis presented.

Following the May 2005 election, the Labour Party was re-elected (although with a post-election majority of 66, down from 167) and reintroduced what was effectively the same Bill. On 27 June 2005 the LSE Identity Project released its main report (LSE Identity Project 2005b), the day before Parliament revisited the Bill. This report was over 300 pages long and concluded that while an identity card system could offer some public interest and commercial sector benefits, there were a number of areas of major concern with the government's existing plans (LSE Identity Project 2005b).

Given the many areas of concern identified in the government's proposals, the LSE main report included an alternative blueprint for a national identity scheme and provided an independent calculation of the likely costs of the scheme. The government's regulatory impact assessment (Home Office 2005) had stated that 'the total average annual running costs for issuing passports and ID cards to UK nationals is estimated at £584m' or £5.84 billion over the first ten years. The LSE, however, provided an alternative costing of the scheme ranging from a low estimate of £10 billion, a median estimate of £14.5 billion and a high estimate of £19.2 billion over ten years. Whilst some of the differences reflected different cost bases (i.e. total costs not just average running costs, costs to government not just to the Home Office) there were also differences associated with estimates of the likely costs of using biometrics and technology infrastructure for the scheme. The decision to present the costs to the Home Office only is arguably disingenuous as most of the claimed benefits can only be realised by integrating Home Office systems with those in other government departments.

Shortly before the report was formally released, a version of the part of the report on costs found its way into the press and the then Home Secretary Charles Clarke went on a Radio 4 news programme to dismiss the LSE's costings as 'simply mad' (BBC News 2005a). The then Prime Minister, Tony Blair, told a press conference that 'some of these figures bandied around about cost are absolutely absurd'. On 5 July 2005, Charles Clarke made further attacks on the LSE research, branding it 'technically incompetent', describing the findings as 'fabricated' and singling out one of the project members, Simon Davies, as being 'partisan' because his opposition to identity cards was well known (BBC News 2005b), a claim repeated by the Prime Minister in January 2006 (Davies 2006).

In response to these claims the Director of the LSE, Howard Davies, wrote to The Times on behalf of the LSE's governing council upholding academic freedom to analyse government policy without personalised political vilification.

He continued noting that 'it is unfortunate that, on an issue where the civil liberties concerns are so serious, the government should have chosen to adopt a bullying approach to critics whose prime motivation was to devise a scheme which might work, at an acceptable cost' (Davies 2005). He later wrote to a member of the House of Lords saying 'we have had some extraordinary responses to our work from the government, who appear to think that they can deal with a report from a group of academics from a university in the way they would a submission from the official opposition' [Quoted by Lord Phillips, Hansard 19 December 2005, Column 1551].

After an extended Parliamentary debate and a ping-pong battle between the House of Commons and the House of Lords over the meaning of the phrase 'initially on a voluntary basis' (and in the context of the Salisbury Convention, which restricts invocation of the Parliament Act to manifesto commitments, see Whitley and Hosein 2009), the legislation was finally passed in March 2006, following an amendment proposed by the former Cabinet Secretary Lord Armstrong which offered the concession that, for a period until the next general election, a person could choose not be issued with a card although obtaining a passport would remain conditional on biometric registration in the database. A further key amendment (section 37) required the government to provide reports on the likely costs of the scheme every six months.

The new Identity and Passport Service was created on 1 April 2006, replacing the earlier Passport Agency and in October 2006, James Hall, formerly of Accenture, was appointed as the IPS Chief Executive.

On 9 July 2006 a leading Sunday Newspaper ran a front page headline story entitled 'ID cards doomed' based on leaked emails sent between senior officials from the Office of Government Commerce and the Identity and Passport Service. These emails had been exchanged on 8 and 9 June 2006.

The first email, from OGC Mission Critical Director David Foord, warned:

> Even if everything went perfectly (which it will not) it is very debatable (given performance of Govt ICT projects) whether whatever TNIR [Temporary National Identity Register] turns out to be (and that is a worry in itself) can be procured, delivered, tested and rolled out in just over two years and whether the resources exist within Govt and industry to run two overlapping procurements. What benchmark in the Home Office do we have that suggests that this is even remotely feasible?
>
> I conclude that we are setting ourselves up to fail. (*The Sunday Times* 2006)

The response, from Peter Smith, Acting Commercial Director for the Identity and Passport Service indicated what was likely to happen next:

> The procurements we will (we hope) launch in the next few months – not the TNIR but things like APSS and contact centre – are all necessary (essential) to sustain IPS business as usual, and we are designing the strategy so that they are all sensible and viable contracts in their own right EVEN IF the ID Card gets canned completely. So also less dependence on business case approval etc. (*The Sunday Times* 2006)

Following these leaks the recently appointed Home Secretary John Reid delayed all aspects of the procurement process and ordered a full scale review of the proposed scheme. As a result of this review, a new Strategic Action Plan (UKIPS 2006) was released in December 2006. This proposed an apparently radical redesign of the scheme, for example by dropping the mandatory use of iris biometrics and reusing three existing government databases rather than designing a new National Identity Register from scratch.

There was a further redesign of the scheme in March 2008, when a new Delivery Plan was issued that delayed the roll-out of identity cards to ordinary citizens, focusing instead on key workers and young people (UKIPS 2008).

Civil liberties concerns with the scheme

The design of the Identity Cards Scheme included three elements that raised particular concerns about privacy and surveillance. These are the role of the National Identity Register and particularly the audit trail associated with using it to verify formally an identity; the role of biometrics in the scheme and the security issues associated with scheme.

Although the act is called the Identity Cards Act, it is the National Identity Register that is most troubling from a civil liberty as well as a technological perspective. The Register will contain the details of all British citizens aged sixteeen and over, as well as details of all non-EEA visitors who are planning to reside in the UK for a period of more than three months.[2] As such, it is potentially one of the largest registers of individuals in existence and it has even been proposed that the NIR be used as a national population register (see Pounder 2007). In addition, surveillance capabilities have been hard-coded into the legislation (LSE Identity Project 2007) as it specifies that the Secretary of State 'establish and maintain a register of individuals' that includes 'information about occasions on which information recorded about him in the register has been provided to any person' (i.e. the audit trail). It also specifies other audit details that are recorded on the register including: the date of every application by him for a modification of the contents of his entry; the date of every application by him confirming the contents of his entry (with or without changes); particulars of every occasion on which information contained in the individual's entry has been provided to a person; particulars of every person to whom such information has been provided on such an occasion; and other particulars, in relation to each such occasion, of the provision of the information (see also LSE Identity Project 2008; Wadham et al. 2006). The Act also allows identifiers from 'designated documents' pertaining to other government permits and licenses to be added, thus potentially creating a master index for cross-referencing to other systems.

A second major concern relates to the collection and use of biometrics for the scheme. The use of biometrics is intended to ensure that no individual can enrol in the scheme more than once (i.e. by faking a biographical identity). A recent parliamentary answer has indicated that it is the government's intention to 'record ten fingerprint images which will be stored on the national identity register with two of the holder's fingerprints stored on the chip on the identity card. This is also the procedure planned for the identity card to be issued to foreign nationals' [Meg Hillier, written answer to question 210838]. In addition to the use of fingerprints for the enrolment process, one of the 'benefits' of the scheme is that this fingerprint data will also be shared with the police force to match against their records of unresolved crime scene fingerprints (Whitley and Hosein 2008).

Unlike passwords and PINs, biometric identifiers cannot be revoked if they are compromised. It is for this reason that the independent review of identity assurance undertaken by Sir James Crosby on behalf of Gordon Brown, recommended that:

> As a matter of principle, the amount of data stored should be minimised. Full biometric images (other than photographs) should not be kept. Only non-unique digital representations of biometric images should be stored.
>
> (Crosby 2008)

A third major concern with the scheme is the security risks associated with the storage of vast amounts of personal biographical and biometric data on the National Identity Register. During the parliamentary debates about the scheme, Microsoft was one of many companies that warned of the security risks of a centralised database (Young 2005) contrasting this approach with modern 'user-centric' architectures designed to maximise transparency, security and citizen control.

The shift to three separate databases as part of the Strategic Action Plan only mitigates this concern somewhat, if at all and could be regarded as an expedient repurposing of existing systems, saving direct costs at the expense of data quality, without offering the resilience and flexibility of truly decentralised architectures.

In 2006, the Department of Constitutional Affairs issued an 'Information Sharing Vision Statement' which acknowledged that:

> the more we share information, the more important it is that people are confident that their personal data is kept safe

and secure. This government has an excellent track record of strengthening individuals' right to privacy.

(DCA 2006)

As is noted below, confidence in government's abilities to manage personal data securely dropped significantly following a series of high profile data breaches. In particular, on 20 November 2007 the Chancellor Alistair Darling informed Parliament that a data breach involving 'personal data relating to child benefit' had arisen in Her Majesty's Revenue and Customs (HMRC). On 18 October 2007, in response to a request from the National Audit Office for data in relation to payment of child benefit, a civil servant at HMRC sent a copy of the full database on two compact discs, using an obsolete version of compression software with weak encryption. The discs were sent using HMRC's internal mail service, operated by TNT. The package was not recorded or registered and failed to arrive at the NAO. When the requested discs did not arrive, a further set of discs were sent, this time by recorded delivery and these did arrive. Senior management at HMRC were not told about the lost discs until 8 November 2007.

The discs, containing details of all child benefit recipients, records for 25 million individuals and 7.25 million families, have still not been recovered. The records included the names of recipients and the names of their children as well as address details and dates of birth, child benefit numbers, national insurance numbers and, where relevant, bank or building society account details.

This incident resulted in a series of reviews of government data handling, all published on the same day, some seven months later. They pointed to chronic 'cultural failings' and processes that were 'woefully inadequate'. They also recommended stringent new handling procedures only for new (rather than legacy) systems (Cabinet Office 2008a, 2008b; IPCC 2008). The link back to identity cards was made when it was reported that PA Consulting, who had been paid £24 million between 2004 and 2006 for advising the Identity and Passport Service about the scheme, had lost a memory stick containing the details of 84,000 prisoners (Lomas 2008).

Public opinion

When the Identity Cards Bill was being debated in Parliament, much was made of public support for the scheme, with the Home Office quoting research it had sponsored which suggested that 73 per cent of the UK public support the introduction of identity cards [Baroness Scotland, Hansard, 31 October 2005 Column 13]. As Gandy (2003) notes, information about the attitudes and opinions of ordinary citizens can be particularly relevant for the formation of policies in areas like identity cards. For example, if the proposals are or become unpopular with the general population, a party that pushes them as part of its policies may face an electoral backlash (Burstein 1998). Indeed, the opposition parties have labelled the Identity Cards Scheme a 'plastic poll tax' to emphasise the similarities with the unpopular 'community charge' policy that the Conservatives introduced in the late 1980s and which is believed to have been instrumental in removing Prime Minister Margaret Thatcher from power.

With public opinion potentially playing such a leading role in the eventual success of the scheme, both the Home Office and the independent campaigning organisation opposed to identity cards and the database state No2ID (2008b) have conducted a series of opinion polls about public perceptions of identity cards.

The Home Office has commissioned a series of studies examining public attitudes to the National Identity Scheme and ID cards by the Central Office of Information (Identity and Passport Service 2008). To date, there have been six such studies (February 2007, October 2007, January/February 2008, May 2008, August 2008 and November 2008). These studies involve adding questions to Taylor Nelson Sofres' general public omnibus survey. The questions are intended to elicit awareness and attitudinal data about identity cards and the National Identity Scheme and have a sample weighted to represent the adult population aged 16+. The questions cover topics such as awareness of the scheme, support for the scheme, the reasons for introducing the Scheme and proposed benefits of the scheme (Identity and Passport Service 2008). In this stream of research, support for the scheme in the samples remains statistically stable at around 60 per cent.

No2ID has also organised a series of public opinion polls that it has commissioned from ICM research (No2ID 2008a). Its research has asked the same question over time, namely 'The government has proposed the introduction of identity cards that, in combination with your passport, will cost around £93. From what you have seen or heard do you think that this proposal is a ... [good ... bad idea]?'[3]. In contrast to the Home Office sponsored research, this stream shows a decline in the net scores for the Identity Card Scheme being 'a good idea', down from 81 per cent in December 2004 to less than 50 per cent in June 2008 with a sustained drop following the HMRC data breach.

The difference in these measures of 'public opinion' scores cannot be explained away in terms of sample size as both studies are implemented by recognised polling organisation (the IPS study has a sample of around 2000 representative individuals, whilst the No2ID study has a sample size of around 1000), so the explanation is more likely to arise from the nature of the questions being asked (Gandy 2003; Haggerty and Gazso 2005).

For example, it is unlikely that the IPS survey questions emphasise the unprecedented privacy impact of a lifelong 'audit trail' and the capture and storage of large numbers of biometrics. Similarly, there are known issues with potentially 'leading' survey questions that include price in the question.

In June 2008, No2ID asked a second question that did not mention Identity Cards but did describe the National Identity Register on which the scheme is to be built.[4] This resulted in 63 per cent of the respondents thinking this was a net bad idea.

A further factor that might influence public (and political) opinion is the editorial position taken by leading newspapers and magazines. The Financial Times, for example, has been consistent in its opposition to the scheme:

> In the two years since legislation for a UK national identity card scheme gained Royal Assent, the case against the multi-billion pound programme has become overwhelming. The Government's arguments in favour have crumpled. ... Gordon Brown inherited this deeply flawed plan from his predecessor as prime minister. He should follow his instincts and abandon it altogether.
>
> (Financial Times 2008)

The Economist, in contrast, was initially mildly in favour of the scheme:

> At worst, identity cards will embarrass the government as did the Millennium Dome. ... Nevertheless, identity cards will probably eventually become part of the landscape. They will be accepted, though not loved – and certainly more useful to the government than the Dome has been.
>
> (The Economist 2005)

By 2008, however, it had changed its view markedly:

Although Britons are already among the most-watched people in the world, ID cards are a step too far for some. Nick Clegg, the Liberal Democrat leader, has said that he would go to jail rather than carry one.[5] Judging by opinion polls and widely circulated pledges to disobey, a significant fraction of his countrymen feel the same way.

(*The Economist* 2008)

In addition, one of the key amendments introduced into the Identity Cards Act was the need to report on the ongoing estimates of the costs of the scheme every six months. Even if there were no other issues associated with the scheme, the earlier row about costs has meant that every six months the story of the likely costs of the scheme reappears in the press. Moreover those news stories that go beyond reporting official press releases are overwhelmingly critical, meaning that virtually every publication by the Identity and Passport Service now results in a detailed analysis that is at best sceptical and usually hostile.[6] For a detailed example, see Appendix 1.

Identity cards, privacy and surveillance in the public consciousness

Following from the debates about the Identity Cards Scheme, stories about privacy and surveillance have become increasingly high profile in British newspapers. The themes have also become the focus of a number of editorial statements in the leading broadsheet newspapers.

For example, early in 2008, it was revealed that the conversations between an MP (Sadiq Khan) and one of his constituents (Babar Ahmad) had been surreptitiously recorded whilst Khan visited Ahmad in HM Woodhall prison. The communications of MPs were normally considered a matter of parliamentary privilege and, in the case of telephone communications, were covered by the 1966 'Wilson Doctrine' that prevented phone tapping of MPs' conversations.[7] Although the bugging took place in a face-to-face meeting, the issue of surveillance caused a number of newspaper commentators to react.

For example, an editorial in the Independent stated:

A much-needed public debate about covert surveillance has begun, thanks to the allegation that counter-terrorism police officers secretly recorded discussions between the Tooting MP, Sadiq Khan, and a constituent, Babar Ahmad. Secret surveillance is obviously necessary in counter-terrorism and organised crime operations. … But the proliferation of eavesdropping and secret information gathering has taken on a sinister momentum of its own. This is part of a trend that has seen Britain acquire more CCTV cameras than anywhere in the world and brought us the prospect of biometric ID cards. If anything good can come out of this row, it will be that we wake up to the casual and dangerous erosion of our privacy.

(Independent 2008)

According to Gareth Crossman, Liberty's Director of Policy:

The past decade has brought many threats to personal privacy. However, over the last two years in particular, growing nervousness in Westminster, the media and wider public opinion suggests that the time may be ripe for broad and balanced debate about this important democratic value.

(Crossman 2007)

Both of these quotations suggest that the issues of privacy and civil liberties have become increasingly high profile in recent years. Crossman's suggestion that this issue has risen in importance in the past two years (i.e. since 2005) places this renewed debate about civil liberties contemporaneously with the debate about the UK Government's proposals to introduce biometric identity cards.

This view of the recent surge in privacy related media coverage is shared by numerous civil society and privacy activists. There have been some historical studies of media coverage of privacy issues, especially in relation to direct marketing activities (Petrison and Wang 1995; Roznowski 2003). These studies focus on trends and coding of samples of papers. Neither of these studies make particular mention of front page, headline stories which suggests that privacy issues have not been such lead stories. In contrast, during the period that this paper was being revised (the so-called quiet news period of July–September 2008), privacy related stories have been the main front page news on a number of occasions.[8]

As well as editorials, newspaper commentators of all political persuasions have written extensively about the scheme and civil liberties more generally. Henry Porter, columnist for the left-of-centre Observer newspaper, has written numerous columns on the topic.[9]

In the right-of-centre *Daily Telegraph*, columnist Philip Johnston also frequently writes in this area.[10]

In July 2007, Johnson was awarded The Charles Douglas-Home Memorial Trust Award, an annual essay prize established in honour of the former editor of the Times. His award winning essay reflects on the erosion of civil liberties under the Labour Government including CCTV cameras, identity cards, the DNA database and other surveillance technologies and is based on his earlier columns (Johnson 2007). That a columnist writing in this area is recognised in this way both reflects the status of writing on this topic and contributes to the ongoing public scrutiny of the scheme.

As well as these columnists, a number of other reports and inquiries have also been undertaken. In September 2006 the Information Commissioner's Office published a report by the Surveillance Studies Network on the Surveillance Society (ICO 2006) thus officially coining the phrase 'surveillance society' as an alternative to the over-used 'Big Brother' imagery.

Shortly afterwards, the Royal Academy of Engineering (RAE) published a report entitled *Dilemmas of Privacy and Surveillance: Challenges of Technological Change* (RAE 2007).

The RAE report argued that 'the collection, storage and processing of personal data can be of great benefit to citizens, but that users' privacy must be protected' and suggested that 'engineers have some responsibility for designing systems that enhance data protection'. It also encouraged data minimisation and made recommendations about the design of systems that would minimise the risk of privacy related failure.

These reports helped trigger two Parliamentary inquiries. The first, by the Home Affairs Committee, into 'A surveillance society?' has recently reported its findings (Home Affairs Committee 2008) in which it suggests that whilst the UK cannot currently be characterised as a surveillance society, the government should take active steps to ensure that this does not come about. The committee also advocates the principle of data minimisation that was highlighted by the RAE report. The second, by the House of Lords Constitution Committee is looking at 'The Impact of Surveillance and Data Collection upon the Privacy of Citizens and their Relationship with the State' and is due to report soon.

With the heightened awareness of privacy and surveillance issues, both the Parliamentary oral evidence sessions for the inquiries and publication of the final reports generate considerable media interest. Once again, however, it is not immediately apparent what the causal relationship is here (Gandy 2003; Leff *et al.* 1986): is the media reporting stories that are believed to be of interest to the public or are they attempting to shape opinion by their choice of emphasis (Callaghan and Schnell 2001)?

Discussion

The current media coverage and public debates about identity cards, surveillance and privacy raise important questions about the kinds of issues they are, the role that the media plays in presenting them and the effects this has on public policy. For example, in their classic paper, Gamson and Modigliani (1989) suggest that every policy issue has 'a culture' that helps frame how the public understand and cope with it (Wagner *et al.* 2002). This culture provides an 'interpretive package' consisting of many different elements associated with the topic. Indeed, for controversial topics such as identity cards, there may be competing elements that are trying to determine which interpretive package predominates (Callaghan and Schnell 2001).

In this context, the media plays an important role in the social construction of meaning (Wagner *et al.* 2002). For example, whilst much of the British press has, as was noted above, become hostile towards the proposals for identity cards, there is less agreement about other issues such as CCTV. Moreover, much of the mainstream coverage has typically focused around the 'card' itself, rather than the databases underlying the National Identity Register (Martin and Whitley 2007).

Another key element in the media coverage of the topic has been the imagery and cartoons used to accompany news stories (Gamson and Modigliani 1989). In the case of identity cards and surveillance, much of the coverage of the RAE report used its iconic cover image of a CCTV pole with four cameras, whilst the HMRC data breach brought forth a series of cartoons about data losses, including one of Father Christmas admitting that he had lost the disc containing every child's name and address. The cartoons would again keep the issue in the public imagination and develop their understanding of the consequences of the event.

Although public concern and media coverage of privacy and surveillance has been high over the past three years, it is unclear whether this interest will remain over the long term. For example, Downs (1972) argues that public attention rarely remains focused on any one issue for an extended period of time, suggesting that the issue goes up and down in attention over time. Thus, after an initial period where the issue has not captured much public attention, it might move to a period of 'alarmed discovery' or 'euphoric enthusiasm' before practical issues come to the fore and intense public interest gradually declines. He suggests that this is particularly likely to be the case where only a minority of individuals are facing the issue or where the benefits to the majority outweigh the hardships to the minority. Issues will also decline if the problem has 'no intrinsically exciting qualities'. Put another way, for media coverage to remain high, the story must continue to be dramatic and exciting because news is 'consumed'.

In these terms, with identity cards and surveillance affecting the entire population and government mismanagement of personal data affecting an increasingly large proportion of the population it can be argued that the topic is likely to remain as a topic of interest. Moreover, the technological basis of many of the issues (from Google recording street images for its Street View system, councils monitoring how much rubbish families throw away to the collection of fingerprints for biometric identification) is likely to make 'exciting' news stories with an easy angle for broadcasters and publishers to use. In so doing, it raises the question of the relationship between news reporting, 'infotainment' and the political process (Brants 1998)

Jasper (1988), in contrast, argues that technological controversies have a variety of 'life cycles' with different forces at work at different stages. He therefore distinguishes between issues that address so-called 'basic values' and those that have interest (to the media initially) because they arise from disagreements between scientific experts (as was the case with the LSE analysis). Basic values, such as concerns for equality and justice, are assumed to change far more slowly than issues that are more media-driven.

Issues of privacy and surveillance, however, do not fall neatly into either category. Whilst privacy campaigners often argue that privacy is a basic value or a human right, there is considerable evidence that it is generally not viewed as such, with examples of individuals handing over vast amounts of personal data in exchange for a chocolate bar or nominal discount at a supermarket (although see Felten 2008). The ongoing and diverse coverage of the issue, in the UK at least, suggests that, having reached a certain level of awareness, the issue is becoming one which shares many of the characteristics of a basic-values issue as defined by Jasper.

Conclusions

This chapter has argued that there has been a marked shift in media coverage of issues of privacy and surveillance. This shift is contemporaneous with the UK Government's plans to introduce biometric identity cards in the UK and suggests that the early debates about the scheme has placed the broader issues of civil liberties onto the mainstream media agenda. The resulting increased and prominent coverage of privacy related news stories appears to have had an effect on public opinion with some polls indicating a gradual decline in support for identity cards alongside growing unease about the 'surveillance society'. This decline is somewhat lower, however, than might have been expected following events like the HMRC data breach suggesting that privacy and surveillance have not fully achieved the status of 'basic values'.

With some of the variance in public opinion attributable to the wording of the questions being asked, the role of awareness and understanding of surveillance technologies becomes important, suggesting that the UK is following a similar path to that found elsewhere (e.g. the experience of the Australia card in the late 1980s) where increased awareness and understanding leads to changes in attitudes. Thus, in common with other issues (like environmental issues), there is an important role for the academy to play in informing public debate about important, technologically based issues.

All technological systems are open to social shaping and government technologies are particularly so. With the design of government systems driven by the values of elected officials, there is a clear role for public opinion in shaping the potential design of systems like the Identity Cards Scheme through the public's choice of parliamentarians and parties to represent them.

Acknowledgements

The arguments in this chapter have been extensively road tested and I am grateful to the organisers of the various events where I've had an opportunity to present these ideas for the feedback received. These organisers are: Martin Bauer and Jane Gregory, Steven Akehurst, Peter Walley, Toby Stevens and Daniel Neyland. Thanks, as ever, to Aaron Martin, Gus Hosein, Phil Booth, the book editors and the other unnamed individuals who have given helpful feedback on this work.

Appendix

As this chapter was being completed, on 25 September 2008 the UK Government announced the design of the identity cards that would begin to be issued to foreign nationals from mid November (see note 2). This provided an ideal opportunity to 'test' empirically some of the claims made in the chapter. Based on an initial analysis of the news reports the following themes are apparent.

The 'launch' of the new cards has been reported in over 70 news outlets (including newspapers, online and paper only), specialist trade outlets and political news websites. These have included the broadsheet as well as the tabloid newspapers. The launch made the front page of one (evening) newspaper.

Much of the coverage that goes beyond the simple reporting of the official press release is critical of the plans with headlines like 'ID card scheme faces new stumbling block over fingerprinting' (*Daily Mail*), 'ID card unveiled with Euro bull but minus Union Flag' (*Mirror*), 'Jacqui Smith unveils the UK's new identity card – with no sign of Britain' (*Daily Telegraph*), 'New ID card unveiled amid criticism' (Reuters), 'Smith dismisses ID card fingerprint problem' (*Independent*) and 'Boost to security, or threat to liberty?' (*The Herald*).

The technical press is also critical, with CIO News View reporting 'The ID card honeypot' and PublicTechnology.net reporting 'First ID card unveiled by Home Secretary – not everyone's happy, though' and Silicon.com reporting 'ID card "will drown in a billion mismatches": Won't somebody think of the elderly?'.

The launch triggered two more editorials with the Independent editorial entitled: 'An assault on our freedom' arguing 'Talk about an unwelcome arrival. The government has unveiled a small piece of plastic which represents a big threat to our historic liberties'. In the tabloid Mirror newspaper the editorial states: 'The look of the first national ID card was revealed yesterday and it is not a pretty sight. ... The expense of ID cards is bad enough. Using them to stigmatise the poor is just unacceptable'. The Herald, under the heading 'Rejecting ID cards' writes 'Soft colours and symbolic flowers may suggest little sister rather than big brother, but the pink and blue card complete with rose, thistle, daffodil and shamrock, to be issued to foreign workers from November, is unlikely to reassure opponents of the government's multi-billion-pound identity card scheme'.

Notes

1 This work was partially supported by the Technology Strategy Board; the Engineering and Physical Sciences Research Council and the Economic and Social Research Council [grant number EP/G002541/1].

2 Under the terms of the UK Borders Act 2007, the government was given the authority to start issuing identity cards to foreign nationals. It intends to do so from 25 November 2008 (UK Border Agency 2008).

3 The one exception is the first poll, before the government had come up with a likely cost for the card. This time the wording was 'The government has proposed the introduction of compulsory identity cards. Which of these statements comes closest to your view?'.

4 The question asked was 'You may have heard that the government intends to collect information about citizens and store it on large computer systems which can then be used for a wide range of purposes. Do you think storing information and sharing it between different parts of government in this way is a … [good/bad idea]?'

5 The government has always said that whilst it plans to make it compulsory to have an identity card, it would not be compulsory to carry one. The final Act introduces civil rather than criminal penalties for failing to enrol in the scheme so Clegg would, in fact, be fined rather than imprisoned.

6 Recent examples include Lettice (2008) on the IPS Annual Report, BBC (2008a) on the Biometrics Advisory Group Annual Report and Watt (2008) on the Independent Scheme Assurance Panel Annual Report.

7 The BBC states the Wilson doctrine was 'first introduced in 1966 under the then Prime Minister Harold Wilson to assuage concerns that MI5 might be monitoring politicians with no oversight or authorisation. Mr Wilson gave an undertaking there would be no tapping of MPs' phones. This was later widened to include all forms of communication and to include peers in the House of Lords. The doctrine has been confirmed by subsequent prime ministers' (2008b). The Report on the matter by the Chief Surveillance Commissioner (Sir Christopher Rose 2008) suggests that it is unclear whether the Wilson Doctrine applies in this case. In addition, he called for greater clarity about the relationship between the Doctrine and existing surveillance legislation (the Regulation of Investigatory Powers Act).

8 In July these front page stories included the privacy issues associated with Viacom's law suit against Google (*Guardian*), use of surveillance powers by local government (*Daily Telegraph*) and the government's proposals for a database of communications (*Daily Mail*). In August, front page stories included the breach of data about prisoners (*Daily Mail, Daily Telegraph*), Bank details being sold on eBay (*Daily Mail*) and the identity fraud risks after hackers hit a hotel chain (*Daily Telegraph*). September stories include companies being able to access your medical files (*Sunday*

Telegraph), government surveillance of all car journeys (*Guardian*) as well as a breach of data, this time about prison warders (*Sunday Telegraph*).

9 A selection of titles of his recent articles (Porter 2008) includes: Panopticon highway; Is liberty in Peril?; We can't leave David Davis to carry the fight on his own; A magnificent gesture that we must support; Why I told Parliament: you've failed us on liberty; MPs must thwart the dark plans of the state; A mass movement is needed to tackle the state's snoopers; Each DNA swab brings us closer to a police state; Liberty's wake-up call; This contempt for liberty that Brown must sweep aside; After a sinister year, it's down to us to protect our freedoms; There's just no escape from these snoops; Hands off our fingers!; We don't need ID cards; We are already at the gates of the surveillance society; Government property: your identity; This ID project is even more sinister than we first thought.

10 A selection of his recent articles (Johnson 2008) includes: David Davis struck a blow for liberty; David Davis is tilting at real giants; MPs must act now to set limits on snooping; We'll be able to sign up for ID cards at Tesco; We don't need a high-tech Domesday Book; Just because it's digital doesn't mean it's safe; Why I am prepared to break the law; Tap-dancing around phone tapping; Innocent – but on a criminal database; Here is your passport to penury; The end of privacy as we know it; Balancing our rights against their wrongs.

References

BBC News (2005a) *£300 price tag on ID cards 'mad'* [Online]. Available at: http://news.bbc.co.uk/1/hi/uk_politics/4099356.stm [accessed 3 December 2008].

BBC News (2005b) *ID cards academic attacks Clarke* [Online]. Available at: http://news.bbc.co.uk/1/hi/uk_politics/4651299.stm [accessed 3 December 2008].

BBC News (2008a) *ID card fingerprint errors fear* [Online]. Available at: http://news.bbc.co.uk/1/hi/uk_politics/7484853.stm [accessed 3 December 2008].

BBC News (2008b) *Q&A: MP bugging row* [Online]. Available at: http://news.bbc.co.uk/1/hi/uk_politics/7225871.stm [accessed 3 December 2008].

Brants, K. (1998) 'Who's afraid of infotainment', *European Journal of Communication*, 13(3): 315–5.

Burstein, P. (1998) 'Bringing the public back in: should sociologists consider the impact of public opinion on public policy?', *Social Forces*, 77(1): 2–62.

Cabinet Office (2008a) *Cross Government Actions: Mandatory Minimum Issues* [Online]. Available at: http://www.cabinetoffice.gov.uk/~/media/assets/www.cabinetoffice.gov.uk/csia/dhr/cross_gov080625%20pdf.ashx [accessed 3 December 2008].

Cabinet Office (2008b) *Data Handling Procedures in Government: Final Report* [Online]. Available at: http://www.cabinetoffice.gov.uk/~/media/assets/www.cabinetoffice.gov.uk/csia/dhr/dhr080625%20pdf.ashx [accessed 3 December 2008].

Callaghan, K. and Schnell, F. (2001) 'Assessing the democratic deficit: how the news media frame elite policy discourse', *Political Communications*, 18(2): 183–212.

Crosby, S.J. (2008) *Challenges and Opportunities in Identity Assurance* [Online]. Available at: http://www.hm-treasury.gov.uk/d/identity_assurance060308.pdf [accessed 3 December 2008].

Crossman, G. (2007) *Overlooked: Surveillance and Personal Privacy in Modern Britain: Liberty* [Online]. Available at: http://www.liberty-human-rights.org.uk/issues/3-privacy/pdfs/liberty-privacy-report.pdf [accessed 3 December 2008].

Davies, H. (2005) 'Letter: LSE report on ID cards cost', *The Times* [Online]. Available at: http://www.timesonline.co.uk/tol/comment/letters/article539428.ece [accessed 3 December 2008].

Davies, H. (2006) *Letter to the Prime Minister* [Online]. Available at: http://identityproject.lse.ac.uk/daviestoblair.pdf [accessed 3 December 2008].

Davies, S. (2004) *The Loose Cannon: An Overview of Campaigns of Opposition to National Identity Card Proposals* [Online]. Available at: http://www.privacy.org.au/About/Davies0402.html [accessed 3 December 2008].

Davis, D. (2008) *It is Incumbent Upon Me to Take a Stand* [Online]. Available at: http://www.conservatives.com/News/Speeches/2008/06/David_Davis_It_is_incumbent_upon_me_to_take_a_stand.aspx [accessed 4 December 2008].

DCA (2006) *Information Sharing Vision Statement* [Online]. Available at: http://www.foi.gov.uk/sharing/information-sharing.pdf [accessed 3 December 2008].

Downs, A. (1972) 'Up and down with ecology: The "issue-attention cycle"', *Public Interest*, 28(1): 38–50.

Felten, E. (2008) *It Can be Rational to Sell Your Private Information Cheaply, Even if You Value Privacy* [Online]. Available at: http://freedom-to-tinker.com/blog/felten/it-can-be-rational-sell-your-private-information-cheaply-even-if-you-value-privacy [accessed 4 December 2008].

Financial Times (2008) 'Editorial', *Financial Times*, 27 January.

Gamson, W.A. and Modigliani, A. (1989) 'Media discourse and public opinion on nuclear power: a constructionist approach', *American Journal of Sociology*, 95(1): 1–37.

Gandy, O. (2003) 'Public opinion surveys and the formation of privacy policy', *Journal of Social Issues*, 59(2): 283–99.

Haggerty, K. and Gazso, A. (2005) 'The public politics of opinion research on surveillance and privacy', *Surveillance and Society*, 3(2/3): 173–80.

Haggerty, K.D. and Ericson, R.V. (2000) 'The surveillant assemblage', *British Journal of Sociology*, 51(4): 605–22.

Home Affairs Committee (2008) *A Surveillance Society?* [Online]. Available at: http://www.publications.parliament.uk/pa/cm200708/cmselect/cmhaff/58/58i.pdf [accessed 3 December 2008].

Home Office (2005) *Regulatory Impact Assessment*. London: Home Office.

ICO (2006) *A Report on the Surveillance Society* [Online]. Available at: http://www.ico.gov.uk/upload/documents/library/data_protection/practical_application/surveillance_society_full_report_2006.pdf [accessed 3 December 2008].

Identity and Passport Service (2008) *Tracking Research* [Online]. Available at: http://www.ips.gov.uk/identity/publications-research.asp [accessed 3 December 2008].

Independent (2008) 'Leading article: Is something bugging you?', *Independent*, 5 February.

IPCC (2008) *IPCC Independent Investigation Report into Loss of Data Relating to Child Benefit* [Online]. Available at: http://www.ipcc.gov.uk/final_hmrc_report_25062008.pdf [accessed 3 December 2008].

Jasper, J.M. (1988) 'The political life cycle of technological controversies', *Social Forces*, 67(2): 357–77.

Johnson, P. (2007) 'Are we a free country any more?', *The Times*, 19 July.

Johnson, P. (2008) *Articles*. Available at: http://www.telegraph.co.uk/opinion/main.jhtml?menuId=6795andmenuItemId=10340andview=PICHEADLINE

Leff, D.R., Protess, D.L. and Brooks, S.C. (1986) 'Crusading journalism: changing public attitudes and policy-making agendas', *Public Opinion Quarterly*, 50(3): 300–15.

Lettice, J. (2008) *IPS Finds No Nuggets in ID Checking Goldmine* [Online]. Available at: http://www.theregister.co.uk/2008/07/04/ips_validation_service/ [accessed 3 December 2008].

Lomas, N. (2008) *Home Office Loses Data on 84,000 Prisoners* [Online]. Available at: http://www.silicon.com/publicsector/0,3800010403,39274254,00.htm [accessed 3 December 2008].

LSE Identity Project (2005a) *Interim Report* [Online]. Available at: http://identityproject.lse.ac.uk/interimreport.pdf [accessed 3 December 2008].

LSE Identity Project (2005b) *Main Report* [Online]. Available at: http://identityproject.lse.ac.uk/identityreport.pdf [accessed 3 December 2008].

LSE Identity Project (2007) *Submission to the House of Lords Constitution Committee Inquiry into the 'Impact of Surveillance and Data Collection'* [Online]. Available at: http://identityproject.lse.ac.uk/HoLConst.pdf [accessed 3 December 2008].

LSE Identity Project (2008) *Analysing the Home Office's May 2008 Identity Cards Cost Report: A Report by the LSE's Identity Project* [Online]. Available at: http://identityproject.lse.ac.uk/s37Response4.pdf [accessed 3 December 2008].

MacKenzie, D. and Wajcman, J. (1999) 'Introductory essay and general issues' in D. Mackenzie and J. Wajcman (eds) *The Social Shaping of Technology* (2nd edn). Buckingham: Open University Press.

Martin, A.K. and Whitley, E.A. (2007) 'Managing expectations of technological systems: a case study of a problematic government project', *Spontaneous Generations*, 1(1): 67–77.

No2ID (2008a) *No2ID Press Releases* [Online]. Available at: http://www.no2id.net/news/pressRelease/ [accessed 3 December 2008].

No2ID (2008b) *No2ID Website* [Online]. Available at: http://www.no2id.net/ [accessed 3 December 2008].

Osborne, T. and Rose, N. (1999) 'Do the social sciences create phenomena?: the example of public opinion', *British Journal of Sociology*, 50(3): 367–96.

Petrison, L.A. and Wang, P. (1995) 'Exploring the dimensions of consumer privacy: an analysis of coverage in British and American Media', *Journal of Direct Marketing*, 9(4): 19–37.

Porter, H. (2008) *Articles* [Online]. Available at: http://www.guardian.co.uk/profile/henryporter [accessed 3 December 2008].

Pounder, C. (2007) *Evidence Submitted to Home Affairs Committee Inquiry into 'A Surveillance Society?'* [Online]. Available at: http://www.publications.parliament.uk/pa/cm200708/cmselect/cmhaff/58/58ii.pdf [accessed 3 December 2008].

RAE (2007) *Dilemmas of Privacy and Surveillance: Challenges of Technological Change* [Online]. Available at: http://www.raeng.org.uk/policy/reports/pdf/dilemmas_of_privacy_and_surveillance_report.pdf [accessed 3 December 2008].

Roznowski, J.L. (2003) 'A content analysis of mass media stories surrounding the consumer privacy issue 1990–2001', *Journal of Interactive Marketing*, 17(2): 52–69.

Sir Christopher Rose (2008) *Report on Two Visits by Sadiq Khan MP to Babar Ahmad at HM Prison Woodhill. Report of Investigation by the Right Honorable Sir Christopher Rose, Chief Surveillance Commissioner* [Online]. Available at: http://www.official-documents.gov.uk/document/cm73/7336/7336.pdf [accessed 3 December 2008].

The Economist (2005) 2 July.

The Economist (2008) 24 January.

The Labour Party (2005) *Manifesto 2005* [Online]. Available at: http://www.labour.org.uk/index.php?id=manifesto [accessed 3 December 2008].

The Sunday Times (2006) *Emails from Whitehall Officials in Charge of ID Cards* [Online]. Available at: http://www.timesonline.co.uk/tol/news/uk/article684968.ece [accessed 3 December 2008].

UK Border Agency (2008) *Identity Cards for Foreign Nationals* [Online]. Available at: http://www.ukba.homeoffice.gov.uk/managingborders/idcardsforforeignnationals/ [accessed 3 December 2008].

UKIPS (2006) *Strategic Action Plan for the National Identity Scheme: Safeguarding Your Identity* [Online]. Available at: http://www.homeoffice.gov.uk/documents/strategic-action-plan.pdf [accessed 3 December 2008].

UKIPS (2008) *National Identity Scheme: Delivery Plan 2008* [Online]. Available at: http://www.ips.gov.uk/identity/downloads/national-identity-scheme-delivery-2008.pdf [accessed 3 December 2008].

Wadham, J., Gallagher, C. and Chrolavicius, N. (2006) *Blackstone's Guide to the Identity Cards Act 2006*. Oxford: Oxford University Press.

Wagner, W., Kronberger, N. and Seifert, F. (2002) 'Collective symbolic coping with new technology: knowledge, images and public discourse', *British Journal of Social Psychology*, 41(3): 323–43.

Watt, N. (2008) 'ID cards may put poorer people at risk of fraud', *The Guardian* [Online]. Available at: http://www.guardian.co.uk/politics/2008/may/16/idcards.ukcrime [accessed 3 December 2008].

Whitley, E.A. and Hosein, I.R. (2008) 'Departmental influences on policy design: how the UK is confusing identity fraud with other policy agendas', *Communications of the ACM*, 51(5): 98–100.

Whitley, E.A. and Hosein, I.R. (2009) *Global Issues in Identity Management*. Basingstoke: Palgrave.

Whitley, E.A., Hosein, I.R., Angell, I.O. and Davies, S. (2007) 'Reflections on the academic policy analysis process and the UK Identity Cards Scheme', *The Information Society*, 23(1): 51–8.

Young, K. (2005) *Microsoft Slams UK ID Card Database: Central Database Could Lead to 'Massive Identity Fraud'* [Online]. Available at: http://www.vnunet.com/vnunet/news/2144113/microsoft-slams-uk-id-card [accessed 3 December 2008].

Part 3

Surveillance futures

Chapter 7

'Ten thousand times larger ...': anticipating the expansion of surveillance

Kevin D. Haggerty

Thinking about thinking about the future of surveillance

Contemplating the future frees an author from the narrower dictates of the scientific axiom that they should stay close to their data and concentrate on such things as validity, reliability and generalisability. While evidence must still be marshalled, thinking about the future provides greater latitude to speculate, and to use your full intellectual palate to paint on a broader canvass. At the same time, this is a daunting prospect. Early sociological figures unabashedly engaged in what is now called 'futurology,' predicting possible social formations based on current trends. In the 1970s, this reached its zenith when prominent figures such as Daniel Bell (1973) and Alvin Toffler (1970) engaged in an ambitious form of futurology that advanced radical visions of potential social developments. Contemporary sociologists tend to be more circumspect. To the extent that we talk of the future it tends to involve narrower forms of social forecasting that extrapolate from existing (often statistical) trends to anticipate the challenges officials will face in the future – the most common example being discussions about the policy implications of demographic transformations.

More conjectural forms of futurology have become a whipping boy for sociologists who prefer more circumspect disciplinary ambitions and for those blessed with hindsight. Futurology is easy to dismiss, as its practitioners tend to repeatedly reveal their limited imaginations. *The Oxford Dictionary of Sociology* is unsparing on this point, concluding futurology 'has an almost complete record of predictive failure'.

Being invited to contemplate the future is therefore also an invitation to be profoundly, perhaps even breathtakingly, wrong. Hence, I identify with Professor John Frink of the TV show *The Simpsons* who in his 1970s incarnation confidently made the laughably mistaken pronouncement that: 'within 100 years, computers will be twice as powerful, ten *thousand* times larger, and so expensive that only the five richest kings of Europe will own them'.

Anticipating what is to come would therefore normally be something that I would cheerfully cede to more inspired and thick-skinned literary figures. Nonetheless, my interest in surveillance has solidified a belief that we must seriously contemplate what lies ahead if we are to advance towards collective goals, or identify looming disasters. Indeed, disavowing futurology is disingenuous, as all of our normative positions are informed by at least a tacit understanding of possible future developments – even if we simply hold a naïve faith that life will continue largely unchanged. Moreover, if we abdicate the question of the future the issue falls to the technocrats, imagineers and corporate propagandists who are actively trying to forge futures characterised by such things as more information technology and greater concentrations of capital. It is folly to leave the future in the hands of such visionaries who, as a whole, only tend to address questions of power and inequality when reproducing the shop-worn, and demonstrably false, cliché that new technologies will inevitably undermine concentrations of power and forms of inequality (Andrejevic 2007).

What needs to be explained?

> We may get to a point where we look back and say 'how the hell did we get here?'
>
> Richard Thomas, Information Commissioner
> for the United Kingdom

Surveillance involves the collection and analysis of information about populations in order to govern their activities. While interpersonal surveillance is an inevitable component of human interaction, today informal face-to-face scrutiny has been augmented by a raft of initiatives designed to make people more transparent. Indeed, surveillance is now the dominant organising practice of late modernity, and is used for a multitude of widely divergent governmental projects, by turns both laudable and disconcerting.

So, what does the future of surveillance hold in store? Unfortunately, the specifics are impossible to discern. One reason for this is because surveillance practices will undoubtedly continue to be intimately connected to developments in computing and information processing; areas where remarkable developments arrive with head-spinning speed and regularity. Hence, we can perhaps vaguely anticipate, for example, that current investments in nanotechnology will culminate in an army of microscopic sensing machines embedded in our physical environment (van den Hoven and Vermaas 2007; Wright et al. 2008). Beyond such imprecise scenarios our ability to forecast is so hampered by the dramatic pace of technological change that projections can easily become science fiction.

When looked at from a broader level, and forgiving the pun, the future of surveillance is entirely transparent. Western nations are undergoing a world-historical transformation in the dynamics of social visibility. Institutions recognise that they can capitalise on technologically enhanced scrutiny of different classes of people (citizens, motorists, workers, students, consumers, voters, military adversaries, welfare recipients, and assorted other groupings) to enhance such things as rational governance, corporate profit, social regulation, entertainment and military conquest. Consequently, we have seen the progressive formalisation and intensification of the 'visible imperative,' which refers to the institutional expectation that individual's lives will be ever more open to scrutiny. For the foreseeable future surveillance will continue to expand, becoming more pervasive, penetrating and prosaic. This overall development will advance in fits and starts, becoming established more or less quickly and smoothly depending on the processes and populations being targeted. Nonetheless, our future is clearly in sight.

This expansion cannot be attributed to any single factor, but is made possible by the potentialities for greater transparency inherent in developments operating across a range of domains. New information technologies are a vital precondition for these transformations, but such tools only have serious consequences when aligned with changes to such additional factors as ideologies, laws, market structures, governmental logics, public sensibilities and risk perceptions.

The pivotal question, then, is temporally the exact opposite of the one the Information Commissioner anticipates at the head of this section. Rather than wait until we find ourselves in a 'maximum' or 'total' surveillance society (Norris and Armstrong 1999; Whitaker 1999), bemoaning how this could have happened, better to contemplate how this will, or, more optimistically, could, occur. As surveillance is often understood to be antithetical to democracy, some might suggest that such a future could only unfold in the aftermath of an unprecedented natural or social disaster. So, for example, the maximum surveillance scenario could result from efforts to address a monumental environmental collapse or as a project initiated by heretofore unanticipated totalitarian governments. My sense is we do not need to posit such radical discontinuities to explain the maximum surveillance scenario. The recent past provides numerous examples of more familiar factors that have helped surveillance expand in Western societies; these promise to continue to operate into the future.

As noted, the expansion of surveillance is an over determined process, fostered by processes that operate in different domains and across social registers. What follows, then, is not a catalogue of all of these factors, but a selective discussion of phenomena that I believe to be particularly consequential. It highlights the operation of dynamics of social stigmatisation and also efforts designed to establish 'conditional choices.' We start by addressing how cognitive processes can alternatively encourage citizens to embrace surveillance, or discount the extreme political risks inherent in a transparent society.

Surveillance: the very idea

Analysts have alternatively emphasised how surveillance is a social relationship, a sociotechnical assemblage, a tool of enforced conformity, a means of social exclusion, a racialising and gendering practice, and so on. Little has been said about surveillance's epistemology. Surveillance, fundamentally, operates as an *idea* that draws upon some of the most entrenched and weighty traditions of Western thought.

Surveillance is now the preferred solution to any number of social ills (Haggerty 2009). Governments amass warehouses of data on the scope and dynamics of social problems, hoping to use this information to rectify such issues. Policy advocates regularly champion different manifestations of the 'surveillance solution'; the use of surveillance to try and ameliorate a social ill. Some high-profile examples of the surveillance solution include efforts to reduce cheating in sports by testing for drugs, installing CCTV cameras to manage disorder, and intensifying the documentary regimes for international travellers to try and thwart terrorists. Advocates advance explicit arguments why governmental data collection, or assorted forms of the 'surveillance solution,' might rectify vastly different problems. Over and above such specific rationalisations, it also appears that the public appeal of pleas for greater surveillance is also enhanced by how our culture privileges the sense of sight.

Surveillance tends to make phenomena visible. While some forms of surveillance, such as audio recording, captures other forms of sensory data, even those technologies typically culminate in the production of visible inscriptions such as graphs, tables and charts. Surveillance is therefore the physical manifestation of one of our most common expressions; the trope of visibility. It would be hard to find a better demonstration of the centrality of such ocular metaphors in the English language than in Martin Jay's (1993: 1) magisterial *Downcast Eyes*. Scattered throughout the opening paragraph of that book are 21 visual metaphors:

> Even a rapid glance at the language we commonly use will demonstrate the ubiquity of visual metaphors. If we actively focus our attention on them, vigilantly keeping an eye out for those deeply embedded as well as those on the surface, we can gain an illuminating insight into the complex mirroring of perception and language. Depending, of course, on one's outlook or point of view, the prevalence of such metaphors will be accounted an obstacle or an aid to our knowledge of reality. It is, however, no idle speculation or figment of imagination to claim that if blinded to their importance, we will damage our ability to inspect the world outside and introspect the world within. And our prospects for escaping their thrall, if indeed that is even a foreseeable goal, will be greatly dimmed. In lieu of an exhaustive survey of such metaphors, whose scope is far too broad to allow an easy synopsis, this opening paragraph should suggest how ineluctable the modality of the visual actually is, at least in our linguistic practice. I hope by now, *optique lecteur*, you can see what I mean.

Our language is not just replete with visual metaphors, but vision is consistently valorised. Religious history provides ample examples of sun worship and of theological connections between deities and light.[1] Today, darkness is still associated with evil, and stands opposite the shining illumination of goodness. We reveal truth by pulling back the veil of ignorance, and applaud those who bear witness against evil. Plato's metaphor of the cave stands as the iconic example of the now inescapable connection between sight, knowledge and enlightenment. These associations became even more pronounced during the scientific revolution, when a procession of new scientific technologies of visibility helped render the physical world increasingly knowable (Lynch 1985).

This valorisation of vision is germane to thinking about how surveillance systems will expand in the future because it imperceptibly provides arguments in favour of using surveillance to rectify social problems with a form of 'epistemic privilege,' a concept borrowed from Somers and Block (2005: 265). In their history of the rise of market fundamentalism – the belief in the superiority of organising all dimensions of social life according to market principles – Somers and Block detail how the *idea* of market fundamentalism radically transformed social policy in two very different historical contexts. Their research examines England's *New Poor Law* of 1834 and the *Personal Responsibility and Work Opportunities Reconciliation Act* passed in 1996 in the United States. As they note, these laws were introduced in contexts that differed across every significant sociological parameter except for the nearly identical arguments in favour of market fundamentalism which were skilfully advanced to undermine previous welfare regimes. Cautious to avoid lapsing into idealism, and recognising the importance of other structuring factors, their account nonetheless suggests that it was the ideational privilege of market fundamentalism that brought about these changes, producing policy effects over and above other potential causal factors such as structural transformations in the marketplace or the differential power of political claim's makers.

For our purposes, a modified version of the notion of an ideational privilege is preferable. Where Somers and Block are concerned with how one ideational regime dissembedded its predecessor in two distinct policy domains, I am suggesting that surveillance, operating as an *idea*, has an unarticulated but deep-seated epistemic privilege. The idea of surveillance flows as a cultural undercurrent, percolates into a multitude of policy discussions, and helps buoy arguments in favour of greater surveillance, providing them with a form of intuitive common sense. As such, this notion has affinities which Bourdieu's (1980) concept of doxa, which refers to fundamental deep-founded, unthought beliefs social actors take as self-evident.

Where Sommers and Block attribute causal powers to the ideational regime of market fundamentalism, the idea of surveillance does not preordain any policy outcome, but operates more as a cognitive structure that exerts varying degrees of influence in different contexts, but tends to make arguments in favour of greater scrutiny appear intuitively plausible. People who hold such an orientation to the powers of sight are simply predisposed to accept the proposition that by making something more visible it becomes easier to manipulate, regulate and control.

This also means that individuals are more apt to discount evidence that surveillance will not work. Ideas with epistemic privilege tend to display 'astonishing immunity to the kinds of empirical challenges that should be evidently disconfirming ... even in the face of repeated empirical challenges...' (Somers and Block 2005: 265). Put differently, because citizens tend to unconsciously privilege the idea of surveillance, they can find it counterintuitive when they encounter evidence that a new surveillance regime might not work. Individuals arguing against using surveillance also find themselves positioned on the denigrated half of the dichotomous weighting of visual metaphors as they are unconsciously aligned with darkness, irrationality and ignorance.

Beliefs about the power of vision become even more compelling when combined with the conviction, now widespread, that social problems are best solved through new technology. This view, known as the 'technological fix' (Marx 1995), inclines citizens and officials alike to think that technology is the best and perhaps even the *only* way to address social or political concerns. In the future, as a monitoring function is built-in to ever-more information technologies, the combination of these entrenched assumptions will further predispose individuals to embrace new forms of surveillance. Such beliefs will also reinforce the cognitive tendency to discount the worst case scenario for how officials might use this multiplying surveillance capacity.

Worst cases

Whereas surveillance's ideational privilege tends to make citizens believe that enhanced visibility is an effective solution to any number of social ills, our cognitive relationship to 'worst case' scenarios can foreclose critical thought about the dangers inherent in the contemporary embrace of surveillance.

Surveillance measures are usually evaluated on a case-by-case basis. If there is ever public debate about a new monitoring technology this tends to occur just prior to the tool being incorporated into a concrete governmental initiative or expanded to new populations. Much of this evaluation is narrow and technocratic, focusing on whether the technology will accomplish a prescribed goal. Any discussion about the dangers posed by those tools tends to focus on the implications for the populations that will be immediately targeted, and isolates the proposed initiative from wider political developments. This discourse also has a short time horizon and, crucially, presumes the continuation of a comparatively stable political context. Lost in this case-specific framing is an acknowledgement that surveillance capacity has increased exponentially across almost all institutional domains, *cumulatively* transforming our sociotechnical world, and in the process, posing new political risks.

The unadorned truth is that our wholesale adoption of surveillance carries with it the risk of draconian forms of social control. Not simply that surveillance will infringe on our civil liberties (which is itself a concern characteristic of liberal democratic societies), but that groups will combine and co-ordinate such devices across institutional boundaries, putting them in the service of some of the worst atrocities imaginable. So, whereas I previously indicated that we need not posit the emergence of totalitarianism to explain the intensification of surveillance, the expansive but still loosely co-ordinated surveillance infrastructure we are creating could serve totalitarian ends or even foster the rise of such governmental forms. The thousands of surveillance systems now dispersed across institutions will outlast contemporary political arrangements. Surveillance cameras, electronic databases, integrated bureaucracies, human implants and internet monitoring mechanisms are just a fraction of the technological and informational inheritance awaiting any group that gains power. Once installed, governments will not remove such technologies except to replace them with new and more sophisticated devices.

Citizens of the global north tend to be blinkered about the prospect that their governments (or corporations) could engage in forms of untempered coercion. Westerners tend to dismiss such scenarios out of hand, and distance themselves from the cautionary examples of regimes that have employed surveillance as a basic attribute of despotic rule (Klein 2008; Black 2001), preferring to see such practices as resulting from a weak rule of law, lack of democratic traditions or an authoritarian culture. Such a Panglossian position almost willfully ignores that political structures are inherently fragile and subject to dramatic transformation. When things go wrong, as happens with disconcerting regularity, little in the way of international agreements, legality or democratic sensibilities has proved capable of thwarting single-minded ruthlessness. If we contemplate political structures in the context of a world-historical timeframe, it seems inevitable that at least some liberal democratic societies will devolve into forms of authoritarianism. Should that happen, individuals who now embrace, or are indifferent towards, the ongoing manufacture of a surveillance infrastructure could awake to find themselves singled out by such devices because they look or act in ways now entirely unobjectionable. People who discount such a scenario out of hand are whistling past a graveyard.

When asked to contemplate the future, Westerners tend to envision a world that looks remarkably like the present. Citizens rarely acknowledge the prospect of drastic political or social upheaval, making it difficult for them to appreciate the dangers inherent in an extensive surveillance infrastructure. This shortsighted public imagination inadvertently allows surveillance to expand into the future by foreclosing consideration of some of the most dramatic perils created by these developments.

Why individuals and institutions tend to be complacent about worst case scenarios has been the subject of much academic debate.[2] Here, I follow Cerulo (2006) to emphasise how the routine operation of 'positive asymmetry' in human thought processes tends to foreground only the best characteristics of a phenomena. While this might seem a curious proposition in the context of a mass media dominated by doom and gloom accounts, she presents compelling examples drawn from personal relationships, child rearing and disaster planning to demonstrate how we routinely discount the prospect that the very worst might occur. To appreciate why this is the case requires a brief excursion into cognitive science.

Our brains use mental categories to classify and process information (Cerulo 2006: 6–10). We distinguish between a phenomena's sameness or difference along a number of axes in relationship to a category ideal. This comparative process extends to making reference to other members of that class of phenomena. In so doing, the brain amplifies or exaggerates the category ideal, meaning that an example of a phenomena that only has a few of the concept's ideal attributes will be included in the category, but mentally distanced from the 'best case' specimen. So, for example, our category for 'houseplant,' might have a fern coming closer to that ideal than the insect-eating Venus flytrap. The extent to which any individual case fits as an instance of a conceptual category is a matter of degrees, making asymmetry the brain's normal operating practice. Given that the worst-case example of any concept is only minimally similar to the category ideal, the brain routinely distances such instances from active consideration.

As the brain moves along a quality continuum toward the worst-case example, it does not simply proceed toward another well-articulated pole of meaning. Rather, movement results in a marked loss of definition. In this way, proceeding toward the worst requires an adjustment of both relativity and clarity, of both position and accessibility. The worst-case pole of the quality continuum is simultaneously oppositional and remote. Backgrounded in this way, the worst becomes vague and muted. Absent the articulation of the category ideal, the worst-case is relegated to the fringes of consciousness.

(Cerulo 2006: 10)

Biology does not provide the categories used by the brain, and hence we must appreciate how social factors also contribute to asymmetric thinking. Humans draw upon a cultural repertoire of categories to discriminate among different stimuli. We interpret the world with reference to such culturally-generated ideal concepts, a process which itself involves a tendency to emphasise the best or most positive cases of a categorisation. However, not everyone uses the same interpretive scheme. Members of different thought communities interpret reality from a similar vantage point, and all such communities have their own biases, emphasising and prioritising some factors over others. Amongst such groups, '[t]he best is continually defined as the most immediate and familiar dimension of quality. In contrast, the worst is distanced and blurred, perhaps completely blocked by images of perfection and excellence. Thus, the worst evolves as a minimal presence to seemingly myopic community members' (Cerulo 2006: 12).

That culture plays a role in this process suggests that concerted efforts by communities to foreground the worst prospect can result in a greater sensitivity to disastrous possibilities. In some contexts of personal protection individuals have cultivated a sensibility towards bleak potentialities and justify their efforts to mitigate against extremely remote risks by noting that they are trying to avoid worst cases (Haggerty 2003). To take a more concrete example, since the terrorist attacks of September 11, 2001, there has been an official effort to nurture the ability of institutions and citizens to imagine and plan for horrific worst case scenarios. This started almost immediately after the attacks, but was given a major boost when the 9/11 Commission concluded that one of the four causes of that tragedy was an organisational failure to imagine novel and unprecedented terrorist threats (Kean and Hamilton 2004). In the ensuing years governments have nurtured official imaginaries of disaster, trying to foster an ability to contemplate the very worst terrorist scenarios (de Goede

2008). However, such speculations have themselves been consciously steered down narrow and officially signposted avenues. Security planners are encouraged to contemplate co-ordinated, simultaneous, multi-site and multi-scale terrorists attacks conducted by foreign adversaries. Citizens are subjected to a pedagogy of paranoia, being trained to perceive danger masquerading as an unattended backpack or tourist photographing a national monument. No official effort has been expended to encourage citizens to contemplate how the official turn to surveillance (for anti-terrorist among many other purposes) itself provides fodder for a different variant of worst-case scenario. Hence, the cognitive and cultural tendency to discount worst cases means that the nightmare of new informational and visualising devices being deployed tyrannically is marginalised, dismissed as the fevered fulminations of fanatics.

The stigmatised

While citizens are directed away from contemplating the worst case scenario of a surveillance society, anxiety still plays an important role in the expansion of surveillance. Again, stepping back from the specifics to analyse these developments from a higher vantage point, we can anticipate that processes of stigmatisation will also contribute to the expansion of surveillance.

Every society stigmatises some groups, singling them out for elevated public censure. As such populations become the focus of public anxiety they are also routinely subjected to greater official scrutiny. It is impossible to say exactly what behaviours or groups will become the most vilified, but 'criminals' will undoubtedly figure prominently in this process. Since the Reagan presidency political posturing about coddled criminals has proven to be an effective vote-winning strategy, and as such, is reborn every election season. In the United States this has culminated in such things as the return of chain gangs, the introduction of three strikes legislation, hardened attitudes towards criminals and a mind-boggling increase in the prison population, now the largest of all democratic societies (Mack 2007). The decline of the rehabilitative ideal among policy élites (Garland 2001a; Loader 2005) has tended to reduce prisons to stark racialised warehouses devoid of programming, training or treatment (Garland 2001b).

While the official response to deviance is multi-faceted, surveillance figures prominently in the war on crime, and will undoubtedly continue to be a proving ground for new practices and technologies of visualisation. To date, the criminal justice system has helped legitimate the introduction and/or expansion of such things as CCTV systems, drug testing, metal detectors, DNA databases, Internet monitoring, biometrics, electronic bracelets and refinements in dataveillance. There is recurrent talk about plans to implant inmates with microchips and subject them to voice stress analysis and brainwave monitoring. All of this is accelerated by efforts to deal with 'terrorists,' a figure that straddles the threshold dividing criminals from soldiers, and which is now routinely used to justify new surveillance measures (Haggerty and Gazso 2005; Lyon 2003; Ball and Webster 2003).

Criminals and terrorists are just some of the stigmatised groups who promise to figure prominently in the ongoing broadening of surveillance. Under neoliberalism indigent populations have been stigmatised as lazy and undeserving. In an extension of longstanding practices, we can expect that people on social assistance will be subjected to new forms of scrutiny. Poor people have little option but to expose the specifics of their lives and documentary identities if they want to receive assistance.

Of the numerous examples of state co-ordinated surveillance of the poor, one of the most notorious involved variations on the 'man in the house' rules. Starting from the patriarchal assumption that a man should financially support a women with whom he is intimately involved, these regulations prohibited women in such relationships from collecting benefits. Hillyard Little (1998) provide an unsettling account of the lengths to which zealous authorities in Ontario, Canada, would go in trying to detect male breadwinners. It involved a band of welfare workers engaging in what was colloquially known as the 'manhunt'; scrutinising women's homes for telltale signs of masculine domesticity, such as shaving cream, extra toothbrushes and razors. 'Social workers have also been known to check for tire tracks in the snow, examine fridge notes, search for hunting equipment and evidence of dogs, stake out parking lots at night, throw sand on the doorstep in order to trace footprints – all in an effort to confirm that a man is living in the home' (Hillyard Little 1998: 174).

Today, officials have turned to information technology to conduct a more categorical scrutiny of the poor, in the process also reducing the need for expensive social workers. John Gilliom's (2001) research on Appalachian women receiving social assistance demonstrates how this new surveillance operates. With little prospect of employment, these women collect social assistance in order to survive and raise their children. Tragically, everyone – from senior officials to front-line welfare workers – acknowledges that the women simply cannot live on the funds they are provided. This also places claimants in an agonising Catch-22 because if caught earning additional income their desperately needed state support will be suspended.

While the state's rules for social service eligibility are often Byzantine, the use of information technology gives the process of monitoring for rule violation a series of new dynamics. In their interviews with Gilliom's researchers, these Appalachian women inevitably complained about the ubiquitous presence of CRIS-E in their lives. The acronym stands for 'Client-Registry Information System – Enhanced', a computer system that integrates vast stores of personal data drawn from different state databases dealing with issues of identity, paternity, health, employment and educational history and financial need. The computers subject the informational spoors of these women's lives to the continuous scrutiny of state and national fraud control programs, a process all the more intensive because it combines the monitoring capacity of myriad previously discrete systems. All of this subjects the women to an ever-tightening regulatory weave, making it difficult for them to find alternative sources of income or engage in the pedestrian types of rule violation that can be necessary to survive on social assistance.

Beyond the government's constant concern that too much money is spent on welfare, questions about effectiveness and efficiency in service delivery have become paramount (Gross Stein 2001). There is now a sense that services are going to the wrong people, being delivered at the wrong time and in the wrong ways. In light of such concerns Britain, for example, has sought to direct extra attention to what are called 'high cost, high risk' groups. Individuals are assigned to this category if they are more likely to be incarcerated, use health services, be on social assistance, not pay taxes, and so on, all of which translates into extra costs for the state. Consequently, government service delivery now aims to single out individuals who might disproportionately need such assistance – now or in the future – and to reduce or eliminate these risks. To do so, officials must know, and know in considerable detail, everyone's risk profile. Extensive data is compiled about where people live, their biographical details, medical profile, social service history, criminal history (and, ideally, the comparable histories for parents, siblings and friends). Official ministries tirelessly churn such information to try and determine which factors, alone or in combination, predict that a person will be at greater risk of being socially excluded or reliant on governmental services.

The profiling practices required to single out 'at risk' citizens therefore depend upon a massive integrated governmental infrastructure of data collection and monitoring *of the entire population*. Here, people are not scrutinised because they have behaved in a suspicious or problematic fashion, but simply because they are a member of a population. People deemed to be 'at risk' are singled out on the basis of their statistical profile. Risk, so understood, is always relative to something else. A person can only be more or less at risk as compared to some other individual or group. Hence, awareness that someone is 'risky' emerges against a background knowledge of the statistical profile of the entire population. Consequently, social welfare policy in the United Kingdom now *'depends* on surveillance – it has an internal logic that necessitates surveillance in order to function' (Pleace 2007: 948).

In the future, other groups will undoubtedly rocket up the official 'hit list' of suspicious populations. The Los Angeles' Police Department's recent proposal to map the city's Muslim communities is a reminder that as authorities come to see groups as a problem they also seek to scrutinise them in greater detail (Winton, Watanabe and Krikorian 2007). Unless the symbolic economy of the stigmatized undergoes an unforeseeable change, surveillance will continue to expand disproportionately among groups perceived to be marginal, risky, immoral or simply unpalatable. We can expect that wide swathes of the population will be scrutinised by efforts designed to detect and monitor the stigmatised, given that the boundaries of such categories are fluid, malleable and indistinct; that such designations rely on a comparison with wider population groups; and that membership in a stigmatized category is increasingly akin to having a kind of 'spectrum disorder' where we are all located on a continuum of deviance, rather than positioned on one or the other side of a distinct evaluative dichotomy.

Conditional choices and lesser options

Citizens must increasingly provide institutions with greater access to assorted informational traces in order to take advantage of governmental programming and private sector services. Such data speaks to their past behaviour, future inclinations and wider social networks. People unwilling to reveal such information can find it difficult, if not impossible, to travel, use credit, receive electricity, and so on. The costs of going completely off the surveillance grid and extricating oneself from official scrutiny are already so high – necessitating that people forego the institutional and informational conduits of late modernity – that few are willing to follow that path.

As noted, I call this institutionalised expectation that people will reveal ever more information about themselves the 'visible imperative'. Occasionally its dynamics are unambiguously coercive, as in Canada where citizens who refuse to complete the census can be criminally charged. On a routine basis the subjective experience, and legal framing, of the visible imperative is more likely to be a form of 'conditional choice'. Organisations present citizens with the option – albeit a highly circumscribed option – to surrender information in exchange for assorted perks. Hence, people can – at least theoretically – maintain their data privacy by foregoing such benefits.

Configuring surveillance as the result of an individual choice has proved to be a key means to legitimise such practices in liberal democratic societies where it is axiomatic that people should have maximum latitude to select their leaders, occupations, romantic partners and the like. Organisations look at these situations differently, seeing the conditional choice as a form of exchange, where, in return for surrendering personal data, citizens are provided something in return, such as the convenience of shopping on line, or a 1 per cent discount on their grocery bill. Consequently, organisations are refining efforts to calibrate the exchange thresholds where individuals will opt to surrender their information. Rather than establish opportunities for free and informed choices, institutions have instead sought to structure the context of decision-making to preordain that people will opt to surrender their information. This can be done by offering a desirable 'free' service, the costs of which are paid for through the profits gained from advertising and from exploiting the user's information. In such situations incomprehensible and non-negotiable legal minutia are used to obfuscate that data is being collected and how it is used. Alternatively, organisations make it so costly to avoid scrutiny that few would choose this route, as in the United Kingdom where customers of SKY TV satellite service are charged £248 if they refuse to activate the features that allow the service provider to monitor the minutia of their viewing patterns (Tinic 2006: 318).

Organisations aim to put forward a publicly acceptable and legally defensible façade of choice. Still, even the best corporate spokesperson sometimes cannot sugar-coat the compulsions that lurk behind this illusion. Consider China's plans to provide high technology residence cards to the approximately 50 million people who do not have permanent residency in the city where they live. Michael Lin, a vice president at the company providing the cards, makes the coercive aspects of this choice clear: 'If they do not get the permanent card,' Mr. Lin enthuses, 'they cannot live here, they cannot get government benefits, and that is a way for the government to control the population in the future' (Bradsher 2007). Organisations find it beneficial to frame surveillance as resulting from an individual's choice because, for them, choice is entirely compatible with the lack of any meaningful alternative. The demonstrated successes of establishing situations where conditional choices operate will ensure that this dynamic also continues into the future.

Note as well that for the conditional choice to work its information-generating magic, the 'lesser option' must be maintained at a suitably unpalatable level. Organisations keen to encourage larger percentages of the population to surrender their personal information must ensure that the option to *not* do so is always suitably expensive, inconvenient, and disagreeable. Hence, efforts to improve the lives of disadvantaged groups are subtly constrained by how the daily inconveniences and extra costs that they face are used to entice more privileged individuals to use 'premiere' services. Advantaged groups can avoid these lesser options, but in so doing they subject themselves to new configurations of bureaucratic monitoring.

A final attribute of the conditional choice worth accentuating is that it expands the dynamics of surveillance to non-stigmatised targets. Whereas governmental surveillance has historically been disproportionately directed at the 'dangerous classes,' today more powerful segments of society are also scrutinised. This includes a form of 'synopticism' (Mathiesen 1997) where the mass media allows the many to see the few, but also involves the powerful exposing themselves to bureaucratic monitoring in order to receive a specified service. For the élite, such trade-offs are desirable to the extent that they allow unencumbered transit through the physical and informational corridors of power. In the future, we can anticipate that perks which are now offered to the privileged as an option will tend to become an expectation for the masses, as the benefits of enrolment are reduced and the costs of not subjecting oneself to such scrutiny are ratcheted up.

Conclusion

This account presents only some of the factors that I believe will contribute to an ongoing expansion of surveillance in Western societies. My vision extrapolates a number of contemporary dynamics into the future such that temporalities overlap. A vision of what is to come draws insights from the past to raise contemporary questions.

Notably absent from this portrayal, however, is any discussion of resistance. This important omission can be attributed to the type of story I am telling. Undoubtedly, many citizens and officials in the state's privacy bureaucracy will oppose surveillance's onward march. I have ignored such endeavours because my interest here is in detailing how surveillance tends to expand. Consequently, the above chronicle of cognitive factors, conditional choices and practices of stigmatisation can also be read as a narrative about factors that tend to overcome and overwhelm attempts to resist surveillance.

Readers should also recognise that this is a modest exercise. I expect that many of the processes identified above will hold true, while being fully cognisant that social change is unpredictable. Human existence is too chaotic, and too fascinating, for it to be predicted perfectly. Sociology's subject matter also conspires to make it extremely difficult to anticipate the future. Whereas a researcher in the natural sciences can safely presume the stability of her object of study – cobalt or hydrogen do not change in light of how they are described – this is not the case for the social world (Hacking 1999). Social scientists need to be attuned to how the knowledge they produce can also change society. Anthony Giddens highlights this with his notion of the 'double hermeneutic,' which refers to the tendency of sociologists to draw from concepts used by laypeople in order to develop higher order knowledge about social life. Such higher order concepts tend to enter back into daily existence, changing our objects of study and in the process also constraining a sociologist's ability to produce cumulative or predictive knowledge (Giddens 1990).

Some find the social science's limited predictive abilities exasperating. Looked at differently, the ability for our descriptions to also change the world – hopefully for the better – provides a space for one of the social sciences main reasons for being. Scholarly accounts *can* alter human practice and social policy, even if the routes by which this happens are notoriously difficult to discern. Contemplating the future is therefore far more than an intellectual diversion. Critics who dwell on the tendency for speculative forms of academic futurology to be proven wrong simply miss the point. Nothing could be more perverse than someone being proud that they had accurately predicted how a dystopic future would unfold. Better to forcefully draw attention to the processes whereby surveillance expands and, in the process, hopefully help refute your own claims.

Notes

1 One of the main instances where vision is, in contrast, denigrated is the notion of the 'evil eye' which today can be found in many cultures but is most firmly rooted in the Middle East.
2 A recent volume of the journal *Sociological Inquiry*, 78(2), accentuates some of the reasons why organisations fail to plan for extreme but predictable disasters.

References

Andrejevic, M. (2007) *iSpy: Surveillance and Power in the Interactive Era.* Lawrence, KS: University Press of Kansas.

Ball, K. and Webster, F. (eds) (2003) *The Intensification of Surveillance.* London: Pluto.

Bell, D. (1973) *The Coming of Post-industrial Society: A Venture in Social Forecasting.* New York: Basic.

Black, E. (2001) *IBM and the Holocaust: The Strategic Alliance Between Nazi Germany and America's Most Powerful Corporation.* New York: Crown Publishers.

Bourdieu, P. (1980) *The Logic of Practice.* Stanford, CA: Stanford University Press.

Bradsher, K. (2007) 'China enacting a high-tech plan to track people', *New York Times*, 12 August.

Cerulo, K.A. (2006) *Never Saw it Coming: Cultural Challenges to Envisioning the Worst.* Chicago, IL: University of Chicago Press.

de Goede, M. (2008) 'Beyond risk: premeditation and the post-911 security imagination', *Security Dialogue*, 39(2/3): 155–76.

Garland, D. (2001a) *The Culture of Control.* Chicago, IL: University of Chicago Press.

Garland, D. (ed.) (2001b) *Mass Imprisonment: Social Causes and Consequences.* London: Sage.

Giddens, A. (1990) *The Consequences of Modernity.* Cambridge: Polity Press.

Gilliom, J. (2001) *Overseers of the Poor: Surveillance, Resistance and the Limits of Privacy.* Chicago, IL: University of Chicago Press.

Gross Stein, J. (2001) *The Cult of Efficiency.* Toronto, ON: Anasi.

Hacking, I. (1999) *The Social Construction of What?* Cambridge, MA: Harvard University Press.

Haggerty, K.D. (2003) 'From risk to precaution: the rationalities of personal crime prevention', in R.V. Ericson and A. Doyle (eds) *Risk and Morality.* Toronto, ON: University of Toronto Press.

Haggerty, K.D. (2009) 'Surveillance and political problems', in S. Hier and J. Greenberg (ed.) *Shades of Surveillance.* Vancouver, BC: University of British Columbia Press.

Haggerty, K.D. and Gazso, A. (2005) 'Seeing beyond the ruins: surveillance as a response to terrorist threats', *Canadian Journal of Sociology*, 30(2): 169–87.

Hillyard Little, M.J. (1998) *'No Car, No Radio, No Liquor Permit': The Moral Regulation of Single Mothers in Ontario, 1920–1997*. Oxford: Oxford University Press.

Jay, M. (1993) *Downcast Eyes: The Denigration of Vision in Twentieth-century French Thought*. Berkeley, CA: University of California Press.

Kean, T. and Hamilton, L.H. (2004) *The 9/11 Commission Report*. New York: W.W. Norton.

Klein, N. (2008) 'China's all-seeing eye', *The Rolling Stone*, 29 May.

Loader, I. (2006) 'Fall of the "platonic guardians": liberalism, criminology and political responses to crime in England and Wales', *British Journal of Criminology*, 46(4): 561–86.

Lynch, M. (1985) 'Discipline and the material form of images: an analysis of scientific visibility', *Social Studies of Science*, 15: 37–66.

Lyon, D. (2003) *Surveillance After September 11*. London: Polity Press.

Mack, A. (ed.) (2007) 'Punishment: the US record', *Social Research*, 74(2).

Marx, G.T. (1995) 'The engineering of social control: the search for the silver bullet', in J. Hagan and R. Peterson (eds) *Crime and Inequality*. Stanford, CA: Stanford University Press.

Mathiesen, T. (1997) 'The viewer society: Michel Foucault's 'panopticon' revisited', *Theoretical Criminology*, 1(2): 215–34.

Norris, C. and Armstrong, G. (1999) *The Maximum Surveillance Society: The Rise of CCTV*. Oxford: Berg.

Pleace, N. (2007) 'Workless people and surveillant mashups: social policy and data sharing in the UK', *Information, Communication & Society*, 10(6): 943–60.

Somers, M.R. and Block, F. (2005) 'From poverty to perversity: ideas, markets and institutions over 200 years of welfare debate', *American Sociological Review*, 70: 260–87.

Tinic, S. (2006) '(En)Visioning the televisual audience: revisiting questions of power in the age of interactive television', in K.D. Haggerty and R.V. Ericson (eds) *The New Politics of Surveillance and Visibility*. Toronto, ON: University of Toronto Press.

Toffler, A. (1970) *Future Shock*. New York: Random House.

van den Hoven, J. and Vermaas, P.E. (2007) 'Nano-technology and privacy: on continuous surveillance outside the panopticon', *Journal of Medicine and Philosophy*, 32: 283–97.

Whitaker, R. (1999) *The End of Privacy: How Total Surveillance is Becoming a Reality*. New York: The New Press.

Winton, R., Watanabe, T. and Krikorian, G. (2007) 'LAPD defends Muslim mapping effort', *Los Angeles Times*, 10 November.

Wright, D., Gutwirth, S., Friedewald, E. and Punie, Y. (2008) *Safeguards in a World of Ambient Intelligence*. Germany: Springer.

Chapter 8

Since *Nineteen Eighty Four*: representations of surveillance in literary fiction

Mike Nellis

Introduction

This chapter explores the representation of surveillance practices in (mostly) contemporary 'literary fiction', a term used here in the sociological sense, to denote novels in general, including genre novels (and short stories), not just the putatively 'highbrow' writing to which critics usually restrict the term. It examines the way in which novelists present surveillance as an issue, and identifies some of the cultural resources which the (admittedly segmented) 'reading public' might be using to make sense of the emergent 'surveillance society'. It extends David Lyon's (2007: 145) recent comments on the subject, which suggest that while 'the novel may be being supplanted by the film as a means of understanding surveillance ... the key question of the surveillance metaphor ... will still have to be sought in literary contexts'. The intimation that cinematic (and televisual) fiction is superseding literary fiction as a source of knowledge about surveillance rests on clear evidence that 'blockbuster movies' like *Enemy of the State* and *Minority Report* became significant reference points in popular debate upon it, in a way that no *recent* novel has (see Kammerer 2004). For better or worse, George Orwell's (1948) *Nineteen Eighty Four* still remains a touchstone in this respect, although the concepts it bequeathed to us – 'Big Brother', 'thought police' and 'telescreen' – long ceased to be adequate for grasping the varied forms, political complexity, multiple uses, ambivalent intentions and contradictory consequences of contemporary surveillance.

The u–surveillance novels – *We*, *Nineteen Eighty Four* and *The Castle*

Orwell's *Nineteen Eighty Four*, Yevgeny Zamyatin's (1924) *We*, which influenced Orwell, and Franz Kafka's (1922) *The Castle* were the three novels – published in the first half of the twentieth century and all written in oblique response to an emergent totalitarianism – which gave contemporary conceptions of the surveillance society its inalienably sinister tone. *The Castle*, admittedly, is open to a range of readings, not all of which privilege surveillance, although the comments of the superintendent (a Castle functionary) to the novel's bewildered lead character, K – 'You ask if there are control officials ... There are *only* control officials' (quoted in James 2008: 346) – ensures that it is never wholly outwith the territory. I will dwell here on Zamyatin, because his work is the least celebrated, and because not all of it is echoed by Orwell.

We – a mortifying satire on the dangers of untrammelled Taylorism as much as a veiled indictment of Stalinism – envisages control via the regimentation of labour, propaganda, leader worship, public executions and the creation of popular fears about imminent dangers – all of which occur in *Nineteen Eighty Four*. The 'One State' stifles imagination using neurosurgery rather than Orwell's 'newspeak', while the Bureau of Guardians are the precursors of Orwell's 'thought police'. The Guardian's covertly infiltrate the population and observe them from flying cars equipped with 'spying tubes', or via mechanical 'ears' in public thoroughfares. Domination in Zamyatin's dystopian city, however, is both augmented and symbolised by buildings whose walls, floors and ceilings are made of toughened glass, and whose occupants are forever on display. Only a residual interest in privacy survives – citizens can temporarily screen off their rooms at set times in order to have sex with officially sanctioned lovers, but the subjects of the 'One State' accept that everything is known about them, and cannot imagine it otherwise.

Both Orwell's and Zamyatin's narrators are initially system-insiders who become (doomed) dissenters. Zamyatin's is a senior mathematician 'named' D503, who takes a certain pride in knowing that it is his profession's work – the construction of mathematical formulae – which underpins and makes possible the hyper-regulated social order in which he lives. He rejoices in 'the mathematically perfect life of the One State' (1924: 4) and in 'the glass walls of my algebraic world' (1924: 32) through which everything becomes clear, certain and orderly. 'When a man's freedom is reduced to zero', he reasons, 'he commits no crimes. That's clear. The only means to rid man of crime is to rid him of freedom'. Yet the highly cerebral D503 guiltily knows himself to be attracted by the apparent chaos prevailing among the barbarian-humans in the 'wild world' beyond the city walls, and because he fails to suppress his more unruly emotions he believes himself to be an unworthy subject of the One State, deserving of his eventual punishment.

D503 anticipates that his secret memoir might one day be read by those outside the city walls, and struggles to explain to a less educated, less modern, consciousness what the experience of being totally known by the state felt like. At one point he compares it to the intimacy of being watched by one's own shadow. Later, ruminating on the ever-presence of undercover Guardians in their midst, he asks 'Who knows, maybe it was the Guardians that ancient man foresaw in his fantasy about the "archangels", both stern and tender, that were assigned at birth to every human' (1924: 49). Scrutiny by a real Guardian actually feels anything but tender – 'his eyes flashed: two sharp gimlets, quickly revolving, boring deeper and deeper and now screwing into my deepest depths, where they will see what I myself won't even' (1924: 32) – but later he tells himself:

> It strengthened me, I'd say. It's so nice to feel that someone's keeping a sharp eye on you, kindly protecting you from making the slightest mistake, the slightest misstep. This may sound sentimental, but the same analogy occurs to me: the guardian angels that the ancients dreamed about. So much of what they merely dreamed about has materialised in our life.
>
> (1924: 65)

Contemporary stories about people who find themselves in indecipherable environments, at the mercy of unseen but seemingly omniscient powers necessarily owe a debt to Kafka. Serbian fabulist Zoran Zivokovic's (2003) promisingly entitled – but ultimately tedious – *Hidden Camera* is one such. It concerns a somewhat prissy citizen who discovers that he has been secretly filmed while sitting in a park and immediately assumes not that he is the victim of state surveillance, but of a reality TV show. Rather implausibly, he spends the next twelve hours trying to find out who is filming him and simultaneously to avoid embarrassing himself on camera. He resigns himself to the ubiquity of the invisible cameras, but is nonetheless discomforted by the surveillant gaze, and tries, probably forlornly, to make his 'indisposition as unnoticeable as possible' (2003: 217). There are resonances here with Milan Kundera's (1985: 109) observation in *The Unbearable Lightness of Being* that 'the moment someone keeps an eye on what we do, we involuntarily make allowances for that eye, and nothing we do is truthful' [in the sense of authentic] and indeed with Vaclav Havel's (1986) broader indictment of having always to 'live a lie' in totalitarian societies. This characteristically East European view of surveillance's effects – self-diminishment, suppression of oneself as a public being – remains an important, although not universal, motif in surveillance fiction (but see also Kadare's (1993) satire on totalitarian power, in which the objects of surveillance are people's nightly dreams).

Science fiction

In a multiplicity of idioms – scientific, surreal and satirical – science fiction sought throughout the twentieth century to imagine possible, probable and preferable futures for mankind, near and distant. Whilst by no means exhausting all that science fiction has attempted to do, extrapolations of existing technologies and explorations of their social consequences, have been legion. Surveillance technology – particularly of the visual kind – has been a recurrent theme, rooted in the pre-twentieth century utopian, dystopian and speculative fiction from which science fiction itself sprang. One of the earliest references occurs in a Jules Verne-influenced novel called *The Land of the Changing Sun* (1894), by a neglected but once popular American writer W.N. Harben.[1] In it a group of Victorian-era travellers discover a 200-year-old, technologically advanced utopian city beneath the Arctic. The ruler explains to them that order is in part maintained by police who have access to a glass disc on which a detailed simulation of the city and its people are displayed:

> The most remarkable feature of the invention was, that the instant the eye rested on any particular portion of the whole that part was at once magnified so that every detail of it was clearly observable ... No sooner does anything go wrong than a red signal is given on the spot of the trouble and the attention of these officers is immediately called to it. A flying machine is sent out and the offender is brought to the police station, but trouble of any nature rarely occurs, and the duties of our police are merely nominal; my people live in thorough harmony.
>
> (Harben 1894)

The basis of Harben's imagined device was probably a Camera Obscura, which were widely used as popular public entertainments in the nineteenth century, and which had been envisaged by engineers as a means of urban crime prevention as early as 1824 (*Glasgow Mechanics' Magazine* No XXXII, cited in Jennings 1985: 164). Scottish dystopian James Leslie Mitchell (1934) (though better known as Lewis Grassic Gibbon) may himself have been extrapolating from this (and periscope) technology in *Gay Hunter*, whose future rulers of Britain relay visual images of what their enemies are doing over great distances. The technological mechanism is not precisely explained; 'what if?' is usually more important to science fiction novelists than 'exactly how?' Orwell did not explain how 'telescreens' worked, although Phillip Dick (1967: 238) made it a little clearer in one of his dystopias, where 'each TV set came equipped with monitoring devices to narrate to the Security Police, whether its owner was bowing and/or watching' when the Absolute Benefactor of the People was addressing his subjects. A strand of modern American science fiction was much influenced by *Nineteen Eighty Four*; in the Cold War era the idea of the omniscient tyrant who sees and knows everything became commonplace in the genre (see, for example, van Vogt 1973). Nonetheless, among right wing libertarian writers, long before the 'war on terror', heroes rather than villains were becoming enamoured of surveillance technology – as a means of securing personal liberty. Larry Niven's (1972), for example, imagined basketball-size 'copseyes' floating twelve feet above ground patrolling a California park, allowing all manner of libertine behaviour but zapping all perpetrators of violence; when an antiauthority activist misguidedly disables them disorder erupts and civility crumbles.

More total forms of surveillance – the amassing and mining of unimaginably vast tracts of information, for example – were arguably imagined by H.G. Wells (1898/2004: 5), whose prospective Martian invaders – 'intelligences greater than man's' – had 'scrutinised and studied' the Earth for many years before attacking, 'perhaps almost as narrowly as a man with a microscope might scrutinise the transient creatures that swarm and multiply in a drop of water'. The link to the contemporary practice of dataveillance – perhaps to the darker ideal of what has later been called 'total information awareness' – is made clearer in Iain M. Banks 'Culture' novels, in which a benevolent despotism of Minds (the Culture) seek to know everything about, and sometimes to manipulate, the species living on other planets. In one novel a gigantic Culture spacecraft unobtrusively orbits Earth throughout the year 1977, dredging an 'avalanche of data' into its computers. The precise means by which this is done is left unclear, although it includes the use of miniature drones and bugs, some of which were 'so small the main problem with camera stability was Brownian motion' (Banks 1991: 134).

'Smart dust' – 'autonomous computer[s] with a volume of around one cubic millimetre sensing and communicating information wirelessly' (O'Hara and Shadbolt 2008: 188) had barely been conceived when Banks wrote this, but the idea of microscopic surveillance devices suffusing whole environments might first have been suggested in the last of Bob Shaw's 'slow glass' stories. Shaw had envisaged an accidentally invented transparent metal, formally called Retardite but nicknamed 'slow glass', through which light passes slowly – how slowly depending initially on how thickly and densely the glass is engineered – thereby preserving an image of whatever happens in front of it. The invention, initially used by artists to make pictures, is adapted by the American Government for surveillance purposes. Once it is discovered that a 'usable image could be obtained from a particle a few microns in diameter … each speck invisible to the naked eye' the government manufactures slowglass dust and sprays it everywhere from aircraft: 'the slowglass micro-eyes were … released from high up so that they would cling to everything – trees, buildings, telegraph poles, flowers, mountain slopes, birds, flying insects. It would be in people's clothing, in their food, in the water they drank' (Shaw 1972: 157). The chagrined inventor of slowglass anticipates a totalitarian future: but we are told in the conclusion that, in later decades, 'men were to come to accept the universal presence of Retardite eyes, and they learned to live without subterfuge or shame as they had done in a distant past when it was known that the eyes of God could see everywhere' (1972: 158).

In their homage to Shaw, *The Light of Other Days*, Arthur C. Clarke and Stephen Baxter (2002) substitute 'wormhole cameras' for slowglass particles, microscopic devices which can literally expose anything anywhere instantaneously. This technology is initially exploited by a global news corporation, but subsequently made cheaply available to everyone. This novel explores the social and psychological consequences of total mutual surveillance, fleshing out David Brin's (1998) 'transparent society' (which he envisages as not far off) with descriptions of shame-free public nudity and public sex. Although he is in no sense a futurist, in M. John Harrison's (2002; 2006) recent imagining of the twenty-sixth century, variants of 'smart dust' are still the surveillance technology of choice, in routine use by spaceship captains and police officers, but no such transformations of sexual expression are in evidence, and governmental omniscience is limited simply because, then as now, for want of proper maintenance, technologies sometimes break down. Despite the distant future setting, Harrison is speaking to the way we live now – or at least soon, but in a fabulist idiom. Yet while science fiction writers do not necessarily aim to be predictive, it is in the nature of their craft to envisage possibilities outwith the interest of more realist writers, and by dint of that avid science fiction readers have been imaginatively prepared for many of the twenty-first century's surveillance practices. Something akin to the now widespread electronic tagging of offenders was imagined by Piers Anthony and R.E. Margroff (1968), and now it figures in conventional realist crime fiction (Leonard 1992 – see Nellis 2003 for a fuller account). Implant technology (to read minds, modify moods and track bodies) was envisaged by Phillip Dick (1966), among many others of his generation, and later by cyberpunk writers, but already it is shifting into realist comic thrillers (Llewellyn 2002; see also Seed 2002).

Spy novels

Spies as information gatherers have a long history in literature, but the post-nineteen sixties espionage novel – typified by Ian Fleming, John Le Carre and Len Deighton – drew attention to surveillance largely in terms of what might be called 'the psychology of spycraft' (the effect of the job on the person doing it) and gadgetry (usually in the form of eavesdropping and tracking devices, and miniature weaponry). Deighton's first major novel, *The Ipcress file* (1962), apart from containing an appendix with technical information testifying to the author's supposed insider's expertise in spycraft, contended that however substantial external threats may be, 'one's real enemy [was] behind one, in the upper echelons of the British secret service, not across the Iron Curtain' (Sutherland 2006: 69–70). Different authors have toned the 'intelligence community' in different ways, but whether glamorous or seedy, heroic or – in Jerzy Kosinski's (1976) explicit conflation of surveillance and voyeurism – depraved, this widely read genre has cumulatively fed into popular culture the idea that there were arms of government in all major nations – 'a secret state', perhaps beyond democratic control even in democratic nations – whose work was largely unknown to their respective general publics and who had, whenever they needed it, means of accessing information about whatever they wanted to know.

Even in the hiatus between the ostensible ending of 'the cold war' and the beginning of the 'war on terror', the popularity of 'secret agent'/'secret state' stories never died, in literature, film or TV, but the post-9/11 world has further boosted their significance, and the surveillance technologies available to them – near instantaneous access to a range of databases and real-time tracking of individuals – has become immensely sophisticated. It resembles the technology routinely found in 'technothrillers' (a genre with which spy novels overlap) and even in the more realistic science fiction novels – the average reader cannot know whether such technological expertise really is available to the security services: and somewhat like the prisoner in Bentham's panopticon, sheer uncertainty as to whether one is 'being watched' or not may intensify feelings of paranoia.

Eoin McNamee is a relative newcomer to spy fiction, specialising in 'fictionalising' real events. In *12.23* (McNamee 2007) the event is the 'assassination' of Princess Diana in a Paris car crash. His security operatives, of a generation who learned their 'dark craft' (as he calls it) in Belfast in the 1970s, are as seedy and downbeat as Le Carre's, but – unlike them – they are matter of factly aware of globe-spanning information-gathering technologies than can either enable or thwart them. *12.23* is replete with men who position themselves so as to avoid being seen face-on by CCTV cameras and who use mobile phones with caution. McNamee does not celebrate or exaggerate the flashiness of the technology, but he is alert to its presence and demystifies its purpose. He goes behind the walls of listening stations like GCHQ and Menwith Hill, into the minds of the people who sift the datastreams, and speculates a little on the nature of the human/machine interface. The following is typical:

> It felt like the times at GCHQ when they knew that something was going on, signal traffic building in the east, nothing defined, but you could feel the anxiety out there in the networks, the deep unease. Operators bent over their screens, Transmissions coming in in dense clusters. If you touched one of the cables you could almost feel it, the coaxial hum. A feeling that events were moving on the ground. Everyone getting connected. Trying to access the information clusters. Knowing that they had to get beyond the commonplace, that powers akin to divination were required, that you had to use the ancient parts of the cortex, access the primordial neural pathways. They were trying to filter out the clutter and find their way to the pure message.
>
> (McNamee 2007: 73)

Many people on the receiving end of such surveillance will never know that they are so positioned, but for those who do, what does it mean to have become 'data'? Don DeLillo (a 'highbrow' novelist, whose work nonetheless sometimes touches on espionage, and other ostensibly genre themes) offers an intriguing description in *Mao II* of a political activist mentally reconstructing the processes by which he'd become inscribed in security service databases:

> In the beginning there were people in many cities who had his name on their breath. He knew they were out there, the intelligence network, the diplomatic backchannel, technicians, military men. He had tumbled into the new culture – the system of world terror – and they'd given him a second self, an immortality, the spirit of Jean Claude Julien. He was a digital mosaic in the processing grid, lines of ghostly type on microfilm, They were putting him together, storing his data in starfish satellites, bouncing his image off the moon ... He sensed they'd forgotten his body by now. He was lost in the wave bands, one more code for the computer mesh, for the memory of crimes too pointless to be solved.
>
> (DeLillo 1993: 12)

Police procedurals

Police procedurals focus on the *methodical* way in which policemen solve crimes, narrowing down the list of suspects, marshalling evidence, catching the villain (or not). The process always involves information gathering and exposure ('Private eye' novels do the same thing, less methodically). Ian Rankin's seventeen-book series about an Edinburgh police Inspector, John Rebus, written between 1987 and 2007, implicitly traces the way in which technology has developed to augment the information gathering process. In the very first book, *Knots and Crosses*, a colleague explains to a sceptical Rebus how he is beginning to make informal, unofficial use of a new police computer, and speculates on the shape of things to come:

> I know one of the guys who work in the computer room. Comes in handy, you know, having one of those terminal operators in your pocket. They can track down a car, a name, an address, quicker than you can blink. It only costs an occasional drink ... Give them time, John. Then *all* the files will be on computer.

And a while after that, they'll find that they don't need the work horses like us any more. There'll just be a couple of DI's and a desk console ... It's progress, John. Where would we be without it? We'd still be out there with our pipes and our guess-work and our magnifying glasses.

(Rankin 1987: 32)

By the time of the last book, twenty years later, newer technologies are both embedded in policing, and completely taken for granted. Characters banter about the ubiquity of CCTV cameras – joke about them being fitted in winebars – and get annoyed when they don't work. Human capacities to detect nonetheless still matter to policemen, especially to one of Rebus's generation – 'One of the things [he] liked best about bars was the urge to eavesdrop on other people's lives' (Rankin 2007: 167) – but he now comfortably scans CCTV tapes in the Edinburgh Central Monitoring Facility to ascertain the movement of a car on a particular night. He reflects on the place:

There was something soothing about the unhurried voyeurism going on around him. One act of vandalism reported, and one known shoplifter tracked along George Street. The camera operators seemed as passive as any daytime TV viewers, and Rebus wondered if there might be some reality TV show to be made from it. He liked the way the staff could control the remote cameras using a joystick, zooming in on anything suspicious. It didn't feel like the police state the media were always predicting. All the same, if he worked here every day, he'd be careful of himself on the street, for fear of being caught picking his nose or scratching his backside. Careful in shops and restaurants, too.

(Rankin 2007: 202)

CCTV is not portrayed in any way problematically in the Rebus novels. It is mere background to character-driven and plot-driven stories. It is no panacea in respect of crime control, but it has its uses – although on the night in which Rebus is interested, not all the cameras are operative. In terms of his own personal reaction to the monitoring facility Rebus is doing no more than Zivokovic's character, resolving to make his 'indisposition as unnoticeable as possible', but it is not a major issue. Rankin's later Rebus stories can legitimately be read as state of the nation novels, but surveillance is not something that either Rebus or his creator urge us to worry about. The prospect of further technological developments does not preoccupy Rankin/Rebus – even though the novels have traced just such development, and shown the relative ease with which people adapt and accept it. Paul McAuley's (2001) *Whole Wide World* is a police procedural crossed with a technothriller – the murder of a young woman is connected to the installation of a sophisticated new police CCTV system in a near-future London, whose computer controlled cameras can automatically track identified individuals. Watching an array of swivelling cameras track a fox in a park late at night, their underslung spotlights 'finger[ing] the darkness with unforgiving precision', McAuley's policeman protagonist becomes aware early on 'of something new and non-human at play in the world: an intelligence vast and cold and unsympathetic testing the limits of its ability' (2001: 5).

Technothrillers

Technothrillers are a very literal type of science fiction (often blended with spy fiction), set in the present or recognisable near future, quite often with a specific aim of educating the public (in an entertaining way) about the significance of a particular scientific advance or environmental development, e.g. DNA, computerised financial transactions, nanotechnology or climate change. They epitomise what literary critic John Sutherland (2006) calls 'info-fiction' because however much the narrative may accord with thriller conventions the author has usually undertaken detailed research into the topic being written about, and may even provide an appendix explaining the issues.

The Traveller *(2006) John Twelve Hawks*

The Traveller, the first volume in a projected trilogy, is set a few years hence. An ancient Illuminati-like secret society is on the brink of achieving complete but mostly covert control of western populations through a capacity to access, integrate and if necessary hack the world's burgeoning surveillance systems. Various characters, and Twelve Hawks himself, disparagingly portray it as a colossal electronic version of Bentham's panopticon. Its enemies – the handful of people who even know of its existence – call it the 'vast machine', and try, with ever increasing difficulty to live 'off the grid', beyond its reach. The plot concerns the efforts of Maya Thorn, a 'Harlequin' (a highly trained order of bodyguards), to find and protect two young men who may be 'travellers', a dying breed of mystics who have the power to cross dimensions – to truly evade the power of the 'vast machine', which understandably regards them as a very distinctive kind of threat, and wants them eradicated. *The Traveller* works well enough as a thriller, it teaches a great deal about integrated surveillance systems and sometimes conveys rather well what it might be like to be tracked in realtime by an assemblage of monitoring devices.

The pseudonymous Twelve Hawks – who garners kudos by living 'off the grid' himself[2] – is consciously reaching for Orwell's mantle and dreads the imminence of total control. He explains in a concluding essay that he has written the novel to awaken readers to the dangers of surveillance in a post-9/11 world. The concept of the 'vast machine' (a term appropriated from William S. Burroughs 1990: 71) is simply extrapolated from the Bush/Poindexter Total Information Awareness project inaugurated in 2002. Twelve Hawks' essay explains the coming integration of facial recognition software in CCTV systems, biometric, RFID chipped passports, infrared and X-ray machines, online detection packages whose algorithms distinguish what is normal and what is suspicious:

> two modern conditions – a generalised fear coupled with sophisticated electronic monitoring – shapes the world of *The Traveller*. The novel is set towards the end of this decade, but all the technological aspects described in the book are either in use at this moment or far along in the development process. I didn't write to predict the future. I wanted to use the power of fiction to describe how we live now.
>
> (Twelve Hawks 2006: 592)

The imminent integration of computer systems means that Bentham's 'panopticon is going to be established throughout our society' (2006: 598). 'If privacy truly disappears freedom will vanish with it' (2006: 599). The novelist draws on Barry Glassner's (2000) *The Culture of Fear* to show how fears are created and sustained by politicians and media. He admits he does not 'believe that a shadowy group of illuminati are guiding the industrial world, but I think it clear that a variety of institutions use fear to manipulate public opinion' (2006: 602). He wrote the book to shatter the complacency towards surveillance and to inspire resistance to it, admitting that 'no outside force will save us. We must look into our own hearts to find the Travellers and Harlequins – the prophets and warriors – who will keep us free' (2006: 605). *The Dark River* (Twelve Hawks 2007) continues the story.

The Pixel Eye *(2003) Paul Levinson*

The Pixel Eye, a technothriller combined with a police procedural, is the third in a series of full-length novels featuring Phil D'Amato, an NYPD detective operating approximately ten years from now, in the city's 'security governance' department. It was one of the first novels in any genre, to deal with the ongoing development of surveillance technology in the post-9/11 era. Its plot hinges on the development of a covert surveillance programme within the Department of Homeland Security, which turns urban squirrels into living cameras by implanting miniaturised telecom equipment in their brains, and retrieving any visual images recently stored there. This 'panopticon of squirrels', as D'Amato dryly calls it (2003: 296) enables Homeland Security to scan public spaces – or windows from adjacent trees – without visible hardware, and without arousing suspicion.

One of the novel's strengths is its depiction of the way that D'Amato comes to terms with the ostensible absurdity of the 'squirrel-cams'. Like most lay people (us, the readers) he is actually quite ignorant of what is technologically possible, or even 'in development' on his own, law-enforcement, side: geopolitically, he knows that he lives in a world whose murky heart – and whose engines of change – he can barely fathom. A plausible context-of-emergence for the squirrel-cam technology is also provided, in experimental neuromusicology – studying how rodents remember visual and aural images, then converting the neurochemical braincode for such memories into computer readable algorithms. Security services co-opt the research to help develop 'total information awareness':

> The goal of course is first to have images, [an operative tells D'Amato] then reliable images, then legally reliable images. Imagine the benefit to national security of having millions of extra eyes, unobtrusive, that can see for us, but send back recordable images of what they see.
>
> (Levinson 2003: 60)

Even without squirrel-cams, surveillance technologies infuse D'Amato's world: 'authorisation codes' of one sort or another govern movement and communication in the city. Swipe cards on subway turnstiles, police scannable ID cards, voice authentication technologies, biometric locks', figure in his daily routine. Humans outperform automated surveillance – facial recognition – but only for the time being. Large crowds can be subject to automated retinal scans using 'cyberspotlights' linked to 'powerhouse computers' (2003: 267). None of this is foolproof and D'Amato knows that 'digital records could be expunged as easily as people' (2003: 162). In addition, every advance in surveillance technology seems to be matched by an advance in deception and encryption technology – ways of fooling eyes, ears and minds, even technologically augmented ones – and the denouement of *The Pixel Eye* reveals that the squirrel-cam project has already been corrupted and subverted. The novel accepts that the dangers facing post-9/11 America are real enough and that security will require some sacrifices of liberty. D'Amato (and maybe Levinson himself) is a reluctant liberal convert to this view, but he worries as to where the limits of security might lie:

> Everyone's DNA in some national archive, matchable to DNA embedded and scannable on a card? Government access to everyone's potential for whatever genetic tic? Would that be worth the chance to stop the ticking bomb of a terrorist?
> (Levinson 2003: 168)

The (self-defined) literary novel

Contemporary 'literary fiction' – in the highbrow sense – explores the consciousness and lived realities of people in the here and now, notionally without recourse to the conventions of genre. As such it comments on the state of the psyche, the nation and the world; the way we live now. Arguably, in the past, literary fiction evinced a certain disdain for questions concerning technology, but now, if it is to remain true to its ethos, it can hardly avoid them, and 'we will', as one noted author/critic has claimed, 'see more engagement with scientific and technical themes before the decade is out' (Foden 2008). It is in this spirit that a number of literary novelists have already begun exploring what living in a surveillance society means and feels like.

The Seymour Tapes *(2005) Tim Lott*

To date, all Lott's novels (and a memoir) deal with dysfunctional families. This cunningly entitled work (Seymour = see more) is no different. Alex Seymour, a London GP, installs covert miniature CCTV in his living room because he suspects his adolescent son is stealing from around the house, and also that his wife is having an affair. The American woman entrepreneur from whom he buys the kit – her shop is based on a real one, cited by Lott in the acknowledgements – turns out to be a sleazy voyeur – and after a series of painful exposures within the family, dysfunctionality is seriously intensified. Lott's underlying argument is that the desire for surveillance is grounded in insecurity and control addiction – the belief that one can shore up one's power, make oneself more secure, if one can only see what others are doing, without them seeing you. For him, voyeurism – at root a characteristic of people with a fragile and uncertain sense of their own identity, and deficiencies in their capacity to make relationships – emerges from this insecurity. A therapist in the novel explains:

> Voyeuristic activity fulfils a sense of adventure and participation missing in 'real' life. The subject is usually introverted, timid, over-controlled and socially isolated … voyeurism is not simply about sex. Voyeurs … are stimulated or satisfied by covert observation of many kinds. The main thing is that people are being watched in secret. It gives the voyeur a sense of power. But at the same time, like any compulsion, it leaves the sufferer feeling empty and hopeless. As an alcoholic needs more and more alcohol, the voyeur needs to witness deeper and deeper secrets, you might say.
>
> (Lott 2005: 163)

Lott (and the therapist) debate whether voyeurism has now become a 'national trait' (or a 'national sickness') in Britain. The concluding pages – chillingly written from the standpoint of a 'sentient' but emotionless camera – 'I see you … Nowadays, I have no limits' (Lott 2005: 242) make clear that Lott believes his insights can be generalised out to larger CCTV systems, and to recognise that just as surveillance fails to solve the relationship problems in this family so it will also fail to solve society's disorders – and may well aggravate them. This shift of register comes a little abruptly, and it is debatable whether the loathing readers will likely feel towards the players in the domestic drama will translate into civic anger towards public space CCTV, but it is a commendably ingenious attempt to foster revulsion towards pervasive surveillance systems. Like Michael Haneke's (2006) film *Hidden*, the novel convincingly questions whether CCTV images ever contain much 'truth'; the meanings imputed to merely visual representations of people's private behaviour are likely to be erroneous (see also Meek 2007). In addition to all this, Lott also argues – by way of further explanation as to why the invasiveness of surveillance seems not to bother us – that in contemporary culture media-stimulated narcissism is turning privacy into a tradable commodity; people are increasingly willing to market themselves to the tabloids or to publishers of fashionable 'tell all' memoirs for the sake of tawdry fame and transient fortunes. *The Seymour Tapes* is actually a damning spoof of that kind of book.

Surveillance *(2005) Jonathan Raban*

Surveillance concerns the permeation of surveillance technologies and mentalities into the everyday lives of ordinary Americans in the early twenty-first century, focusing on the lives of four people in a very near future Seattle. Lucy is a freelance journalist writing a profile about an ageing neocon writer, August Vanags, who has achieved fame with a holocaust memoir; Alida is her almost-teenage daughter; Ted a middle-aged, politically radical family friend and Charles Ong Lee is the landlord wanting to evict them all from his apartment block. The novel opens with a mock-terrorist attack on the city, orchestrated by the Department of Homeland Security to test civil defence procedures. The putative threat of Islamist terrorism is ever present, and an easy mental separation between reasonable vigilance and creeping paranoia becomes difficult to sustain. Lucy listens uneasily to radio bulletins covering the hunt for an Algerian who seemingly fits the 'terrorist' profile, and twigs the presence of an undercover marshall aboard a ferry. She recognises 'the fright-machine at work, cogs and wheels relentlessly revolving from sea to shining sea' (2005: 144) but simultaneously, mostly for Alida's sake, she seriously contemplates moving from the potentially dangerous city to the probably safer countryside. Ted stokes her anxieties with talk of black helicopters, ECHELON[3], and the expanding 'machinery of tyranny' (2005: 227), warning her of:

> a huge programme to renew reflective lane-markers on highways, ostensibly the baby of the Department of Transportation but known by Tad to have originated in the National Security Agency. These weren't just any old lane-markers, they were clandestine – you might say clairvoyant – lane-markers that

would track the number, make and colour of your car as it went by when the system was complete, they'd be able to bug the exact movements of every vehicle in the US. It was, Tad said, all done by microchips and wireless technology.

(Raban 2005: 220)

But surveillance is ubiquitous. Alida and her schoolfriends observe 'the angled barrel of the spy camera that had just recently gone up over the doors of the gym, one of the many that had appeared around the school since the winter break' (2005: 34). They joke about the possible whereabouts of the watchers, trading on popular stereotypes – 'underground, in a secret cellar, somewhere downtown'. The landlord proposes installing CCTV in the apartments, so that tenants can be alert to the 'lowlife' in the rear alley. Investigative journalists like Lucy utilise surveillance tools to good ends, paralleling the government's more sinister use of them. As Ted tells her:

We're all spooks now. Look at the way people Google their prospective dates. Everybody does it. Everybody's trying to spy on everybody else. At least you know you're a spook, which is something. Most people are in denial.

(Raban 2005: 225)

Raban is actually moot on the extent to which surveillance protects us from terrorism, but the earthquake/tsunami which devastates Seattle at the novel's end effectively says that, all along, the real danger lay elsewhere. Satellite surveillance (and advance warning) of tectonic plate activity may have saved more lives than tooling up for a 'war on terror'. Echoing Zamyatin, Raban mocks the view that technoscience and risk management strategies have wrought 'the end of nature' – in both novels, in different ways, resurgent nature ruthlessly reclaims the formerly surveilled spaces. Somewhat sardonically, he also confirms Zamyatin's belief that mathematical formulae appeal to those who desperately want order and predictability in their lives – in this instance, twelve-year-old Alida, who likes algebra because in it:

unknown quantities revealed their true identities ... $6 - 2y = 7y + 13$ made perfect sense to Alida but what she really wanted was a system of human algebra. It'd be incredibly cool if you could only figure people out like this, isolating their variables to just one side of the equation, adding positives to negatives to make zeros, until the problem disentangled into one clear statement; this means that.

(Raban 2005: 53)

People, Raban suggests, cannot entirely be figured out like this, reduced to algorithms – but while insecure children can and do outgrow the need for complete order and predictability, insecure states progressively demand more of both. Raban clearly challenges this, whilst recognising that many instances of modern surveillance technology has its uses. Tad's diligent computer searching, for example, does eventually expose Charles Ong Lee as an illegal immigrant with a stolen identity, giving him and Lucy the leverage to thwart his plan to evict them (2005: 251). At root, though, in Raban's view, not everything is knowable, or traceable online. Lucy concludes that despite all her Internet searching, the truth about Vanags' background remains shadowy, and she builds that unfathomability into her profile, deliberately writing 'an ambitiously inconclusive piece … for these inconclusive times' (2005: 308). Surveillance itself is pitched the same way, provoking thought rather than supplying answers.

What Was Lost (2007) Catherine O'Flynn

What Was Lost is set in and around the fictitious Green Oaks shopping mall in Birmingham, alternating between 1984 and 2003/4. It is, on one level, a mystery story which resolves, some twenty years after the event, the fate of a missing little girl. It is also a sombre commentary on working life in a modern shopping centre, and a critique of contemporary consumerism. Kurt is one of 200 security guards on the four square kilometre site. He mostly patrols the mall and its labyrinth of service corridors. Sometimes he takes his turn manning the banks of CCTV monitors. He is singularly bored:

He never expected to see anything on the CCTV. No one ever did on the night shift … He'd been looking at the same monitor screens for the past thirteen years. When he closed his eyes he could still see all the empty corridors and locked doors in soft grey-scale tones. Sometimes he thought maybe they were just flickering photographs – still lives that would never change.

(O'Flynn 2007: 71)

Ruminating on the expansion of shopping centres in Britain generally:

> Kurt wondered how much of the country had now been split off into these security fiefdoms. Patches of scorched earth almost bleached white by the constant surveillance of so many eyes. He thought of his grandmother who had been badly beaten up in her own flat last year, and wondered when she might be considered as worthy of protection as a range of Nike baseball caps.
>
> (O'Flynn 2007: 84)

Lisa is a young woman who works in Green Oak's Your Music store. She is as despondent about the banality of her job as Karl is with his, and equally as uncomfortable with the ubiquity of surveillance. Like Zivokovic's character she makes her 'indisposition as unnoticeable as possible', but embellishes it with a mildly satisfying fantasy drawn from the surveillance fictions suffusing popular culture:

> Lisa was keenly aware of the hidden security presence in the centre. Every morning she felt those tired eyes upon her and was hyperconscious of her every movement. The constant weight of surveillance made her feel suspicious, and over time, this sense of guilt had developed into a little game she liked to play. She imagined that inside her bag, instead of an aged satsuma and seventeen empty envelopes, she carried something clandestine; a small timed device, a secret message, an illicit package – it didn't matter what. In her head various genres had been mixed up to create some incoherent spy/terrorist/resistance fighter fantasy – it changed from day to day, but always with the hidden security guards cast as Nazis.
>
> (O'Flynn 2007: 74–5)

There is a great deal in *What Was Lost* about the desolating experience of being managed, manipulated and watched as employees and customers of the shopping centre, but no grand political theme, and no dramatic human consequences. Being subject to constant surveillance has the effect of making people feel under suspicion, wary rather than safe, but in the main ordinary life goes on relatively unchanged. Control is far from total – people (Lisa's estranged brother) still go missing, and manage to live under assumed names – but CCTV is a fixed presence in the workplace, and the novel captures exactly what John McGrath (2004: 186) means when he calls shopping mall security guards an embodiment of 'peculiarly abject authority'.

Conclusion

Literary fiction – in the broadest sense – has tackled the theme of surveillance in a way that parallels and complements (and quite possibly draws from) ideas being developed in the social sciences. It does so in a somewhat more nuanced way than cinematic fiction, and it acknowledges the increased complexity of surveillance since *Nineteen Eighty Four* appeared. Yet no single surveillance story has emerged to supersede this iconic novel, although the majority of the texts mentioned here are among the few to have been publicised in press reviews. No claims can be made as to how audiences have received them, and it is unlikely that any readers yet have a sense of 'surveillance novels' as a distinct literary grouping; at present, for now, that is a purely academic construction. The gist of the novels, taken collectively, is indeed that burgeoning surveillance technologies are to be feared, although if psychoanalyst Adam Philip's (2007) insightful epigram – 'Paranoia is the self-cure for insignificance' – is valid, our fear is arguably functional, perhaps even agentic. In a globalised world where we occasionally sense that the control of events is beyond us, shaped by unimaginably powerful institutions, in whose machinations we might at any time be caught up, surveillance stories *both* legitimate our suspicions and also hint, rather reassuringly, that, in our fumbling quest to understand who our masters are, we are at least on the right track, even if we cannot be certain about their exact organisational forms, or their capabilities and reach.

In at least some surveillance stories, a new variant of the traditional adventure story hero is our surrogate in this quest – a person who, despite everything, still manages to live anonymously, invisibly, 'off the grid', without leaving traces, and onto whom we can project our dwindling hopes of freedom. In Ken Macleod's (2007) technothriller *The Execution Channel*, for example, a security operative frustratingly learns:

> from MI5's London HQ that all the face recognition software, all the trawling and tracking and surveillance of the British state, couldn't find a trace of the face, card transactions, or vehicle registrations of a man who evidently went by many names, only one of which was James Travis.
>
> (Macleod 2007: 107–8)

In broad terms, this type of character is not wholly new in Western literature. Joseph Conrad's (1915) Axel Heyst was 'invulnerable because elusive' but the Malay archipelago in the late-nineteenth century afforded more opportunities for reclusive Europeans to vanish than the present day western world affords to anyone[4]. From the Scarlet Pimpernel onwards, in traditional crime and spy thrillers, insouciant and ingenious heroes routinely stay 'one step ahead' of powerful opponents, but twenty-first century heroes require quite specific counter-surveillance skills to achieve this. Anonymity must now be worked at, via easy access to forged identity documents, the capacity to route untraceable phone calls through the net and, when necessary, an ability to anticipate and dodge the swivel and tilt of CCTV cameras. Maya and the two young men she protects in *The Traveller* (Twelve Hawks 2006) epitomise the type, but there are more mundane, realistic examples. They can comfortably take on new identities, remain anonymous despite remorseless scanning and cannot be 'mined' out of databases, at least not in real-time, not until it is 'too late' for whatever authority-subverting action the plot requires. The Harlequins' austere protocols for survival amidst the tendrils of 'the vast machine' – keep on the move, defy predictability and order, cultivate randomness – speak, in fantasy form, to the latent fears and desires of at least some late modern people.

But, for ordinary mortals, is ever greater self-diminishment before the gaze and reach of surveillance, all we have to fear? Is that the only subjectivity that surveillance produces in us? In J.G. Ballard's idiosyncratic oeuvre, the sterile, alienating domains in which the contemporary middle class lives and moves – suburbs, science parks, leisure complexes and shopping malls, in which surveillance is ubiquitous – call forth psychotic violence, before – or more precisely, at the very point at which – subjugation of their occupants is almost achieved. Such are the aggressive traits that evolution has left us with, overlain by the restless, thrill-seeking consciousness fostered by consumer society, that the discomfort of 'indisposition' is neither as passively borne (in the West), nor as easily suppressed, as Zoran Zivokovic imagined. Not everyone succumbs easily to control by impersonal systems – although the means by which it is resisted may be far from the convivial liberal understanding of rational revolt espoused, say, by Tom Paine. In much of Ballard's work psychosis is the consequence of over-control. It is invariably represented as a twisted and destructive affirmation of basic human impulses for freedom and meaning in the soulless landscapes of modernity – and given the insidiousness of the controls to which we are subject, he sees this as this no bad thing. *Running Wild* – one of Ballard's (1988) masterpieces – offers a variant of this view. It begins in a luxurious gated community in southern England whose affluent parents benignly use technology to surveil every moment of their precious children's time, fatally but unknowingly eroding their capacity for affection and empathy – and are systematically massacred by them as a result. Here the childrens' psychosis is portrayed less as a *reaction against* the 'surveillance of the heart' (1988: 37) and more as its terrifying corollary, an outworking in particularly brutal form of the same inhuman, unloving logic that misguidedly inspired the parental imposition of panoptic surveillance in the first place (see Gasiorek 2005: 161–8).

Margaret Atwood's (2003) *Oryx and Crake*, is less concerned with the consequences of what surveillance seeks to repress, and more concerned with its misapplication. Like Jonathan Raban's *Surveillance* she insists that investment in contemporary forms of anti-terror surveillance, directed at an external 'other', deflects our attention away from far more pressing dangers, closer to home. Her novel is set at two points in the future. In the first, humanity has been rendered all but extinct by an orchestrated bioterrorist attack from within rather than without the western world. The second – nearer to us in time – depicts the police state in which the virus responsible for the man-made pandemic is first cultivated. The security services in this earlier era – the CorpSeCorp – make full use of CCTV, biometric access controls, automated motion sensors and lie-detection, but none of this hardware identifies where the real danger lies – a misanthropic scientist, emblematic of western nihilism – let alone saves the world. In the later future, the ailing lone survivor of the pandemic shambles disconsolately into the ruins of the laboratories where he had once worked:

> He passes the first barricade with its crapped out scopers and busted searchlights, then the checkpoint booth. A guard is lying half in, half out … No trees here, they'd mowed down everything you could hide behind, divided the territory into squares with lines of heat and motion sensors. The eerie chessboard effect is already gone; weeds are poking up like whiskers all over the surface … He continues on, across the moat, past the sentry boxes where the CorpSeCorps armed guards once stood and the glassed – in cubicles where they'd monitored the surveillance equipment, then past the rampart watchtower with the steel door – standing forever open, now – where he'd once been ordered to present his thumbprint and the iris of his eye.
>
> (Atwood 2003: 225–7)

Such may be one future for the particular forms of surveillance technology with which we surround ourselves now. As the review in this chapter has shown, there are numerous others, and many idioms in which surveillance is being discussed. How much such fiction contributes to a critical consciousness in the wider public is uncertain, but it is of significance in itself that major novelists like Atwood, Lott, Ballard, Raban and DeLillo think surveillance is worthy of serious intellectual attention. Genre novels are important too – perhaps more important, given their mass readership – because whether surveillance is merely part of the backdrop or the specific focus of the story, they are registering its presence in the world. The distinction between genre fiction and literary fiction is in any case permeable, and increasingly spurious. Atwood, like Orwell before her, recognised that the idiom of 'speculative fiction' has much to offer as a means of engaging with the challenges of late modern life. Several hitherto literary writers e.g. Michael Cunningham (2005); Jeannette Winterson (2007) have in fact tried their hand at science fiction (and addressed surveillance in passing) and this genre – the very first to see surveillance coming – will continue to be a key source of critical thinking on the subject. J.G. Ballard, on the other hand, famously made the transition the other way – from science fiction to literary fiction, and in *Running Wild* he produced a classic of 'surveillance literature' which has yet to be recognised as such, and which may indeed have anticipated the very neglect into which its searingly unpalatable truth about contemporary surveillance would fall.

Notes

1 I am grateful to Dietmar Kammerer for the reference to Harben's work. He also drew my attention to a recent German novel by Ulrich Peltzer's (2007) *Teil der Losung (Part of the Solution* – although it is as yet not translated into English) – which explores the surveillance society through the eyes of a contemporary young journalist seeking to make contact with the still 'underground' members of the former Red Brigades. Doubtless there is a case for comparative literary studies of surveillance representations, and different stories are perhaps being told outside the mostly Anglophone literature covered in this chapter.

2 There is inevitably much speculation on the Internet as to Twelve Hawk's 'real identity'. One suggestion, currently ascendant, is that he is Michael Cunningham, a literary novelist seeking to reach a wider audience with his concerns about surveillance with a potentially bestselling genre

novel. Cunningham (2005) has written a serious literary/science fiction novel, *Specimen Days*, passages of which do indeed register some of the same concerns as *The Traveller* – but the same might be said of many contemporary writers.

3 ECHELON is a primarily US/UK satellite-based eavesdropping network run by the National Security Agency (NSA) which sifts 'economic intelligence' from global telecommuncations traffic that may be of benefit to Anglo-American commercial enterprises. It originated in 1971, was greatly expanded in the 1975–1995 period and may serve covert military or other governmental purposes. A considerable amount of mystique, fostered by both champions and critics, once surrounded it (Todd and Block 2003: 44–7)

4 There is a general fascination with people who live 'off the grid', precisely because it is getting harder to do. Osama Bin Laden is a case in point. More mundanely, John Darwin faked his own death in a canoe accident near Hartlepool in March 2002, lived 'off the grid' thereafter (secretly renewing contact with his 'widow' after a year, but not his grieving sons), finally handing himself into London police in December 2007. One journalist described it as 'a story that has gripped the imagination of the British. A story of greed, lies, subterfuge and betrayal. But perhaps most of all a story about escape' (Richard Elias, 'Living a Lie', *Scotland on Sunday*, 9 December 2007).

References

Anthony, P. and Margroff, R.E. (1968/1986) *The Ring*. New York: Tom Doherty Associates.

Atwood, M. (2003) *Oryx and Crake*. London: Bloomsbury.

Ballard, J.G. (1988) *Running Wild* (reprinted in 1997). London: Flamingo.

Banks, I.M. (1991) *The State of the Art*. London: Orion.

Bell, E. (2006) 'We're all reporters in the digital democracy', *The Guardian*, 20 March.

Brin, D. (1998) *The Transparent Society: Will Technology Force Us to Choose Between Privacy and Freedom*. Reading, MA: Perseus Books.

Burroughs, W.S. (1990) *Interzone*. New York: Penguin.

Clarke, A.C. and Baxter, S. (2002) *The Light of Other Days*. London: Harper Collins.

Conrad, J. (1915) *Victory*. Harmondsworth: Penguin.

Cunningham, M. (2005) *Specimen Days*. London: Fourth Estate.

Deighton, L. (1962) *The Ipcress File*. London: Harper Collins.

DeLillo, D. (1993) *Mao II*. London: Vintage.

Dick, P. (1966) 'We can remember it for you wholesale', *The Magazine of Fantasy and Science Fiction*, April 1966. Reprinted in P. Dick (2002) *Minority Report (and other stories)*. London: Gollancz.

Dick, P. (1967) 'Faith of our fathers', in H. Ellison (ed.) *Dangerous Visions*. Reprinted in P. Dick (2002) *Minority Report (and other stories)*. London: Gollancz.

Elias, R. (2007) 'Living a lie', *Scotland on Sunday*, 9 December.

Foden, G. (2008) 'The book', *Guardian Society*, 2 January.

Gasiorek, A. (2005) *J.G. Ballard*. Manchester: Manchester University Press.

Glassner, B. (2000) *The Culture of Fear*. New York: Basic Books.

Harben, W.N. (1894) *Land of the Changing Sun*. Dodo Press.

Harrison, M.J. (2002) *Light*. London: Gollancz.

Harrison, M.J. (2006) *Nova Swing*. London: Gollancz.

Havel, V. (1986) *Living in Truth*. London: Faber and Faber.

James, C. (2008) 'Franz Kafka', in *Cultural Amnesia: Notes in the Margin of My Time*. London: Picador.

Jennings, H. (ed.) (1985) *Pandaemonium: The Changing Face of the Machine as Seen by Contemporary Observers*. London: Andre Deutsch.

Kadare, I. (1993) *The Palace of Dreams*. London: Harvill.

Kafka, F. (1922) *The Castle*. Munich: Kurt Wolff Verlag.

Kammerer, D. (2004) 'Video surveillance in Hollywood movies', *Surveillance and Society*, 2(2/3): 464–73.

Kosinski, J. (1976) *Cockpit*. London: Corgi.

Kundera, M. (1985) *The Unbearable Lightness of Being*. London: Faber and Faber.

Leonard, E. (1992) *Maximum Bob*. Harmondsworth: Penguin.

Levinson, P. (2003) *The Pixel Eye*. New York: Tor Books.

Llewellyn, R. (2002) *Brother Nature*. London: Flame/Hodder and Stoughton.

Lott, T. (2005) *The Seymour Tapes*. London: Viking.

Lyon, D. (2007) *Surveillance Studies*. Cambridge: Polity Press.

Macleod, K. (2007) *The Execution Channel*. London: Orbit.

McAuley, P. (2001) *Whole Wide World*. London: Harper Collins.

McGrath, J.E. (2004) *Loving Big Brother: Performance, Privacy and Surveillance Space*. London: Routledge.

McNamee, E. (2007) *12.23*. London: Faber and Faber.

Meek, J. (2007) *Surveillance*. Edinburgh: Long Lunch Press.

Mitchell, J.L. (1934/1989) *Gay Hunter*. Edinburgh: Polygon.

Nellis, M. (2003) 'News media, popular culture and the electronic monitoring of offenders in England and Wales', *Howard Journal*, 42: 1–31

Niven, L. (1972) *Cloak of Anarchy* (Analog March 1972). Reprinted in L. Niven (1975) *Tales of Known Space*. New York: Ballantine Books.

O'Flynn, C. (2007) *What Was Lost*. Birmingham: Tindall Street Press.

O'Hara, K. and Shadbolt, N. (2008) *The Spy in the Coffee Machine*. Oxford: Oneworld Publications.

Orwell, G. (1948) *Nineteen Eighty Four*. London: Secker & Warburg.

Peltzer, U. (2007) *Teil der Lösung*. Zurich: Ammann Verlag.

Phillips, A. (2007) *Side Effects*. London: Penguin.

Raban, J. (2006) *Surveillance*. London: Picador.

Rankin, I. (1987) *Knots and Crosses*. London: Orion.

Rankin, I. (2007) *Exit Music*. London: Orion.

Seed, D. (2004) *Brainwashing: The Fictions of Mind Control – A Study of Novels and Films since World War II*. Kent, OH: Kent State University Press.

Shaw, B. (1972) *Other Days, Other Eyes*. London: Pan.

Sutherland, J. (2006) *How to Read a Novel: A User's Guide*. London: Profile.

Todd, P. and Block, J. (2003) *Global Intelligence: The Worlds Secret Service's Today*. London: Zed Books.

Twelve Hawks, J. (2006) *The Traveller*. London: Corgi.

Twelve Hawks, J. (2007) *The Dark River*. London: Transworld.

van Vogt, A.E. (1973) *Tyranopolis*. London: Sphere.

Wells, H.G. (1898/2004) *The War of the Worlds*. London: Phoenix.

Winterson, J. (2007) *The Stone Gods*. London: Hamish Hamilton.

Zamyatin, Y. (1924/2007) *We*. London: Vintage.

Zivokovic, Z. (2003) *Hidden Camera*. Champaign, IL: Dalkey Archive Press.

Index

accountability *see also* de Menzes, Jean Charles
  improving 54–5
  judicial authorisation 55–8
  oversight 51–4
  overview xxiii, 107–12
  parliamentary oversight 61–3
Acquisition and Disclosure of Communications Data Code of Practice 45–6
age of data 93–4
al-Qaeda 74, 76
Anthony, Piers 184
Anti-Terrorism, Crime and Security Act 2001 47, 59–60, 90
Ashworth, A. 87
Asset Recovery Agency 59
Atwood, Margaret 199–200
authorisation
  executive authorisation 55, 66–7, 81–2
  judicial authorisation 55–8
  self-authorisation procedures 60
  USA 55–6, 66–7

Ballard, J.G. 198–9, 200
Bankers' Books Evidence Act 1879 59

Banks, Iain M. 182–3
Baxter, Stephen 183
Bell, D. 159
Bell, Dr Sandra 126
Bennett, C. xviii, 20, 25, 109
Bentham, D. 185, 188, 189
biometric access systems 36n11
biometric identifiers 75, 135, 138, 140
Blair, Sir Ian 115, 116, 117, 127
Blair, Tony 68, 137
Block, F. 164
Blunkett, David 56, 135
Bourdieu, P. 164
Brin, David 183
Brown, I. xx, xxi
bugging 44–5, 56, 59, 144–5
Burket, H. 36n10
Burroughs, William S. 189
Bush, George W. 66, 68

Campbell v United Kingdom 91
Canada 170
Castells, M. xvii
The Castle (Kafka) 179
Cavada, Jean-Marie 93–4
Central Office of Information 142
Cerulo, K.A. 167–8

Chakrabati, Shami 127
checks and balances 63–5
Chief Surveillance Commissioner
    22, 52
Chilcot Review 44
child benefit data discs 141
China 173–4
CIA 66
civil liberties
    Data Retention Directive 78–9
    identity cards 135–6, 137, 139–41
    media coverage 145–6, 149
    sacrificing xvi, xx
Clarke, Arthur C. 183
Clarke, Charles 137
Clegg, Nick 126, 144
CNIL 15–16
Code of Practice on Data Retention
    48
Communications Assistance to Law
    Enforcement Act 1994 43
Communications Data Bill 64–5
communications surveillance
    access to 41–7
    background 39–41
    data access 45–7
    data retention 47–9
    European Union 82–3
    interception of communications
        42–4
    Interception of Communications
        Commissioner 47, 51–2, 60,
        61–3
    legislation 45–7, 82, 83
    merging regimes 58–61
Computer Misuse Act 1990 44
conditional choices 172–4
Conrad, Joseph 197–8
consensus xxi, 7–9, 18–19
constitutive accountability
    attempts at accountability 115–16
    explanation of 109–10
    failings report 126
    language 124
    overview 128–9

visual images 121
consultation xxi–xxii
consumer credit 4–5, 7–14
Convention on Mutual Assistance in
    Criminal Matters 42
converged networks 39–41
Copland v United Kingdom 80
core principles 5–10
costs of retention 94–5
Council of the European Union 89,
    92
credit information 9, 12–13
Criminal Justice (Terrorist Offences)
    Act 2005 90
criminal rehabilitation 169
CRIS-E 171
Crosby, Sir James 140
Crossman, Gareth 145
The Culture of Fear (Glassner) 189
cybercrime 92

Daily Telegraph 146, 150
Darling, Alistair 141
data minimisation 24–5, 31
Data Protection Act 1998 18–19,
    35n9
Data Protection Technical Guidance
    Note 36n11
Data Protection Working Party 93
data retention
    costs of 94–5
    minimal retention 25, 31
    overview xx
    Service Providers 48–9
    timing 93–4
Data Retention Directive
    in accordance with the law 80–5
    civil liberties 78–9
    Code of Practice 48
    European Data Protection
        Commissioners 64
    introduction of 75–8
    justification 80
    necessity 85–7
    overview 74

proportionality 87–95
Data Retention (EC Directive)
Regulations 2007 37n19
Davies, Howard 137
Davies, Simon 137
Davis, David 133–4
de Menzes, Jean Charles
attempts at accountability 115–16
Cressida Dick's story 113–14
failures 124–8
Jean Charles de Menezes' story
113
language 121–4
moment to moment detail 118
overview xxiii, 128–9
surveillance officer's story
112–13
surveillance team's story 114–15
units of responsibility 116–17
visual images 118–21
Declaration on Combating Terrorism
(European Council) 78, 95
Defence Intelligence 42
deficit models xxi–xxii
Deighton, Len 184
DeLillo, Don 186
demonstrative accountability
attempts at accountability
115–16
explanation of 110–11
failings report 126
language 124
overview 128–9
visual images 121
Denmark 93
Department of Constitutional Affairs
140–1
detention without charge 133
Dick, Commander 122, 124
Dick, Phillip 182, 184
Dilemmas of Privacy and Surveillance
(RAE) 146, 147
Dizaei, Ali 53
double hermeneutic 175
Downcast Eyes (Jay) 163

Downs, A. 147–8
doxa 164
DRM technology 37n20
Drug Trafficking Act 1994 59
Duvall, Len 127
Dworkin, R. 78

Economist 143–4
electronic tagging 184
email protection 80
Emmerson, B. 87
encryption 49–51, 64, 89
engagement-based accountability
129n1
entitlement cards 135
epistemology 162–5
ethics 3–4, 15–16
European Arrest Warrant 89
European Commission 27–8
European Community 5
European Convention on Human
Rights 54, 74, 80
European Court of Human Rights
in accordance with the law 80–5
democratic institutions 40
executive authorisation 55
judicial authorisation 56
necessary in a democracy 85–7
proportionality 87–95
European Data Protection
Commissioners 64
European Telecommunications
Standards Institute 43
European Union 42
evidence 57–8
The Execution Channel (Macleod)
197
executive authorisation 55, 66–7,
81–2

Fair Credit Reporting Act 1970 5
FBI 66
Financial Service Authority 50
Financial Times 143
FISA Amendments Act 2008 55–6

Flynn, Catherine O' 195–6
Foord, David 138
Foreign Intelligence Surveillance Act 1978 40, 66
foreign nationals, identity cards 150, 151n2
Foundation for Information Policy Research 63
France 15–16, 82, 83
future of surveillance 160–2
  conditional choices 172–4
  epistemology 162–5
  idea of surveillance 162–5
  overview xxiv–xxv, 174–5
  worst cases 165–9
futurology 159–60

Gamson, W.A. 147
Gandy, O. 142
Gay Hunter (Mitchell) 182
GCHQ 42, 50, 53–4, 67
Germany 44–5, 49, 57, 89–90, 93
Giddens, A. 175
Gilliom, J. 170
Glassner, Barry 189
Goold, B.J. xx, xxi
Griesemer, J. xxiv
Guerin, Veronica 92
Gun, Katherine 67

Haggerty, K.D. xviii, xxiv
Halford v UK 41
Haneke, Michael 192–3
Harben, W.N. 181–2
Harrison, M. John 183–4
Havel, Vaclav 181
Hayman, Assistant Commissioner 116
Health and Safety at Work Act 1979 117, 127–8
Henriques, Mr Justice 126
Herald 150
Heymann, P.B. 75, 76
Hidden Camera (Zivokovic) 180–181
Hidden (Haneke) 192–3

HM Revenue and Customs 42, 44, 141
Home Affairs Committee 146
Hoover, J. Edgar 66
House of Lords Constitution Committee 146
Hughes, Simon 126–7
human dignity 79
Human Rights Act 1998 xix
Hume's guillotine xxiii
Hussain Osman 119, 120

idea of surveillance 162–5
ideational privilege 164–5
Identity and Passport Service 138
identity cards
  civil liberties concerns 139–41
  costs of 136–7, 144
  discussion 147–8
  key events 135–9
  launch of 150
  overview xxii, 134
  public consciousness 144–7
  public opinion 141–4
Identity Cards Act 135–6, 139, 144
Identity Project (LSE) 134, 136
illegal surveillance, detecting 21–2
Independent 144–5, 150
Independent Police Complaints Commission (IPCC) 115–17
  failings report 125–6
individual choice 173–4
Information Commissioner 20, 65, 146, 160
'Information Sharing Vision Statement' (DCA) 140–1
insurance companies 15
intelligence agencies 42, 44
  oversight 53–4
Intelligence and Security Act 1994 54
Intelligence and Security Committee 53–4, 61
Intelligence Services Act 1994 44

Intelligence Services Commissioner
52
intelligence states 75–6
interception of communications
see communications surveillance
Interception of Communications
Commissioner 47, 51–2, 60, 61–3
interconnection xvii–xviii
Internet protection 80
invasions of privacy, detecting 21–2
Investigatory Powers Tribunal 52–3,
54, 58
The Ipcress File (Deighton) 184
Ireland 83, 90
is/ought xxiii

Jasper, J.M. 148
Jay, M. 163
Johnson, Lyndon 66
Johnston, Philip 146
Joint Committee on Human Rights
56, 58
Jones, Ken 128
judicial authorisation 55–8, 60

Kafka, Franz 179
Katz v United States 40
Kennedy, John F. 66
Khan, Sadiq 144–5
King, Martin Luther Jr. 66
*Klass and others v the Federal Republic
of Germany* 40, 55, 60–1
Kopp v Switzerland 84
Kosinski, Jerzy 184
Kundera, Milan 181

The Land of the Changing Sun
(Harben) 181–2
language 121–4
Lapperrière, R. 35n4
Latour, B. xxiv
law, in accordance with 81–5
Leander v. Sweden 86
Leavis, F.R. xxiv
Lee, N. xx

legislation 4–6, 20–1
in accordance with the law
81–5
costs of 22–3
inadequacies of 19–24
market fundamentalism 164
Lessig, L. 25, 41
Levinson, Paul 190–1
Lex Informatica model 36n13
liberal democracy xx
Liberty 145
Liberty and Others v UK 23, 35n8
Lin, M. 173–4
literary novels 191–6, 197–200
literature 178–81
Little, M. 170
Livingstone, Ken 128
local authorities 60
London Assembly 115
London bombings 76, 93
London School of Economics (LSE)
134, 136
Lott, Tim 191–3
Lycos Netherlands v Pessers 82
Lyon, D. 108, 178

McAuley, Paul 188
Macleod, Ken 197
McNamee, Eoin 185
Madrid bombings 76–8, 92–3
Maestri v Italy 81–2
Malone v United Kingdom 58–9, 80,
81
Maras, M.-H. xviii, xx, xxi
Margroff, R.E. 184
market fundamentalism 164
mass surveillance 10–15, 74–5 *see
also* Data Retention Directive
media coverage 144–8, 150
methodology xxiv, 3–4
Metropolitan Police 53
Metropolitan Police Authority 115
MI5 42, 53–4
MI6 42, 53–4
minimal retention 25, 31

Mitchell, James Leslie 182
Modigliani, A. 147
Montgomery, Clare, QC 119–20
MPs communications 144
Mummery, Lord Justice 53

National Black Police Association
    53
National Hi-Tech Crime Unit 92
National Identity Register 135,
    139–40, 143
National Security Agency 66–7
National Technical Assistance Centre
    50
necessity 85–7
Nellis, M. xxiv
neoliberalism 170
Netherlands 82
network society xvii–xviii
New York Times 66
Neyland, D. xxiii
Nineteen Eighty Four (Orwell) 178,
    179, 182
Niven, Larry 182
Nixon, Richard 66
normative questions xxiii–xxiv
notification of surveillance 60–1
No2ID 142–3
novels 178–81, 191–6
    overview 197–200

Observer 145
Omagh bombing 92
Omnibus Crime Control and Safe
    Streets Act 1968 40
Operation Kratos 122–4
organisational failure 124–8
organised crime 76–8
Orwell, George 178, 179–81, 182
Oryx and Crake (Atwood) 199–200
oversight 51–4
    intelligence agencies 53–4
    judicial oversight 55–8, 60
    legislation 51–3, 83
    parliamentary oversight 61–3

strengthening 61–3
USA 62

panopticon 185, 188, 189
passenger name records (PNRs) 75
passports 137–8
personal autonomy 79
Philips, Adam 197
physical searches 59
The Pixel Eye (Levinson) 190–1
Plato 163
Police Act 1997 44
Police and Criminal Evidence Act
    1984 (PACE) 59
police forces, access 47
police procedural novels 186–8
Porter, Henry 145
postal interception 65–6
Pretty Good Privacy (PGP) software
    49, 64, 89
principled restraint 24–30
principles of protection 5–10
Privacy Act 1974 5, 8
privacy, definition of xviii–xix
privacy enhancing technologies
    (PETs)
    examples of 27, 32
    overview xx
    role of 27–30
privacy protection xvii–xxi
privacy, right to
    in accordance with the law 80–5
    European Convention on Human
        Rights 74, 79–80
    necessity 85–7
privacy zones 29, 32, 36n14
private vehicles 44
Proceeds of Crime Act 2002 59
proportionality 86–95
public authorities, access 47
public consciousness 144–8
public opinion 141–4
public participation xxi–xxii

Raab, C. xviii, 25

Raban, Jonathan 193–5
Rankin, Ian 186–8
Raz, J. 79
Rebus novels 186–8
regulation *see also* oversight
    checks and balances 63–5
    mechanisms 41
    model of 30–3
    overview xvii–xxi, 34–5
    parliamentary oversight 61–3
    principled restraint 24–30
Regulation of Investigatory Powers
    Act 2000
    access to communications data
        45–7, 83
    bugging 44
    encryption 50–1
    interception of communications
        42–4
    oversight 51–3
    overview 18–19, 41–2
    puzzling statute 54–5
Regulation of Investigatory
    Powers (Communications Data)
    (Additional Functions and
    Amendment) Order 2006 46–7
Regulation of Investigatory Powers
    (Communications Data) Order
    2003 82
Reid, John 138
Reidenberg, J. 36n13
research assessment exercise 111–12
residential premises 44
resistance 175
risk 171–2
Royal Academy of Engineering
    (RAE) 146, 147
Rule, J.B. xix, xx–xxi
Running Wild (Ballard) 198–9, 200

Salisbury Convention 137
science fiction 181–4
Secret Intelligence Service 42
Security Service 42
self-authorisation procedures 60

self-incrimination 51
serious crime 89–90
Serious Crime Act 2007 90
Serious Organised Crime Agency
    (SOCA) 42
Service Providers
    access to communications data
        45–7
    in accordance with the law 82–3
    checks and balances 64–5
    cooperation 92–4
    data retention 48–9, 75
    encryption 50
    fast-freeze–quick thaw 92
    individual choice 173–4
    interception of communications
        43–4
    overview 40
    service use information 46
The Seymour Tapes (Lott) 191–3
Shaw, Bob 183
shoot to kill 122–4
Silver v United Kingdom 84
single mothers 170
situational crime prevention 36n16
Skype 43–4, 50
Smith, Peter 138
social sciences 134, 175
social services 170–2
Solove, D. 21–2
Somers, M.R. 164
Special Advocates 58
spy novels 184–6
Stalinism 179
Star, S. xxiv
Stichting Brein v KPN Telecom 82
stigmatisation 169–72
Stockwell 1 115
Stockwell 2 115, 116
subscriber information 45–6, 60
The Sunday Times 138
surveillance, broad and narrow
    108–9
Surveillance Commissioners 44, 56,
    61–3

Surveillance (Raban) 193–5
surveillance society 146
surveillance studies xv–xvi
Surveillance Studies Network 146
Sutherland, John 188
Sweden 5, 86
Switzerland 84
systemic failure 127

Taylor Nelson Sofres' survey 142
Taylorism 179
technological fix 165
technologies
    access to 26–7
    limits of privacy protection
        10–16
    overview xx, xxi–xxiv
    worst cases 165–9
technothrillers 188–91
Temporary National Identity
    Register 138
terminology xviii–xix
terrorism *see also* Data Retention
    Directive
Declaration on Combating Terrorism
    (European Council) 78, 95
    legislation 47, 50, 59–60, 78, 90,
        95
    responses to 8
Terrorism Act 2000 59–60
Terrorism Act 2006 50
Terrorist Surveillance Program 55
Thomas, Richard 160
Thwaites, Ronald, QC 119
time of surveillance 93–4
Toffler, A. 159
totalitarianism 162, 166
traffic data 45–6
translation xx–xxi
The Traveller (Twelve Hawks) 188–9,
    198

Twelve Hawks, John 188–9, 198

u–surveillance novels 179–81
UK Borders Act 2007 151n1
The Unbearable Lightness of Being
    (Kundera) 181
units of responsibility 116–17
USA
    executive authorisation 66–7
    judicial authorisation 55–6
    legislation 20, 43
    National Research Council 57
    oversight 62
    privacy 4–5

Vidino, L. 76
visible imperative 161, 173
visual images 118–21
visual metaphors 163
Voice over Internet Protocol (VoIP)
    systems 43–4
voyeurism 192

Walden, I. 88
warrants 42–3, 52f, 55–8
we/us xviii
We (Zamyatin) 179–81
welfare benefits 170–1
Wells, H.G. 182
What Was Lost (O'Flynn) 195–6
whistleblowers 67
Whitley, E.A. xix, xxii, xxiii
Whole Wide World (McAuley)
    188
Wilson Doctrine 144
worst case scenarios 165–9
Wright, Peter 41

Zamyatin, Yevgeny 179–81
Zimmerman, Phil 64
Zivokovic, Zoran 180, 198